Children and
their Primary Schools
A New Perspective

Children and their Primary Schools

A New Perspective

Edited by

Andrew Pollard
Bristol Polytechnic

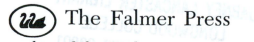 The Falmer Press

(A member of the Taylor & Francis Group)
London, New York and Philadelphia

UK The Falmer Press, Falmer House, Barcombe, Lewes, East Sussex, BN8 5DL

USA The Falmer Press, Taylor & Francis Inc., 242 Cherry Street, Philadelphia, PA 19106–1906

First published 1987

Library of Congress Cataloging-in-Publication Data

Children and their primary schools.

Includes indexes.
1. Education, Elementary — Great Britain — 1965-
I. Pollard, Andrew.
LA633.C49 1987   372.941   87–20130
ISBN 1–85000–320–3
ISBN 1–85000–321–1 (pbk.)

Jacket design by Caroline Archer

Typeset in 10½/12 Caledonia by
Imago Publishing Ltd, Thame, Oxon

*Printed and bound in Great Britain by
Redwood Burn Limited, Wiltshire*

Contents

Acknowledgements

Several of the chapters in this book were presented at a symposium held at the British Educational Research Association Conference in Bristol in September 1986. I am grateful to Maude Brown, Peter Harnett, Bruce Carrington, Geoff Short, Stephen Rowland, Margaret Jackson, Peter Woods and other contributors to the discussions. Thanks also to Paul Croll, Joy Lowe, Maggie Wilson and Sara Meadows and to all the contributors to the collection.

Copyright permission is gratefully acknowledged from:

Collins and A.P. Watt Ltd for material from TIZARD, B. and HUGHES, M. (1984) *Young Children Learning,* Fontana.

Associated Book Publishers Ltd for material from SLUCKIN, A. (1981) *Growing Up in the Playground,* Routledge and Kegan Paul.

Open University Press for permission to reprint POLLARD, A. (1984) 'Goodies, jokers and gangs' from HAMMERSLEY, M. and WOODS, P. (Eds), *Life in School.*

Cambridge University Press for material from BOSSERT, S. (1979) *Tasks and Social Relationships in Classrooms.*

Introduction: New Perspectives on Children

Andrew Pollard

The impertinance of the title of this volume, in reproducing that of the Plowden Report (CACE, 1967), is, I am afraid, deliberate. It is now twenty years since Plowden was published and the chapters in this collection constitute an attempt to present a new perspective on one of the central assumptions which underpinned the Report — on the 'nature' of 'children'.

Within the book there are two themes of particular importance. The first is focussed on how children themselves are perceived, bearing in mind new developments in child psychology and in sociological studies of children's perspectives and behaviour in schools. The second concerns the implications which such developments may have for teaching and learning processes in classrooms.

The medium through which these issues are explored is a series of chapters which report the views and abilities of children, often through reproducing their own accounts and explanations. The volume can thus also be seen as a commentary by children on 'their primary schools' — and perhaps children do remain a significant group of consumers to whom professional educators should respond?

In this introduction, I begin by elaborating the focus on 'children', prior to a review of the chapters. Finally, some of the possible implications are posed.

Children

The Plowden Report contains a number of quotations which seemed designed to inspire. Among them is the following:

> At the heart of the educational process lies the child. No advances in policy, no acquisitions of new equipment, have their desired effect unless they are in harmony with the nature of the child, unless they are fundamentally acceptable to him. (para. 9)

Such views have a history in the 'developmental tradition' in primary education which can be traced back, through Froebel and Pestalozzi to Rousseau. However, they seem, in this case, to have been derived more from the Plowden Committee's understanding of the dominant perspectives in developmental psychology at the time, in particular, that of Piaget which had been widely applied in teacher-education institutions. Thus children, in their cognitive development, were thought to pass through 'stages of thinking' and an invariant, developmental progression in types of cognition was almost universally accepted as reflecting 'the' scientifically documented nature of children's intellectual growth. Running in parallel were other types of developmentalism — for example, Gesell on physical maturation, Kohlberg on moral development — and prescriptive literature which advised on the practical implications of such work abounded. Developmentalism was thus a major foundation of the Plowden Report and this was combined with what some regarded as a degree of saccharine sentiment to produce the view of the 'nature' of children which the quotation above reflects.

Such ideas were quickly criticized as ... 'half-truths that are paraded as educational panaceas' (Peters, 1969, p. 3) and as contributing to an implicit ideology underlying the recommendations of the Report. Despite such objections by philosophers, and indeed, despite the criticisms of many right-wing commentators (for example, Cox and Dyson, 1969), the Report articulated a 'recognizable philosophy' which was well received by an expanding teaching profession in the late 1960s and early 1970s. Thus, developmentalism and assertions about the nature of children have been, and remain, important elements in the professional ideology of primary school teachers.

The problem for teachers is that, despite their pressing need for a clear and accepted legitimation for professional judgment and autonomy at present, child psychology and other types of research on children in school have moved on — indeed, they have moved a long way on. One aspect of this is the appreciation of the cultural relativism of modern, Western perspectives of children and childhood. Beliefs in 'normal' developmental sequences are considerably undermined by studies of children in different historical eras and in different cultures (Kessel and Siegel, 1983). Such work widens the boundaries of what one might expect children to be capable and this revision in expectations has been reinforced by psychological critiques and developments of Piaget's work.

Psychologists initially criticized Piaget on methodological grounds and, in particular, for the abstraction of the tests and activities on which his theory of cognition was based. Donaldson (1978) focussed attention on these issues with her classic book *Children's Minds*. She demonstrated that, if activities and tests are set up in ways which are meaningful to children, then they are able to demonstrate far more competence and cognitive ability than Piagetian theory would predict. According to

Meadows (1983, p. 19) Piaget was simply ... 'too quick to postulate logical inadequacies' and 'overemphasized ... the illogicality of small children'. Awareness of the importance of social context and of children's perceptions was growing, and with it concern about the empirical under-pinnings of previous work. As Bronfenbrenner (1979, p. 19) put it ... 'much of developmental psychology ..., is the science of the strange behaviour of children in strange situations with strange adults for the briefest periods of time'.

A foretaste of this kind of concern had been provided in a collection of papers edited by Richards (1974) on *The Child's Integration into the Social World* and is continued in a more recent sequel (Richards and Light, 1986). In the latter volume Ingleby suggests that the conditions are now right for the emergence of a new paradigm in developmental psychology — a paradigm which he terms 'social constructionist' and which would reflect:

> an approach to human thought, preception and action through meanings, and ...
>
> an acceptance that meanings are created and conveyed through the interaction of people, in particular by using language.

The study of psychology would thus focus on interaction between people and on the 'development of mind' through intersubjectivity rather than on the thought processes of individuals studied in socially artificial settings.

As Ingleby points out, social constructionism hardly represents a coherent paradigm at present. Indeed, he identifies no less than six different theories which might contribute to it — symbolic interactionism, phenomenology, ethnomethodology, analytic philosophy and some forms of Marxism and structuralism. There are serious theoretical, philosophical and methodological differences between these approaches which will probably always produce tensions but they share the conviction that human action is best understood as being meaningful and as a product of social contexts and social interaction. In doing so they, of course, cross the artificial disciplinary boundary between psychology and sociology which in itself provokes much debate.

Sociologists have also developed many new insights into school and classroom processes and into the perspectives of teachers and children. In trends which closely parallel those within psychology, a variety of forms of 'interpretive sociology' have emerged. They also treat the behaviour of people as being meaningful forms of action — and focus, as the first essential for any analysis, on understanding the perspectives of the people who are involved in a particular social situation, (for case studies involving yound children in schools, see, King 1978; Sluckin 1981; Davies 1982 Pollard 1985; Hartley 1985; Lubeck 1986; and Clarricoates, forth coming). Symbolic interactionist theory and ethnographic methods have been particularly significant here, (Hargreaves, 1978; Woods, 1983).

Despite the risks of generalization, I would suggest that the pattern of findings about children in schools is fairly clear. Children tend to feel vulnerable in school. They are aware of the power of teachers, of the personal assessment to which they are subject, of the control which is exercised over them and of the curriculum in terms of which they are expected to progress. Such concerns are reflected in the concepts which children often use to describe teachers — strict/soft, fair/unfair, good fun/boring — or the curriculum — interesting/boring. Of course, children at school also have to cope with their peers and with the social world of the other children. In this regard friendship and membership of a peer-group seem to be particularly important. The factor which appears to underly all these concerns is that of developing and maintaining an identity — a sense of 'self' and a means of effectively presenting that self in school situations. For many children, this will be the means by which they develop a feeling of security and of being valued; for some others the identity may be a means of protecting their dignity in the face of difficulties which they experience at school. For instance, in my own work (Pollard, 1985) children are seen as being active, and examples are provided of the ways in which they act strategically in classroom situations in order to 'cope' with them. By a variety of means children seek to protect their dignity and maximize their enjoyment. They work to learn the tacit rules of the classroom and may become expert at monitoring their teacher's moods and use of power. Children seek respect. They shun the humiliation of being 'told off' and the threat of 'shouting'. They are incensed when they feel they have been treated 'unfairly'.

In reviewing both the psychological and sociological developments it is clear that if the Plowden Committee were taking evidence in the late 1980s on how children learn and how they experience primary schooling then they would be likely to receive very different advice than that which was offered them in the 1960s. And what prescriptions for educational classroom practice would then follow? Perhaps these are the main issues on which the papers in this volume are likely to prevoke discussion.

The Chapters

The first chapter, by Sue Duxbury, has many resonances with the post-structuralist critique by Walkerdine (1984) of the 'normalizing' assumptions of developmentalism and of child-centered pedagogy. Duxbury studied working-class children on entry to nursery school and also documented the social, ideological and economic constraints on their mothers. She argues that childcare ideologies set up idealized expectations of what a 'good mother' should be which are almost impossible to fulfil. Working mothers thus face a dilemma between the need to work and the guilt of doing so and this influences the way their children are treated.

Duxbury then describes the extensive strategies of manipulative resistance which children typically adopt in such situations — behaviour which is regarded as being meaningful in the context of the predicament of the mothers and in the circumstances posed by the ideology of privatised childcare. It is not seen as the consequence of a 'developmental stage'.

The chapter 'The intellectual search of young children' by Barbara Tizard and Martin Hughes is more psychological in orientation and has major implications for Piagetian theory and for teachers. A painstaking and logical struggle to understand is illustrated through transcripts of 4-year-old girls discussing topics such as 'tigers' and 'Father Christmas' with their mothers. Tizard and Hughes argue that the difference between adult's thinking and children's thinking is nothing to do with deficiencies in children's powers of reasoning. It arises because of children's relative factual ignorance and because of the limited conceptual framework within which their experience and thought is organized. The implication is that, rather than 'each child being the agent of his own learning' (Plowden Report, para. 529), there is a vital role for adults in discussion, in giving information and in facilitating each child's own intellectual exploration.

The third chapter in the collection, by Bronwyn Davies, provides a further example of the desire and capacity of young children to 'make sense' of their experiences. It is focussed on pre-school children and on the ways in which they understand and accomplish their 'genderedness' — what it is to be male or female in their everyday world. Arguing that gender is central to each person's identity Davies used a number of 'liberating stories' to discover children's perspectives on various sex-roles. Children who had working mothers seemed to be able to envisage a wider range of roles. Overall though, the embeddedness of sex-based assumptions at such young ages is clear and has important implications for socially-aware teachers.

But what do we offer children when they enter school? The next two chapters, by David Hartley and Margaret Jackson, offer some insights here. Hartley's chapter is based on an analysis of two nursery units attached to primary schools in Scotland. He argues that, whilst the idealism of child-centredness existed, the two classes were far more distinctive for the bureaucratic tendencies which they exhibited. Hidden curricular affecting the use of space, of time and in assessment seemed to 'instrumentalize' the overtly more expressive aims of the teachers. This occurred in ways which Hartley sees as being related to the growth of bureaucratization in society more widely. Jackson reports on her study of 5-year-old children starting at school and demonstrates the ways in which they attempt to 'make sense' of the rules, relationships and procedures which their reception class presented. She sees children as testing and reformulating hypotheses about meanings and behaviour, learning about rules, about teacher power, about collaboration with others and about 'how to be taught' within the constraints of the classroom situation. Children

5

are seen as being active — interpreting, questioning, adapting and formulating new knowledge and understandings as they confront the new situation of school.

Similar skills and abilities are illustrated in the chapter by Thea Prisk on unsupervised groupwork in an infant school. Transcripts of a group of children's conversations when faced with a variety of language tasks over a two-month period showed their capacity to identify and solve problems, to collaborate socially and intellectually, to structure discussions, to evaluate conflicting hypotheses and to develop communication skills. The role of a teacher in providing information at appropriate moments and the importance of group composition are identified, but this does not detract from the evidence of the children's capability.

Peter Woods provides an analysis of the development of a class of children in their transition from infant school to 'the juniors'. He traces the personal challenges which were presented and the changes in skills, attitudes and identities which were made. The children had to 'learn how to learn' by new 'junior' methods and began to establish new identities for themselves. Gender and race were particularly important in this, as they were in parallel social developments with peer groups and friendships. Woods proposes that the development of pupil identities and of 'careers' can be seen as a series of steps. Periods of rapid change, perhaps induced by transitions between institutions, are followed by comparative plateaus of consolidation. He thus sees 'becoming a junior' and developments among 7/8 year olds as being crucial for later progress.

The chapter by Stephen Rowland is an important one in this collection, for it begins to identify the implications which social constructionist psychology might have for children's classroom learning. Rowland examines didactic and the more child-centered 'exploratory' models of teaching and learning but suggests that learning is most effective when the child is 'in control' of the process and when the curriculum is 'owned' by the child. At the centre of this 'interpretive' model of learning is the idea of teacher-child interaction, with the teacher stimulating, acting as a reflective agent and providing instruction as appropriate. The teacher facilitates each child's social construction of understanding and knowledge by sensitively interpreting and acting upon the child's expressed needs.

Sociological research tends to show that, whether or not teachers recognize and capitalize on the sense-making capabilities of children, meanings and perceptions regarding school life will be developed by them. Such perspectives are likely to be influenced by factors such as social class, gender, race, age and progress in school and are often reflected in peer-group cultures or through the social structure which patterns children's social relationships. Such developments often go rather unnoticed, being manifested in the relatively neglected domain of the playground or lost in the challenges and complexities of classroom teaching. However, problems may emerge in that some of the attitudes and perspectives that children develop may be socially divisive or affect teachers' educational aims adversely. Several of the remaining chapters in the collection illustrate these processes and issues.

Steven Bossert's is the first in this group. He reports on the detailed study of four classes: two tightly controlled and organized by their teachers and with an emphasis on question and answer sessions; two using a wider range of organizational strategies and offering the children more choice and control over their learning. In the former classrooms, the children began to form friendship groups which reflected the overt success and failure that they achieved. In the more varied and open classrooms, friendships were more flexible and interest-based and the children were more cooperative.

Such cultural responses do not occur in a social and historical vacuum, as the chapter by Andy Slukin illustrates. Based on long-term observation in primary school playgrounds, Slukin develops the seminal work of Opie and Opie (1959 and 1969) to demonstrate the continuities in the games, rhymes and procedures for governing relationships that go to make up children's culture. Such activities, he argues, are forms of self-motivated learning and an essential preparation for adult life. As such, they deserve greater respect from adults than they often get.

My chapter seeks to break down the tendency to treat 'children' as a homogeneous category and is focussed on the perspectives of various groups of 11-year-old girls in a large middle school. I suggest that three types of friendship groups can be distinguished for analysis; goodies, jokers and gangs. The development of such groups is seen as being greatly influenced by the children's relationships with teachers, with jokers being particularly significant in negotiating classroom understandings and in managing 'laughs'. It is argued that children cope with classroom life by juggling various interests and concerns, particularly those relating to self-image, enjoyment, stress and dignity, and it is suggested that processes of differentiation within children's social relationships could have long-term consequences in the formation of individual identities.

A clash between 'gendered worlds' is the subject of Katherine Clarricoates' analysis. She provides a compelling account of the ways in which gender stereotypes affect status for boys and girls within the social systems of four primary schools and she documents the extent of the spatial and verbal dominance of boys in the playground. Social class differences are revealed but perhaps the most interesting theme concerns the extent of girls' activities as they work to overcome or bypass male domination.

Plenty of evidence of meaningful learning and action is provided in these chapters and much of it raises vital issues for us as teachers. What should our role be and what are our responsibilities, when children's social interaction is shown to involve such basic issues as social differentiation and the development of identities? The question is acutely posed if it is believed that education should be concerned with social justice as well as with effective learning per se. However, an answer has been suggested by the Council of Europe in their recent *Recommendation on Teaching and Learning about Human Rights in Schools* (Council of Europe, 1985) and it is clearly interventionist. Teachers should ensure that the rights and dignity of all people are respected, irrespective of gender, social class, race or belief.

In the heyday of developmentalism the direct introduction of such issues into the primary school curriculum is likely to have been treated very tentatively, if at all. As King (1978) pointed out, 'all things' were supposed to be 'bright and beautiful' and young children were not thought to be at an appropriate 'stage of development' to be directly introduced to such ideas as part of the overt curriculum. However, the chapters of social constructionist psychology and interpretive sociology in this volume clearly show that such attempts to maintain childish innocence are misplaced and can only be based on an ignorance of what children already know and on a lack of awareness of the ways in which their perspectives and meanings develop. One way forward may be through much more frank and open discussion with children, through offering them new experiences and by drawing out, developing and, if appropriate, contesting their existing perspectives. Two chapters in the volume explore such teaching strategies directly with regard to the important topic of race.

'Stories children tell' by Veronica and John Lee with Maggie Pearson, is an account of a programme of coordinated curricular provision and inter-school visiting involving two teachers and their classes from inner-city schools. The racial and cultural mix of a school in an area of poor housing and high unemployment is contrasted with the affluence and racial homogeneity of a school in a fashionable suburb. Both teachers introduced multicultural education programmes and made their commitment to anti-racism clear. Four inter-school visits were made. One fascination of the chapter arises from the ways in which the children showed their awareness of social class and gender as much as they did regarding race. The authors conclude by arguing strongly that new forms of 'progressive pedagogy' are necessary to combat racism and to develop other forms of social awareness.

Geoffrey Short and Bruce Carrington continue these arguments in their case-study report of an anti-racist initiative in an all-white primary school. Developmentalism and child-centredness are challenged directly and it is argued that young children are racially conscious and are certainly capable of racism. However, the case-study of teaching and learning through a topic on events 'In living memory' shows that children can cope conceptually both with individual racism and can also understand the implications of racial inequality.

In the final chapter of the collection, by Sara Delamont and Maurice Galton, much of the recent research on the transfer of children from primary to secondary school is reviewed. Themes of earlier chapters resurface as patterns of children's anxieties and expectations are unfolded. As in the chapter by Woods, there are positive feelings about new opportunities and the new status which is implied by transfer, but this is tempered by the existence of a number of stories and myths which circulate within child culture. Anxieties about the buildings, the curriculum, the teachers and other pupils at the secondary school again cue children's concern with maintaining their dignity and sense of identity when faced by situations which they feel may make them vulnerable.

Implications for Teaching and Learning

I do not propose to attempt to make definitive statements on this topic, for there is much to be discovered and discussed. Many of the implications of constructionist psychology and interpretive sociology can only be teased out by teachers as the practicalities of classroom life are faced. Nor indeed, can such developments avoid the effects of the political and economic factors which have come to have such significance in education in the last few years. However, as I have argued elsewhere (Pollard and Tann, 1987), 'reflective teachers' are likely to want to ensure that classroom judgments are informed by relevant research when it is available.

I therefore set out below a number of issues which seem to me to require consideration by reflective and committed teachers in the light of the arguments contained in their book.

The first concerns control of learning processes. The thrust of social constructionist arguments seems to suggest that children learn best when they feel in control of their own learning, and interpretive sociologists would reinforce this from the motivational point of view. The process of 'intellectual search' cannot proceed fully if adults seek to impose their notions of order or of relevance on it, however good their intentions. How can teachers devise practical ways of organizing classroom activities and managing children so that it is possible to offer such 'control'?

A second implication, in a way, represents a qualification of the first for it concerns the teacher's role. Rowland puts this concisely in his contribution to the volume when he writes of the teacher acting ... 'as a reflective agent, aiming to help the child identify concerns and needs, and also providing positive, yet critical, feedback'. In this way instruction by teachers 'enables' each child's control and achievement. Teachers might thus be seen as being active and as accepting educational and social responsibilities but doing so in ways which preserve the dignity of children and which recognize children's integrity as they seek to know, to understand and to develop new skills. Perhaps we, as teachers, can come to accept and identify with such a role — but can we actually put it into practice?

A third implication concerns the curriculum for it seems clear that, if even very young children are active in piecing together and developing understandings about social issues such as gender, race, unemployment, poverty, or even the possibility of nuclear war, then responsible adults should play a part in discussing and informing children about such issues. How could such issues be considered constructively and responsibly in primary schools?

A fourth implication is posed by the growing understanding of the growth of each child's sense of identity and social development. It can be argued that this may have considerable effect on their future self-esteem and make a direct impact on life-chances. On the one hand children's culture and social activities are a source of self-directed learning, on the other, they may reinforce social inequalities and lead to increasing differentiation. On what basis should teachers make their judgments as they try to resolve the dilemmas which are posed?

A fifth implication concerns relationships with parents. The arguments in this book imply, like so much other recent research, that the education of children, at home and at school, is best thought of as a whole. Children construct their knowledge and develop their attitudes and skills from a wide range of experiences, twenty-four hours a day. How can this breadth and variety in experience be capitalised on in schools?

My final conclusion, to put it frankly, is that teachers face enormous challenges if classroom practices are to be developed to follow up these concerns. We know that, in one sense, the prescriptions of the Plowden Report failed to become an integral part of primary practice, even if the rhetoric has left its mark, (Galton, Simon and Croll, 1980; Alexander, 1984). Perhaps this occurred for practical reasons, as primary school teachers continued to face large classes with strictly limited resources and little provision for professional reflection. Coping in such circumstances has never been easy and the themes of this book are, once more, likely to pose the perennial dilemmas which occur when considering classroom organization and management — between structure and independence, control and freedom. However, there are a number of interesting developments here, for instance, regarding aspects of the National Writing Project, the High/Scope nursery project and moves to increase the amount of problem solving and collaborative group-work which takes place in primary schools.

Nevertheless, the development of classroom practice based on new perspectives on the capacities, awareness and activities of children is likely to remain an area requiring a great deal of professional commitment, collaboration and research for many years.

References

ALEXANDER, R.J. (1984) *Primary Teaching*, London, Holt, Rinehart and Winston.

BRONFENBRENNER, U. (1979) *The Ecology of Human Development*, Cambridge, MA, Harvard University Press.

CENTRAL ADVISORY COUNCIL FOR EDUCATION (CACE) (1967) *Children and their Primary Schools* (The Plowden Report) London, HMSO.

CLARRICOATES, K. (forthcoming) *Gender and Power in Primary Schools*, Cambridge, Polity Press.

COUNCIL OF EUROPE (1985) *Recommendation No R (85)7 of the Committee of Ministers to Member States to Monitor the Teaching and Learning about Human Rights in Schools*, Strasbourg, Council of Europe.

COX, C.B. and DYSON, A.E. (Eds) (1969) *Fight for Education: A Black Paper*, London, Critical Quarterly Society.

DAVIES, B. (1982) *Life in Classroom and Playground*, London, Routledge and Kegan Paul.

DONALDSON, M. (1978) *Children's Minds*, London, Fontana.

GALTON, M. SIMON, B. and CROLL, P. (1980) *Inside the Primary Classroom*, London, Routledge and Kegan Paul.

HARGREAVES, D.H. (1978) 'Whatever happened to symbolic interactionism?' in BARTON, L. and MEIGHAN, R. (Eds) *Sociological Interpretations of Education and Schooling*, Driffield, Nafferton.

HARTLEY, D. (1985) *Understanding the Primary School*, London Croom Helm.

INGLEBY, D. (1986) 'Development in social context', in RICHARDS, M. and LIGHT, P. (Eds) *Children of Social Worlds*, Cambridge, Polity Press.

KING, R. (1978) *All Things Bright and Beautiful? A Sociological Study of Infants' Classrooms*, London, Wiley.

KESSELL F.S. and SIEGEL, A.W. (Eds) (1983) *The Child and Other Inventions*, New York, Praeger.

WALKERDINE, V. (1984) 'Developmental psychology and the child-centred pedagogy', in HENRIQUES, I. *et al.* (Eds) *Changing the Subject: Psychology, Social Regulation and Subjectivity*, London, Methuen.

WOODS, P. (1983) *Sociology and the School*, London, Routledge and Kegan Paul.

LUBECK, S. (1985) *Sandbox Society*, Lewes, Falmer Press.

MEADOWS, S. (Ed.) (1983) *Developing Thinking*, London, Methuen.

OPIE, I. and OPIE, P. (1959) *The Lore and Language of School Children*, London, Oxford University Press.

OPIE, I. and OPIE, P. (1969) *Children's Games in Street and Play-ground*, London, Oxford University Press.

PETERS, R.S. (1969) 'A recognizable philosophy of education: A constructive critique', in PETERS, R.S. (Ed.), *Perspectives on Plowden*, London, Routledge and Kegan Paul.

POLLARD, A. (1985) *The Social World of the Primary School*, London, Holt, Rinehart and Winston.

POLLARD, A. and TANN, C.S. (1987) *Reflective Teaching in the Primary School*, London, Cassell.

RICHARDS, M. (Ed.) (1974) *The Integration of a Child into a Social World*, Cambridge, Cambridge University Press.

RICHARDS, M. and LIGHT, P. (Eds) (1986) *Children of Social Worlds*, Cambridge, Polity Press.

SLUKIN, A. (1981) *Growing Up in the Playground*, London, Routledge and Kegan Paul.

1   Child Care Ideologies and Resistance: The Manipulative Strategies of Pre-school Children

Sue Duxbury

Introduction

The care and education of young children during the twentieth century has been profoundly influenced by development of theories on motherhood, childcare, development and psychology. In this chapter I aim firstly to explore the emergence of these theories and to discuss their impact upon parents, educators and ultimately on children themselves in the 1980s. I will argue that theories which were intended to liberate and individualize children, and to professionalize motherhood, have come to oppress mothers and through them their children.

Secondly, the chapter will examine some distinctive forms of young children's behaviour which are not adequately explained by much of the literature. Many children exhibit a range of manipulative strategies which both challenge the key features of childcare ideologies and establish children's potential for complex behaviour, rather than perceiving it as a deficiency in normal development. This is significant as it demonstrates their competence and skill albeit for negative purposes, and reveals clear indications of the structural difficulties which dominant childcare ideologies place women and children in. Thus young children may be seen not merely as passive recipients of childcare philosophies, but as consciously reacting to the constraints which they and their parents experience in daily life.

The chapter will be illustrated by findings from a recent study of mothers and their pre-school children (Duxbury, 1984),[1] initiated after observing children's behaviour on entry to nursery school. This behaviour was significantly different than the 'norm' perpetuated by child development literature, universal in teacher training. The study attempted to identify by principle social, economic and ideological constraints upon the lives of a group of working class mothers, noting the repercussions on their pre-school children. In particular it identified the consciously adopted manipulative strategies which the children utilized to make sense of their world.

The chapter concludes that if both the needs and rights of children and mothers are to be fully recognized, different types of childcare practices and philosophies will be necessary. These would need to challenge isolated privatized childcare performed principally by women within a society which undervalues children and childcare and perpetuates ideals of competitiveness, aggression and possessiveness.

Childcare Ideologies

This section begins with a brief historical review of the development of childcare ideologies.

The late nineteenth century witnessed a growing belief that high infant mortality was due to the inadequacies of the parents, particularly those of the working classes. The early twentieth century saw the eugenic orientation to pregnancy and the pre-natal period, and the development of a child and maternal welfare movement legitimated by medical jurisdiction over pregnancy and childbirth, (Lewis, 1980). The emphasis was on the authoritarian laws of health and scientific morality, in the belief that the new knowledge would result in the perfect health of all infants, (Graham, 1977). A by-product or accident of the movement was a final step in the male takeover of women's reproductive activities which had begun in the seventeenth century[2] (Oakley, 1976).

Alongside theories of motherhood emerged childcare and education philosophies, and scientific studies of child development. Social poblems came under scrutiny and methods of cure and detection were sought, hoping to nip 'degeneracy' in the bud by regulating the development of children.

The resulting theories encompassed a variety of approaches. Behaviourists advocated an objective structural approach to learning which was popularized by Skinner and Watson in the early thirties. Maturational theorists focussed on the chronological development of the ages and 'stages' of a child's life. This approach was particularly developed by Gessell and Piaget. The psychoanalytic school, emphasizing the interaction of the child with the environment and the development of personality, was associated with Freud.

Perhaps the most influential of these, particularly in relation to modern primary education, was the developmentalism of Piaget. He built upon the work of others such as Darwin, who had identified patterns of growth and patterns of mental functioning many years before. There was also a trend among educationalists, such as Montessori and McMillan, to reject previous authoritarian methods to teaching and to substitute a more child centred, individualized approach in the hope of achieving a more natural, free and 'joyful' type of learning. Thus physical, emotional and mental development were presented side by side in the same terms as newly established 'facts' of child development. Parents and teachers were thought to require scientific training to ensure the normalized development of the next generation.

The rise of such expert opinion and scientific evidence greatly influenced the way children were regarded. For instance, ante-natal literature described in minute detail what 'normal' babies would do at every stage of their life. What is of additional importance is the fact that it was implicitly assumed that part of the necessary provision for 'normal' development was the continuous presence of the mother and her unconditional love for the child. Thus, at the same time as childcare became increasingly professionalized, the responsibility for children's development was placed firmly in the mother's hands, stressing that she had the power to shape the child's future, whilst observing childrearing techniques as an insurance for future healthy development.

In the period following the second World War, women became increasingly isolated from the traditional communities by changes in the family and labour market. The traditional sources of support from other women were thus disrupted and mothers had to learn the art of childrearing secondhand from the experts via books and manuals which, I would argue, reflected a particular childcare ideology which often contradicted working class women's own experiences, (supported by Graham, 1977). This contradiction is similar in some respects to that identified by Walkerdine (1983).

Walkerdine points out that modern educational ideas about what is natural about children are not self evident, but are linked to a particular brand of psychological explanation whose theories and practices become self-confirming. She suggests that developmental psychology is premised on a set of a claims to truth which are not the only or necessary way to understand the child. The emphasis of child-centred education upon observation, classification and monitoring the individual assumes that there exists a set of observational and empirically verifiable facts of child development (Walkerdine, 1984).

In fact, much of Piaget's work has now been questioned as he placed little emphasis on the social context of learning, commenting . . .

> lived experience only plays a minor role, since these structures do not exist in the subject's consciousness but in their operational behaviour (Piaget, 1968, p. 58).

Piaget is criticized by Borke (1978), for his notion of egocentricity, that young children can only see their own point of view. She concluded that children from 3 to 3½ from very different cultural backgrounds could identify happy and sad responses in other people and that to some extent, the ability to recognize sad and fearful situations appeared to be influenced by social class and cultural factors. Borke suggests . . .

that rather than being egocentric, children as young as three years of age show an ability to take another person's perspective (Borke, 1978, p. 35)

This is supported by my own observations of nursery age children who frequently sympathize with another child if hurt or upset, and readily take on another person's role in dramatic play (see also Donaldson, 1978).

Boden (1979) also felt that, despite Piaget's undoubted contribution to child development, he was wrong to assume children of a given age were unable to carry out certain types of more advanced thinking. He suggests that the 'stage' concept has become increasingly dubious. In particular, he disputes Piaget's prediction that the progression of stages would be the same in all cultures with or without schooling. Cross cultural evidence shows that where children are an integral part of the community they learn complex activities, take on responsibility and do not demonstrate negative forms of behaviour (Comer, 1974; Duxbury, 1986). Similarly, some historical evidence also suggests that since the turn of the century the capacities of young children have been progressively underestimated and distorted by the emphasis on the child's dependancy on the mother (Thompson, 1972).

In addition to theories on motherhood and development was the post-war emphasis on the dangers of institutionalized childcare popularised by Bowlby. His *Childcare and the Growth of Love* (1953) implicitly attacked women for working outside the home since this was believed to result in maternal deprivation, despite women's accepted role in the economy during wartime. As Lewis (1980) has stressed, the attack was more attributable to the belief that women should be in the home, rather than any specific proof that by working they caused deprivation or a higher infant mortality rate. However, the coincidence of maternal psychology acted to assist the transition of women back into the home and out of the economy. The maternal deprivation argument has constantly been reiterated when women have not been required in the economy or their unpaid labour has been required at home, (Deem, 1981). For instance, Kitzinger (1978), Leach (1978) and Kellmer-Pringle (1980), stressed the need for the mothers' continuous presence and unconditional love to ensure the child's healthy emotional development.

Such attitudes to childrearing are, according to Rutter (1972), based on little more than myth and propoganda and alternative approaches receive little publicity. Rutter argues that children can be 'mothered' by people of either sex, up to four in number and who may be biologically unrelated to the child. The available evidence shows that the most important factors are quality and consistency of care. Notably, paternal deprivation is rarely cited to deter men from working outside the home yet according to Andrey (1960), it has significant effects on emotional adjustment and delinquency. Maternal employment does not have the adverse effect on children's stability according to the National Children's Bureau[3] and the NSPCC[4]. Oakley (1974) suggests that working parents may actually have more time and interest for their children after having a break from them, whereas a harassed mother forced to stay at home with her child against her wishes may actually become a threat to the child's safety. It is also important to remember the very real financial need of many mothers of pre-school children. For many, paid employment is a necessity at a time of their greatest financial dependency on a partner or the state (Martin and Roberts, 1984).

The twentieth century has thus seen the emergence of prescriptive childcare philosophies which take little account of the reality of socioeconomic circumstances. In addition, ideological pressure for women to fufil their 'natural' destiny has built up within idealized definitions of what a 'good mother' should be. Such ideas have become particular constraints to women in the most disadvantaged groups in society who have to face the contradictions between the economic need to work and the guilt which ensues.

Such are the main ideological and material constraints which structure the experience of many women who both work and accept childcare responsibilities. The next section discusses the outcome of pre-school childcare operated within a multiplicity of constraints, and the resulting behaviour of the children.

Children's Manipulative Resistance

In adopting a developmental, child-centred approach to childcare we have come to accept the behaviour of pre-school children as normal, universal and attributable to their level of maturity. However, I would argue that the more negative and anti-social forms of our children's behaviour need not be universal, as cross-cultural and historical evidence confirms (Mintern and Lambert, 1964; Thompson, 1972; Comer, 1974) and that such behaviours are children's own solutions to the contradictory and restrictive existence which they and their carers experience.

Childcare literature tends to suggest that if 'correct practices' are adopted the child will comply with the desires of the mother. For instance Spock (1945) denied that babies or children can get parents 'under their thumb' stating that . . .

> this isn't true, your baby is born to be a reasonable friendly human being. (p. 123)

Similarly Hadfield (1962) felt that the 4-year-old has willpower and shows positive motivation but . . . .

> no longer has tantrums unless provoked beyond endurance by those treating him as a child. (p. 76)

In contrast to such opinions, in my study of working class mothers of pre-school children (Duxbury, 1984) I found that every mother felt that her pre-school children were capable of 'playing her up' or demonstrating some form of manipulative[5] behaviour to get their own way. Common tactics were disobedience in public places, pretending to be ill or hurt (usually at meal or bed times), playing one parent off against the other, repetitive demands or questions, monotonous voices or high pitched screaming, self-induced vomiting, headbanging, holding breath or aggressive tantrums.

This confirms findings by Andreski (1966) who identified seventeen forms[6] of deliberate behaviour to gain the mother's attention. She questioned whether children may be responsible for the way parents react to them, and suggested that ...

> all infants have to some extent, a pattern of behaviour which can damage parent's attitudes so badly as to repercuss on the child itself. (p. 906)

It seems that a child demanding the total attention of the parent is impossible to ignore yet difficult to satisfy within the confines of an isolated nuclear family.

Actions of a very young baby may be accepted as instinctive, yet later as Andreski pointed out ...

> a number of elaborate techniques for controlling the parent come into play, compared with which the parents or teachers techniques for controlling the child are feeble. (p. 906)

Below are some examples from my study which show how children, confined to one isolated relationship with an adult, can skillfully choose the time and place to be most effective. As one of the mothers interviewed explained, they do it ...

> outside, in front of other people. They know the exact minute to say something wrong, where other people get hold of the wrong end of the stick. It's a knack kids have of making you feel little, especially with other people. (*Paula Maurice*)

Shops were a particular favourite, probably because of their unsuitability for young children. They demanded sweets or toys, played with goods or ran away.... .

> He just bursts into Fine Fare, whizzing all round the place, really making a show of you. They do play you up, there is no doubt about it. (*Fran Longford*)

Eighty-three per cent of the mothers[7] felt their children 'played up' more in public places or other people's houses, the very time when their effectiveness as a parent was under public scrutiny. Several children were so successful in their tactics that their mothers were so humiliated they went home ...

> I've walked out of the Arndale in shame before now because of the way Becky's screamed. I smack her then I've got people saying 'you shouldn't be doing that in the street' ... they all stand there in judgment of you. (*Marie Marsden*)

Most mothers felt their children were manipulative for a particular reason and could be quite ruthless, as the following mothers discussed why their children acted this way.

> She did it because I got upset basically, and because the others took notice. (*Sharon Whitley*)

> Just to get their own way, they know it gets on your nerves. (*Edith Whitchurch*)

> To get what they want, they see a good chance of getting a packet of sweets and they know they can upset you. (*Marie Marsden*)

More seriously, a child could exploit a mother at her most vulnerable, as Paula Maurice's daughter did after her husband left home. She commented:

> They know your weak spots and exactly how to hurt you. Natalie used to say 'I'll eat my tea when my dad gets home', knowing full well he wasn't coming.

Arguably, Natalie was trying to make sense of the fact that it was also her father who had left and hoped her actions may speed up his return.

Children sensing differences of opinions between parents could effectively cause a greater rift by playing one off against the other, usually over matters of discipline as Marie Marsden described:

> They put us up against each other, if she comes in and asks for something and I say 'no', she goes and asks him, and if he says 'yes' that causes another row.

Children of this age can be particularly demanding of their mothers' time, attention, or for food and material goods, 55 per cent of my sample felt that their children constantly demanded all of these things. They described the repetitive stream of demands children made on them:

> If Louise says something and you don't answer her straight away, she goes on 'I wanna cake, I wanna cake, mummy I wanna cake'. I say 'Yes Louise but I'm doing something'. She gives it a break for a few seconds then she starts again. (*Joan Eyres*)

Tracy Hobkirk agreed:

> Our Becky keeps on talking and if you don't answer her she

carries on and on like a record player so you've got to answer her.

Children in this study also utilized a particular intonation of voice, a whine or high pitched screech or reversion to baby talk, which if kept up long enough drove even determined parents into submission:

It's like a voice from the dead, I can't stick it, I go mad and say 'shut up'. Terrible it is, really bad. (*Paula Maurice*).

Fran Langford said her son says 'I want sweets, I want sweets', he just keeps repeating things you feel like doing yourself in.

Clearly, children have great powers of endurance to keep up the tactics for long periods until they work.

The other night Gemma was awake from 1.00 till 3.30 and all she said was 'Mum' she was whining till I answered her. It'd nearly cracked me up in the night. I tried ignoring her then I answered her. She'd stop when I went to her, she'd want a butty or a drink and I'd no sooner get in bed and she'd start up again. It's the droning and she knows it works. It must drive her mad saying it. (*Marie Marsden*)

Andreski (1966) believes such tactics:

resemble both in application and result the more refined methods of interrogation and brainwashing. (p. 706)

Nearly every mother, 93 per cent, felt that their child was conscious of their actions, a perception which would challenge the notion of such behaviour being an inevitable outcome of their stage of development. One mother described her son's behaviour when she brought her new baby home. As his way of regaining attention he developed a stutter and a twitch ...

but he only did it if he thought you were watching him ... first of all we told him to stop it — he looked silly, then we ignored it. A few weeks ago he said 'remember when I used to do that with my eyes?' (twitching), so he did know he was doing it.' (*Viv Fitzmorris*)

Similarly, her daughter later tried holding her breath ...

but only if I was in the room. If I put her upstairs and she was crying she wouldn't do it.

Several children tried vomiting on purpose to distress parents or get their own way:

Sharon's put her fingers down her throat, she sulks first — if you took no notice of the sulk she used to say 'I'll throw up', and I'd say well go on it won't hurt me, and she'd go upstairs and put her fingers down her throat and do it in the toilet. She'd say 'come and see' and I'd say 'I don't want to see', and when you'd flush it without looking she'd go mad. She stopped doing it then. (*Paula Maurice*)

Other children even pretended to hurt themselves to see how parents reacted. Becky, aged 2, copied Gemma, aged 3, banging her head on the floor:

The first time Becky did it a bit too hard and must have thought 'I'm not doing that again, it hurts' so we watched her, she'd pretend to bang her head on the floor and miss it by that much (½") but she'd scream as if she was banging it. (*Marie Marsden*)

Forty-five per cent of the mothers admitted that their children had held their breath, banged their heads or vomited on purpose, the true figure was probably higher. De Lissovoy (1959) noted that the incidence of head banging in children was greater among lighter birthweight babies, mothers with more than average ailments in pregnancy and mothers of higher anxiety scores. All these factors are more likely among women of low socioeconomic groups.

Probably the greatest display of manipulation was the temper tantrum, which the Newsons (1968), believe is the plainest demonstration of defiance and the most shaming of all children's behaviour. They noted that as the social scale descended parents tend to be more 'ad hoc' or indulgent in their childcare practices, and the incidence of tantrums increases. Seventy-two per cent of the mothers in my study had witnessed temper tantrums in their children. Several more had been witnessed by nursery staff in the prescence of the parents, who later denied the behaviour. These outbursts of violent behaviour often frightened inexperienced mothers who felt that they did not know how to handle it.

My data also suggested that once a type of behaviour had proved to be successful the child tended to repeat it. According to Andreski (1966) actions become more sophisticated as a child develops and adapts to the individual susceptibilities of the mother. One mother recalled:

If John didn't get all his own way he used to take a run and throw himself on his stomach and scream and bang his feet and hands. One day I picked him up and smacked him hard and he never did it again. (*Marylin Kearsley*)

Fan Langford found it particularly difficult to control her 3-year-old son; she felt that it was because he had had so much attention as an infant because of a congenital deformity:

with him being the way he is, he's had a lot of attention, usually if he can't get all his own way he does a war dance, he throws things, books and everything, he's very jealous of Michael, if people talk to him Daniel starts getting violent, taking it out on him, hitting out.

Many women had sought the advice of health visitors, doctors or older women who invariably told them to stand up to the child or give him/her a smack. The Newsons (1968), confirm that 'children of 4 are fairly sophisticated social manipulators, capable of consciously exerting social pressure on other people' (p. 427). They agreed that situations of conflict arising between parents and children in our contemporary cultural pattern derive from two facts: that children are fully capable of fighting for their own interests but also that parents are willing to concede to this auton-omous role and may even protect the child's illusions of independence and free will even if they thereby create a more vigorous opposition to their own authority.

Andreski (1966) stresses that manipulative forms of behaviour make mothers feel guilty and inadequate and eventually make them incapable of performing their housework or childcare effectively. Children may succeed in frightening their mothers but may also frighten themelves by turning the game into a crisis. As Sandra Johnson and her sister described:

Sandra wanted Carl to sit in the bath an he wanted to stand, so she forced him to sit and he held his breath. He used to hold his breath that long Sandra used to panic. I did the routine of breath-ing down his mouth and patting him on the back, but he couldn't come out of it, he'd held it that long and passed out.

In this case their doctor was so concerned he sent the child for a brain scan but concluded he was perfectly healthy, 'just a very bad tempered boy'.

Not all manipulative behaviour is so apparently negative. Ninety-seven per cent of the mothers felt that their children could get round them by 'turning on the charm or affection'. This is particularly difficult to resist when affection from the child can also be the greatest reward for a parent. Children quickly learn to use it to their advantage. However as Lesley Finighan pointed out:

They can put a sentence together so nicely and so cutely that you couldn't say no because it's so nice the way they've phrased it and very crafty. You think 'I won't fall for that one again', but you do.

This tactic was often employed to detract from a mothers' annoyance at her child:

The other day I was annoyed at our Louise, I yelled at her and she just sits and talks under her breath, then she comes and puts her arms around me 'I love you mummy, do you love me an all?' and I can't say no. What can I say?, she gets round me that way.

These types of behaviour could not simply be defined in terms of a child's 'stage of development' because their behaviour was seen to alter in different circumstances, for example in public places or at home, with different parents or other people. Nearly all the mothers felt children behaved better for other people and most agreed that fathers were less susceptible to manipulation than mothers, mainly due to the fact that they were not in constant contact with the child who could wear a mother down over long periods. Most felt their children were more open and straight forward with fathers, accepted their word more readily or asked mothers to negotiate for them. The three lone parents in the group felt particularly vulnerable to manipulation as they had no one to hand the child over to at times of stress. Working mothers are also vulnerable, according to Keiran (1970) because they buy sweets and toys to compensate for their guilt at leaving their children, who in turn take advantage of this and demand more compensation.

It seems likely that this type of behaviour is a by-product of modern child rearing in a Western society which, according to Greer (1971) breeds on unhealthy intimacy between mother and child. Comer (1974) adds that because the child is at the mercy of one person's arbitrary authority, the potential for a 'dynamic of mutual tyranny with bribery and blackmail as its central theme' (p. 198) arises. Oakley (1974) stresses that it is in the very position of motherhood in society which causes mothers to avenge their frustration on small children by aggression or smothering affection. It can be argued that such a position has been affected by medicalized childbirth and the privatization of families away from social contact and female support. Other contributing factors may include prescriptive childcare philosophies the focus on child centredness, changing attitudes to discipline and a materialistic society which perpetuates romantic illusions of motherhood. These act to isolate women from the adult world and from participating in the labour market on equal terms, yet fail to provide the resources and facilities to perform their role adequately.

Conclusion

This chapter has outlined the development of theories and philosophies on childcare, motherhood, development and psychology and through the case study I have traced their impact upon parents and children in the 1980s. This focussed particularly on pre-school children and on their demonstration of manipulative behaviour performed within the confines of privatized childcare. The chapter challenges the view that these forms of behaviour are natural, universal and merely an indication of the child's 'stage' of development noting contrary evidence from cross-cultural and historical sources. The argument does not suggest that young children are inherently evil — for these same children are capable of consideration, intelligence, sensitivity and cooperation. Neither does it attribute blame on working class mothers for their so called 'inadequacies' for, as Boulton (1983) pointed out, frustration with pre-school childcare is not confined to any social class, and as Tizard and Hughes (1984) stressed, the working class home can often be a richer source of language and stimulation than the nursery school because it does not restrict children from everyday issues and events.

I would, however, argue that the very theories and philosophies which were supposed to liberate and individualize children, and to sanctify and professionalize motherhood, have become an added constraint particularly upon those in the most disadvantaged groups in society. The 'ideal' created by the literature is impossible to achieve within a multiplicity of social, economic and ideological constraints and creates a seam of guilt and doubt in the mothers' role which is quickly exploited by young children via manipulation, their own conscious reaction to the contradictory position they share with their parents.

In order to fully recognize the structural location and rights of women and mothers and to appreciate the needs and potential of young children, it would be necessary to adopt alternative types of childcare practices and philosophies. These would not perpetuate competitiveness, aggression and possessiveness, nor demand isolated privatized childcare performed principally by women. Instead, positive, sociable and constructive behaviour could be nurtured and the need to resort to manipulative strategies would be invalidated.

Notes

1 The study was carried out when I was a teacher in charge of a nursery class on a Merseyside council estate. It comprised of recorded conversations with sixty working class mothers, over a twelve-month period followed by in-depth tape recorded interviews with a further thirty the following year. The responses and percentages included here are from the latter group and all names are ficticious.
2 Male midwives became associated with surgical and obstetirc techniques leaving female midwives to 'normal' non-surgical deliveries. Women were excluded from medical and surgical training relegating female midwives to secondary status and excluding lay midwives altogether.
3 NCB concludes that pre-school children adjust better to mothers' working than do older children, and that behaviour adjustment is generally unrelated to female employment (1977).
4 According to the NSPCC, only 17 per cent of children on the abuse registers have working mothers compared to 51 per cent national average (in Rutter, 1972).
5 Defined by the Oxford English Dictionary as to 'manage (persons) by dextrous (especially unfair) use of influence. To handle or treat with skill.
6 These included: repetition of syllables in anguished tone; affectation of heavy breathing if mother turns away; throwing objects to be retrieved by parent; touching forbidden objects; demanding food then discarding it; demanding food and refusing to let parents prepare it; jamming adult conversations, precarious

climing; continuous leaping or sittng on parent; continuous questions when uninterested in answers; supernumerary requests for potty; aggressive or monotonous singing; aimless tormenting of younger child or pet; requests for stories not listened to disingenuous requests for affection only if parent is talking to another, continuous chatter at top of voice.

7 Of the thirty women in the final sample group .

References

ANDRESKI, I. (1966) 'The baby as dictator', *New Society*, 15 December, pp. 906–7.

ANDREY, R. (1960) *Delinquency and Paternal Pathology*, London, Methuen.

BODEN, M.A. (1979) *Piaget*, Sussex, Harvester Press.

BORKE, H. (1978) 'Piaget's view of social interaction and empathy' in SIEGEL, L. and BRAINERD, C.J. (Eds) *Alternatives to Piaget*, London, Academic Press.

BOULTON, M.G. (1983) *On Being a Mother*, London, Tavistock.

BOWLBY, J. (1953) *Childcare and the Growth of Love*, Harmondsworth, Penguin.

BROWN, E. and HARRIS, T. (1978) *The Social Origins of Depression*, London, Tavistock.

COMER, L. (1974) *Wedlocked Women*, Leeds, Feminist Books.

DEEM, R. (1981) 'State policy and ideology in the education of women', *British Journal of Education*, 2, 2, pp. 131–44.

DINGWALL, R. *et al.* (1977) *Health Care and health Knowledge*, London, Croom Helm.

DONALDSON, M. (1978) *Children's Minds*, London, Fontana.

DUXBURY, S. (1984) 'An examination of the constraints upon women's lives, with particular reference to a group of working-class mothers of pre-school children', unpublished MLit thesis, University of Lancaster.

DUXBURY, S. (1986) 'A comparative review of contemporary pre-school provision', in BROWN, N. and FRANCE, P. (Eds) *Untying the Apron Strings*, Milton Keynes, Open University Press.

DE LISSOVOY, V. (1959) 'Headbanging in early childhood', unpublished PhD thesis, Cornell University.

GRAHAM, H (1977) 'Images of pregnancy in ante-natal literature' in DINGWALL, R. *et al.* (Eds) *Health Care and Health Knowledge*, London, Croom Helm.

GREER, G. (1971) *The Female Eunuch*, Herts, Paladin.

HADFIELD, A. (1962) *Childhood and Adolescence*, Harmondsworth, Penguin.

HENRIQUES, J. *et al.* (1984) *Changing the Subject: Psychology, Social Regulation and Subjectivity*, London, Methuen.

KELLMER-PRINGLE, M. (1980) *A Fairer Start for our Children*, London, Macmillan.

KEIRAN, P. (1970) *How Working Mothers Manage*, London, Clifton.

KITZINGER, S. (1978) *Women as Mothers*, Glasgow, Fontana.

LEACH, P. (1978) *Who Cares?*, Harmondsworth, Penguin.

LEWIS, J. (1980) *The Politics of Motherhood*, London, Croom Helm.

MARTIN, J. and ROBERTS, C. (1984) *Women and Employement*, London, DES/OPCS.

MINTERN, L. and LAMBERT, W. (1964) 'Mothers of six cultures' cited in BOULTON, M.G. *On Being a Mother*, London, Tavistock.

NATIONAL CHILDREN'S BUREAU (1977) *Development Guide Handbook 0-5 Years*, London, National Children's Bureau.

NEWSOM, J. and E. (1968) *Four Years Old in an Urban Community*, Harmondsworth, Penguin.

OAKLEY, A. (1974) *Housewife*, London, Allen Lane.

OAKLEY, A. (1976) 'Wise women and medicine man' in MITCHELL, J. and OAKLEY, A.

(Eds) *Rights and Wrongs of Women*, Harmondsworth, Penguin.

PENN, H. (1984) 'The Jugoslavian way of looking after children', *The Guardian*, 2 February.

PIAGET, J. (1968) 'Le structuralism', PVF, Paris.

RILEY, D. (1983) *War in the Nursery*, London, Virago.

RUTTER, M. (1972) *Maternal Deprivation Reassessed*, Harmondsworth, Penguin.

SIEGEL, L. and BRAINERD, C.J. (1978) *Alternatives to Piaget*, London, Academic Press.

SPOCK, B. (1946) 'Baby and childcare', excerpts in REBELSKY, F. and DORMAN, L. (Eds) (1970) *Child Development and Behaviour*, New York, Alfred Knopf.

THOMPSON, T. (1972) 'The lost world of childhood', *New Society*, 5 October.

TIZARD, B. and HUGHES, M. (1984) *Young Children Learning*, London, Fontana.

WALKERDINE, V. (1983) 'It's only natural: Rethinking child-centred pedagogy' in WOLPE, A.M. and DONALD, J. (Eds) *Is There Anyone There From Education?*, London, Pluto Press.

WALKERDINE, V. (1984) 'Developmental psychology and the child-centred pedagogy' in HENRIQUES, J. *et al.* (Eds) *Changing the Subject: Psychology, Social Regulation and Subjectivity*, London, Methuen.

2   The Intellectual Search of Young Children

Barbara Tizard and Martin Hughes

Editor's Note

This chapter is derived from a study of the learning of young children funded by the ESRC and DHSS (Tizard and Hughes, 1984). In this research thirty 4-year-old girls were studied in detail. Tape-recordings were made, using radio-microphones, of their conversations at morning nursery school and at home with their mothers in the afternoon. The children attended nine different schools and the sample was designed to enable comparisons between working class and middle class linguistic environments to be made.

Introduction

The following conversation took place while a mother and child were having lunch together, with the baby on the floor. Apprently out of the blue, Mina started to talk about tigers:

Child: Do you like tigers? Do you?
Mother: Tigers?
Child: Mm.
Mother: I like to look at tigers, yeah, they're lovely.
Child: Tigers!
Mother: Yeah, they're lovely to look at, they're really lovely. See them running. Nice to watch them in the zoo.
Child: No, real ones.
Mother: Mm. I don't like to go too near them though in case they try and eat me.

At this point Mina became puzzled. Her puzzlement was probably related to a remark of her mother's a little earlier that the baby couldn't swallow her rattle, since it was too big to go in her mouth. Hence, Mina seemed to be reasoning, a tiger couldn't dispose of her mother.

Child: They won't.
Mother: They might.
Child: Do they ... do they eat you? [Puzzled]
Mother: No, if they were hungry they might try.
Child: Have they got mouths — small mouths?
Mother: No, they've got great big mouths.
Child: Your size?

Mina's question is ambiguous. 'Your size?' could mean either that tigers' mouths are as big as her mother's mouth, or as big as her mother's body. Her mother interprets the question in the former sense:

Mother: Pardon?
Child: Your size?
Mother: What, you think I've got a great big mouth?
Child: No, the tigers.

Mina's reply indicates that there has been a misunderstanding, which her mother, by then asking 'What do you mean?', expects her to clarify. Whether or not Mina was up to this task we shall never know, because her mother makes an imaginative leap to the other possible meaning. Having made this leap, one might have expected Mina's mother to follow up the child's questions, but in fact she allows the conversation to fizzle out:

Mother: What do you mean?
Child: Got a big ...
Mother: Oh, their mouths the same size as me? [Holds her arms to show the size of the whole body rather than just her mouth]
Child: Oh uh um.
Mother: No, not that big.
Child: Why?
Mother: They're just not.

As was often the case, no explicit clarification occurred, and the conversation lapsed. The child's final 'Why?' suggests that she still failed to understand how her mother could fit into the tiger's mouth.

The Concept of Intellectual Search

Mina's conversation about the tiger is an example of what we decided to call *a passage of intellectual search*. This is a conversation in which the child is actively seeking new information or explanations, or puzzling over something she does not understand, or trying to make sense of an apparent anomaly in her limited knowledge of the world. Such episodes are characterized by a sequence of persistent questioning on the part of the child, in which she considers the adult's answers and relates them to her existing knowledge; this in turn may lead to further questions on the same topic. 'Passages of intellectual search' reveal both the strengths of the child — her persistence, her logic, and her ability to assimilate complex ideas — and the frailty of her knowledge, or the naivety of her misconceptions. (see Tizard and Hughes, 1984, chapter 6).

The concept of Father Christmas gave rise to several passages of intellectual search. At this age, children are beginning to puzzle over the multiple inconsistencies in the Father Christmas myth. At the same time, they do not have a firm grasp of some of the basic aspects of the story — for example, that Father Christmas only visits at Christmas time. In the following conversation Penny is mainly concerned to establish what steps are required in order to get the Christmas present she wants. The conversation arose apparently out of the blue, when Penny was making a card for a friend's birthday, and her mother was looking at a catalogue. Penny's mother had promised to buy her a doll's ballerina outfit for her next birthday, and Penny was thinking through the implications of this promise. Presumably she knew from her own experience of getting and giving presents that she would be unlikely to accompany her mother when she bought the ballerina outfit. In this case, she reasoned, someone would have to look after her:

Child: Mummy, who will look after me when you get the 'dancellina' for my birthday?
Mother: Your birthday's not till next year, love.
Child: No, I know, I don't … I mean that …
Mother: Who will look after you? I expect we'll probably get it when you're at school or something.
Child: Oh …
Mother: Might have it from Father Christmas.
Child: No … oh yeah! [Excited]
Mother: You'd have it much sooner.
Child: I'll have to go in his house and ask him.
Mother: You often see Father Christmases in the shops around Christmas time. You could ask him for a ballerina outfit for your little doll.

There is a short digression while Penny and her mother discuss Penny's dressing up as a ballerina at nursery that morning. Penny, however, is still thinking about Father Christmas and the ballerina outfit, and she spontaneously returns to the topic:

Child: Does Father Christmas … give me … does Father Christmas say 'No' if he hasn't got a … hasn't got a … dancellina one?

Mother:	Well, he usually does have those things.
Child:	Will *you* ask him?
Mother:	We'll do what you did last year, and you can write a letter to him. Remember?
Child:	And what will he say if I write a letter to him?
Mother:	He'll say, 'This looks a nice letter, I'll see what I can get. She wants a dancer's outfit.'
Child:	He won't know my name.
Mother:	He will if you put your name on the bottom.

Penny then asks her mother to write to Father Christmas, and her mother explains that it is much too early in the year to do so.

As well as demonstrating Penny's ability to work out what Father Christmas might or might not know, this conversation contains several features which characterize intellectual search in 4-year-olds. First, there is the way in which Penny returns to the topic that is puzzling her, even though the conversation has moved on. We saw several instances of children repeatedly returning to a topic that was preoccupying their thoughts in the course of an afternoon, so that a topic that apparently arose out of the blue might be a throwback to an earlier conversation over which the child had been brooding. Secondly, there is the difficulty which Penny has on more than one occasion in expressing herself. This was not so much a characteristic of Penny — who was normally an articulate child — but more a general feature of intellectual effort. There were a number of occasions when a normally articulate child would become hesitant and inarticulate, and these were usually occasions when she was struggling to express a particularly difficult or novel idea. Finally, there is the logic and consistency which Penny brings to her projection into the future. Clearly she does not subscribe to the idea that Father Christmas is an omniscient figure who knows exactly what every child wants. Rather, she treats him as an ordinary mortal who is constrained by normal human limitations — he might run out of ballerina outfits, he will have to be told by Penny what she wants, and he will not know her name unless he is also given this bit of information.

Susan, also, was confused about several aspects of the Father Christmas story. The following conversation arose when she was playing with a toy handbag, and her mother remarked how pretty it was:

Child:	Did Father Christmas give it to me?
Mother:	Ah, I think he did. Not this Christmas though . . . nor last Christmas.
Child:	Did he give it to me for my birthday?
Mother:	What, Father Christmas? He doesn't come on your birthday.
Child:	When does he come?
Mother:	Christmas. That's why he's called Father Christmas. Did you see him last Christmas?

Child:	No! Did you?
Mother:	No. I didn't see him. I was asleep.
Child:	We wasn't. We was thinking if Father Christmas was out of window.
Mother:	And was he?
Child:	We didn't have a look out of the window. We only thinked.

The conversation moves on to discuss who had been staying with Susan the previous Christmas, and the games they had all played together. But, as with Penny, Susan is still thinking about Father Christmas:

Child:	Mummy?
Mother:	Mm.
Child:	Did you think if Father Christmas was coming here?
Mother:	I knew he was going to come, yeah.
Child:	Did you think he was coming down the chimney?
Mother:	No, I didn't think he was coming down the chimney. 'Cause we haven't got a fireplace.
Child:	Why haven't we?
Mother:	Well, we've blocked them all in ... we left the basement door open, didn't we, so that Father Christmas could come in.
Child:	Last year?
Mother:	Mm.
Child:	Must have been windy.

For some reason, Susan's mother failed to grasp what she meant by this inference, and asked, 'Why must it have been windy?', although it seems clear to us that she was referring to the effect of leaving the basement door open. Susan ignored the question, and returned again to the puzzle of Father Christmas's visit:

Child:	Why did you let Father Christmas in?
Mother:	Well, he had to bring your presents in.
Child:	I didn't know he was coming in here.
Mother:	Well, where did you think he was going to take them?
Child:	Did he, did he, didn't he, know if he, if he know like our house was?
Mother:	Oh, he knows where all the children's houses are.
Child:	I mean, doesn't he know what, what, what like it is?
Mother:	What it looks like? [Child nods] I expect he does. He's been here before hasn't he?
Child:	Had he?
Mother:	Mm, he came the year before.

The conversation continued with further questions from Susan about what Father Christmas brought the presents in (a sack, she was told) and whether the sack was too heavy for him.

This episode illustrates again many of the features of intellectual search we saw in Penny's conversation — the way in which the child returns to the topic that is puzzling her, her occasional lapses from articulateness when she is struggling to express a difficult idea, and the logical and persistent manner in which she pursues the topic. Yet there are differences between the two conversations, particularly in the way in which the child's conceptions of Father Christmas are exposed.

The conversation involving Penny gave us little insight into her conception of Father Christmas, apart from her treatment of him as a fairly human figure. In contrast, Susan's conversation reveals much more of her beliefs. At the start of the conversation she seems to think that Father Christmas gives her birthday presents as well as Christmas presents. Later she wonders if her mother thought he came down the chimney, apparently not having assimilated the fact that the fireplaces are blocked up. She goes on to express surprise that he came into the house at all, and then starts to wonder how Father Chrismas knows what her house looks like. She also does not realize that he is supposed to pay annual visits. Her last questions are indeed very similar to Penny's and suggest that young children start from a more human idea of Father Christmas and work outwards, rather than starting from a more omniscient view of him and then discovering his more human limitations.

Clearly the concept of Father Christmas is not an easy one for children to grasp, given the haziness with which he is surrounded and the lack of logical consistency within the concept itself. It is not at all surprising that they should have misconceptions about the myth, which can only be clarified by the kind of conversations we have quoted. These two conversations also demonstrate the ability of the young child to project imaginatively into another person's perspective, and make realistic assumptions about what that person might or might not be expected to know. We were impressed with how frequently they did this, and by their ready interest in exploring other people's motivations, knowledge, and points of view.

Intellectual Search: Struggling with Several Complex Ideas

The learning potential of what we have called 'passages of intellectual search' is well illustrated in the following long episode, in which the child's confusion about the relationship between money, work and consumer goods was exposed, and to some extent clarified. The conversation started while Rosy and her mother were having lunch, and was triggered off by the appearance of the window-cleaner in the garden. Rosy's mother went off to the kitchen to get him some water, and called out to her neighbour, Pamela.

Child: What did Pamela say?

Mother: She's having to pay everybody else's bills for the window-cleaner, 'cause they're all out.

Child: Why they all out?

Mother: 'Cause they're working or something.

Child: Aren't they silly!

Mother: Well, you have to work to earn money, don't you?

Child: Yeah ... If they know what day the window-cleaner come they should stay here.

Mother: They should stay at home? Well, I don't know, they can't always ...

At this point the window-cleaner appeared at the dining-room window, and cleaned the window while Rosy and her mother carried on with lunch. The conversation switched to what they might have for pudding, and what they might do that afternoon. Rosy, however, was still thinking about the window-cleaner ...

1 Child: Mummy?

2 Mother: Mmm.

3 Child: Umm ... she can't pay everybody's, er ... all the bills to the window-cleaner, can she?

4 Mother: No, she can't pay everybody's bills ... she sometimes pays mine if I'm out.

5 Child: 'Cause it's fair.

6 Mother: Mm, it is.

7 Child: Umm, but where does she leave the money?

8 Mother: She doesn't leave it anywhere, she hands it to the window-cleaner, after he's finished.

9 Child: And then she gives it to us?

10 Mother: No, no, she doesn't have to pay us.

11 Child: Then the window-cleaner gives it to us?

12 Mother: No, we give the window-cleaner money, he does work for us, and we have to give him money.

13 Child: Why?

14 Mother: Well, because he's been working for us cleaning our windows. He doesn't do it for nothing.

15 Child: Why do you have money if you have ... if people clean your windows?

16 Mother: Well, the window-cleaner needs money, doesn't he?

17 Child: Why?

18 Mother: To buy clothes for his children and food for them to eat.

19 Child: Well, sometimes window-cleaners don't have children.

20 Mother: Quite often they do.

21 *Child*:   And something on his own to eat, and for curtains?
22 *Mother*:   And for paying his gas bills and electricity bill. And for paying for his petrol for his car. All sorts of things you have to pay for, you see. You have to earn money somehow, and he earns it by cleaning other people's windows, and big shop windows and things.
23 *Child*:   And then the person who got the money gives it to people . . .

It seems until turn 11 Rosy was under the impression that the window-cleaner pays the housewives, and not the other way round. In the course of the conversation the relationship between work, money and goods is slowly outlined for her, but it is still unclear from her last remark whether she has really grasped all that has been said. The conversation in fact continues later on, after Rosy has watched her mother actually hand over the money to the window-cleaner:

1 *Mother*:   I expect the window-cleaner's going to have his lunch now.
2 *Child*:   He would have all *that* much lunch [stretches arms out wide] because he's been working all the time.
3 *Mother*:   Mm . . . I expect he gets very hungry, doesn't he? I expect he goes to the pub and has some beer and sandwiches.
4 *Child*:   He has to pay for that.
5 *Mother*:   Yes, he does.
6 *Child*:   Not always, though.
7 *Mother*:   Mm, always.
8 *Child*:   Why not?
9 *Mother*:   They won't give him any beer and sandwiches if he doesn't have any money.

At this point Rosy clearly wonders why he cannot do without money to go to a pub:

10 *Child*:   But why doesn't he use his own food?
11 *Mother*:   Well, he might do, I don't know, perhaps he brings his own sandwiches, do you think?
12 *Child*:   He go to a pub and he has his lunch some *and* he has it at his home.
13 *Mother*:   Oh, he wouldn't do both, no.
14 *Child*:   He would do all of those a few times. But he usually go to a pub.

Rosy's mother ends the conversation, with an example of 'planning ahead' child management, (see Tizard and Huges, 1984, chapter 4)

15 *Mother*:   Mm. Come on, sit up. Now I'm going to do the

washing up, then I'll read you a story, and then I'm going to read the newspaper a bit.

Rosy's remarks in this third conversation (especially turn 6, 'Not always, though') suggest that she has only hazily grasped what she has been told, and her understanding of money transactions still seems shaky. This is not because she lacked the intellectual capacity, nor because her mother's explanations were too complex. Rather it seems likely that this conversation reveals something which is characteristic of the slow and gradual way in which a child's understanding of an abstract or complex topic is built up. It may take a considerable time, as well as several more coversatons like the one above, before Rosy has grasped the complexities of the relationships involved, and she may have to return to the same topic again and again before she achieves full understanding.

It is interesting to consider why Rosy keeps asking questions on this topic. Clearly, her initial questions were asked out of curiosity aroused by the unusual event in the daily routine — the arrival of the window-cleaner and the subsequent conversation between her mother and the neighbour. But her later return to the topic suggests something beyond this initial curiosity. Indeed, it suggests that Rosy is at some level aware that she has not grasped the relationships involved, and that her questions are motivated by her desire to clarify her misconceptions. Why she should be aware of her own lack of understanding is not clear — she could perfectly well have stayed with the idea that the neighbour did receive money from the window-cleaner, and got on with her lunch. The fact that she did not suggests that she was at some level dissatisfied with her own grasp of the situation, perhaps because it didn't fit with other facts that she knew, and wanted it sorted out.

Confusion about the relationship between work, money and goods seemed to be less common among the working-class children. Perhaps because their fathers' work was more clearly related to money, rather than to the interest of the job, or because with a more limited income the arrival of the weekly pay packet was a more important event, the relationship between money and work was more often discussed in working-class families.

Intellectual Search: The Power of a Puzzling Mind

It should be clear by now that mothers often gave answers to the children's questions that were less than full, or that failed to meet the central point of the question. Advances in children's understanding seemed to depend as much on their own efforts to achieve greater clarity as on the quality of their mothers' initial explanations. This point is very clearly ex-emplified in the following conversation. Beth, aged 3 years and 10 months, and her mother were having lunch together. The conversation was preceded and succeeded by silence:

Child: Is our roof a sloping roof?

Mother: Mmm. We've got two sloping roofs, and they sort of meet in the middle.

Child: Why have we?

Mother: Oh, it's just the way our house is built. Most people have sloping roofs, so that the rain can run off them. Otherwise, if you have a flat roof, the rain would sit in the middle of the roof and make a big puddle, and then it would start coming through.

Child: Our school has a flat roof, you know.

Mother: Yes it does actually, doesn't it?

Child: And the rain sits there and goes through?

Mother: Well, it doesn't go through. It's probably built with drains so that the water runs away. You have big blocks of flats with rather flat sort of roofs. But houses that were built at the time this house was built usually had sloping roofs.

Child: Does Lara have a sloping roof? [Lara is Beth's friend]

Mother: Mmm. Lara's house is very like ours. In countries where they have a lot of snow, they have even more sloping roofs. So that when they've got a lot of snow, the snow can just fall off.

Child: Whereas, if you have a flat roof, what would it do? Would it just have a drain?

Mother: No, then it would sit on the roof, and when it melted it would make a big puddle.

This episode represents a remarkable attempt by a child not yet 4 to explore an abstract topic. We do not know why she was thinking about sloping roofs in the first instance, as there was nothing in the earlier conversations (which were concerned with how she should eat her lunch and a planned visit to the doctor later that day) which even hinted at this topic. Nevertheless, once the topic was raised, Beth pursues it with a penetrating, remorseless logic. Her mother explains that sloping roofs allow the water the drain off and so prevent rain coming through the roof. However, Beth can think of a counter-example: she knows that her school has a flat roof but rain does not come through the roof there. Beth's mother meets this objection by introducing the idea of a drain, and in the next turn extends the topic by pointing out that countries with a lot of snow need even more sloping roofs. Beth then wonders what happens about snow if you have a flat roof, and reintroduces the idea of a drain: an idea she has assimilated with unusual speed in the short space of time since it was brought up. (Note here her appropriate use of the logical connective 'whereas'.) Her mother explains that the snow melts into a big puddle, although she is perhaps misleading in suggesting that a drain would not be needed to take the melted snow away.

Beth was an exceptionally intelligent and thoughtful child, and it would be wrong to suggest that all the children took part in conversations of this quality. However, the conversation certainly illustrates the potential of intellectual search as a method of learning, as well as demonstrating the power of a very young mind in pursuit of relatively abstract knowledge.

A New Perspective on the Young Child's Mind

Our study of 4-year-old children at home and at nursery school led us to doubt some widely held beliefs and assumptions about the nature of the young child's mind. Most of these beliefs derive from the work of Jean Piaget (for example, Piaget 1926). Piaget's theories are complex, and difficult to present briefly without distortion. Perhaps his major contribution, which is fully supported by our evidence, is that learning is an active process, not a matter of passive absorption. The reader familiar with Piaget's theories will note that the process of intellectual search which we describe, in which the child thinks about the adult's answers to her questions, incorporates them into her thinking and then asks further questions arising from them, strongly resembles Piaget's notion of learning by assimilation and accommodation.

A second major component of Piaget's theory is that the intellectual structures of the child's mind are different from those of an adult. Children think differently from adults, and young children from older children. It is only after innumerable experiences, and reflection on these experiences, that mature forms of thinking develop. Again, we would not dispute this theory. Athough in some of the conversations we have quoted the children are thinking as capably as their mothers, if not more so, in others (sometimes involving the same children) their intellectual limitations are obvious.

However, there are other aspects of Piaget's theory which we, along with a number of other contemporary psychologists, would contest. Piaget held that the active process of learning in childhood is largely dependent on experienceing and responding to innumerable acts of exploration. The process is long and essentially solitary. It follows from Piagetian theory that until the child is six or seven adults can play only a minor part in his or her intellectual development. This notion of the 'exploring' child, learning about the physical world by acting on it, seems to us to capture much of the essence of the very young child. But by the age of 3 or 4, we would argue that dialogue is as important as physical exploration. At this stage the child explores by means of words, as much as through action. And as we have shown, adults can therefore play an important role in advancing the child's understanding through conversation.

Nor do we accept that the young child is as intelletually limited as Piaget believed. According to Piaget, children between the ages 2 and 6 or 7 are at a 'preoperational' stage. They are egocentric, by which he did not mean selfish, but able to see things only from their own perspective. Hence they cannot argue in any real sense, because they do not realize that others may see things differently. They also cannot think logically, because they cannot keep apart statements that exclude or contradict each other. Commonly, they reverse the relation of cause and effect. They have no real understanding of causation, but believe that everything happens because of someone's motivation, or because 'it must be so'.

Our transcripts suggest that young children are much less egocentric and illogical than Piaget believed. We found many examples (as in the 'Father Christmas' conversations) of their awareness of, and interest in, other people's viewpoints. Perhaps the most straightforward example occurred when Ruth had been to the lavatory. She was bending over so that her mother could wipe her bottom. In this position, her mother could not see her head:

Child: Mummy, you lost me.
Mother: I have lost you, yeah.
Child: Can you only see my bottom and legs?
Mother: That's right.
Child: And shoes and pants.
Mother: That's right. Stand up straight.
Child: Here I am.
Mother: That's nice. There she is, back again. Off you go!

This conversation not only revealed Ruth's ability to work out what her mother could see of her, but also showed her expressing this knowledge in a kind of game — 'You lost me' — which her mother readily echoed — 'There she is, back again!' Of course, neither Ruth nor her mother really believed that Ruth had been 'lost', or gone away: rather, the game provided a convenient framework for exploring the situation. There are many parallels here with a task which one of us (MH) devised for studying precisely this ability in preschool children. In this task, the child has to 'hide' a small boy figure from one or more policemen figures who are 'looking for him'. As with Ruth and her bottom, the children in the policemen task found little difficulty in constructing other points of view in the game-like situation.

As well as working out what other people can see, the children frequently demonstrated the ability to calculate or infer what another person might know — or what they might need to know in order to carry out a particular action. Some children are less capable of this than others: we do not want to suggest that these 4-year-olds were as able as adults to look at things or events from another's point of view. In particular, their ability to judge what information must be given to other people so that they could interpret their remarks was not always very well developed. However, this skill is not always deployed by adults: most of us are egocentric from time to time. Our point is that these very young children did not totally lack the ability, but rather seemed to need a good deal more experience in its use.

Moreover, the children seemed extremely interested in other people's viewpoints, and in the way in which they are similar to, and different from, their own. Interest in other people — both children and adults — was a characteristic feature of most of the children in the study, and manifested itself in many different topics: their friends, other members of the family, growing up, birth, illness and death, what people did for their living, and so on. Indeed, it is worth remarking on the breadth of the children's interests, and the complexity of the issues which they raised. It is sometimes supposed that children of this age have special, childish interests, mainly to do with mothers, babies, dolls, teddies and animals, and such a view would be reinforced by most of the picture books published for children of this age. The conversations in our study suggest that, on the contrary, all human experience was grist to their intellectual mill.

Nor can we accept that young children are illogical, or incapable of making reasonable inferences from the information at this disposal. The transcripts — and particularly the episodes of intellectual search — contained many examples of children pursuing a topic that puzzled them with a painstaking and rigorous logic. While we agree with Piaget that young children's thinking is not the same as adult thinking, we do not believe that the essential difference lies in their illogicality. Instead, we would argue that their two major handicaps are their enormous ignorance and the limited conceptual framework within which their experience and thought is organized.

Although it may seem obvious that young children are very ignorant, this aspect of their functioning is rarely discussed by professionals. An imaginative leap is needed to understand their situation, in which almost everything that adults take for granted has yet to be learned. Because they are such active thinkers, children usually construct their own theories to fill the gaps in their knowledge. These theories surface and can be observed when a misunderstanding is apparent. Rosy's belief that tradespeople supply their customers with money, which emerged in the 'window-cleaner' conversation, is widely held by young children, although parents are not always aware of it. One child in our study, Sandra, made it clear by a request to her mother that she believed that the street lights were controlled from a switch in her living room. Another child, Pauline, appeared to believe that people with the same first name also have the same surname:

> *New Teacher*: What's your other name, Pauline who?
> *Child*: Pauline Robinson. I've got two Pauline Robinsons.

Teacher:	Two Pauline Robinsons? Who's the other one?
Child:	Pauline there [pointing to other child called Pauline].
Teacher:	We've got another Pauline? Yes, I don't think she's Pauline Robinson. Got Pauline, the same name as you. I think she has another name that's different from you.

Vida, possibly confused by a well-known children's TV programme, thought that clocks told the day of the week. She was playing with a toy clock, and the day was Wednesday:

Child:	Where's Wednesday?
Mother:	Where's Wednesday?
Child:	Mm.
Mother:	Today.
Child:	Where is it? Which number?
Mother:	It's here.
Child:	Where?
Mother:	Where? Oh, no, don't have it on the clock, you have it on a calendar.
Child:	Oh.

Samantha asked for some cream to put on her face because she felt hot. Her mother spotted the cause of her error and corrected her very clearly: 'You don't put cream on when you're hot. You put cream on when you're sunbathing.'

The apparent illogicality of young children is thus often due, in our view, not to faulty logic, but to the fact that somewhere along the route they have taken on board false assumptions, or lack the experience to reject an implausible implication of a particular line of argument. The conversation below, involving a 4-year-old is a good example of this. Her older sister announced that she was going off to help 'get ready' for the party':

Child:	Whose party is it?
Sister:	Franny's Mum and Dad's party.
Child:	Were Franny's Mum and Dad born on the same day?

The child's conclusion is a valid deduction from her limited knowledge. People have parties on their birthdays, and so if two people are having a party on the same day, they must have been born on the same day. The child did not lack logic, but rather lacked the knowledge that adults hold parties for reasons other than birthdays. For this reason we doubt the current theory that it is children's illogicality that makes them willing to believe in the truth of fairy stories. It seems more likely that they accept the reality of Father Christmas, the recovery of Red Riding Hood from the wolf's stomach, or the world that can be found at the bottom of a well, because they lack the knowledge to rule these events out as impossible.

The children's problem in thinking is not just that they lack useful items of information, as, for example, an older child might not know the name of the prime minister. It is rather that they have an imperfect grasp of a vast range of concepts which an older child or adult takes for granted. Thus we have seen children believing that size and age are associated, that adults can 'grow up', that tradespeople pay their customers, that goods don't necessarily have to be paid for. These ideas are not foolish, but stem from their own experience — for example, of seeing shopkeepers giving change to their mothers. A good deal more experience, together with discussion with adults, will be needed to clarify these issues.

The impression we gained was that the mind of the 4-year-old contains a large number of half-assembled scaffoldings which have yet to be integrated into a more coherent framework. At the same time, this lack of completeness allows the young child a certain degree of mental fluidity, in a way that may characteristically differentiate her from older children or adults. Particular objects or events are not necessarily viewed from a single viewpoint — as they might be by an older child or an adult — but may be seen from a number of different viewpoints, some appropriate, some less so. Thus Ruth, seeing bulbs in the garden, called them 'dead onions'. When her mother corrected her, she still persisted in asking, 'Are they dead?' This is not a question for adults, whose conceptual framework is much more fixed: alive and dead are not categories they would normally apply to either onions or bulbs.

This lack of knowledge, and the mental fluidity associated with it, may explain why questions are so prominent in the nursery years. The children in our study seemed in some sense aware that their conceptual framework was not yet substantial enough to cope with their experiences, and engaged themselves actively in the process of improving their intellectual scaffolding. The passages of intellectual search seemed particularly useful in this process, and indicated that the children were at some level aware that protracted dialogue with adults was a useful way of developing their conceptual knowledge. These issues are not only of interest to psychologists, but have a direct bearing on nursery education, and on the kind of advice that is given to parents.

Overview

We have argued that children of 3 or 4 have an intense need to understand their world, reflected in the large number of questions they ask. Analysis of entire conversations, especially 'passages of intellectual search', rather than individual questions, reveals the persistent and logical way in which they try to extend their udnerstanding. It also reveals extensive areas of ignorance, misinformation and misunderstandings. The Piagetian model of children's minds, in our view, underestimates their thinking capacities, and fails to appreciate the way in which adults can help them to clarify their ideas.

References

HUGHES, M. and DONALDSON, M. (1979) 'The use of hiding games for studying the coordination of viewpoints', *Educational Review*, 31, pp. 133–40.

PIAGET, J. (1926) *The Language and Thought of the Child*, London, Routledge and Kegan Paul.

TIZARD, B. and HUGHES, M. (1984) *Young Children Learning*, London, Fontana.

3   The Accomplishment of Genderedness in Pre-School Children

Bronwyn Davies

Introduction

Gender is a central defining feature of people in our society. In order to interact comfortably we each need to know the gender of the person we are interacting with and we need, in return, to act in such a way that we do not lead others to misconstrue our own gender. Our taken-for-granted knowledge about gender is that maleness and femaleness are the only and mutually exclusive categories relevant to gender. Part of being a competent member of society derives from our capacity to attribute to others, and to aid others in attributing to ourselves, the 'correct' gender identity. The work that we do to cue others to our gender is also done for ourselves in the sense that we each have an emotional commitment to the gender we have been assigned (cf. Kessler and McKenna, 1985). This commitment is developed at a very early age. As Kessler and McKenna (1985) point out:

> Most of the evidence for the development of gender identity during a critical period comes from cases where the initial assignment was deemed in error and an attempt was made to 'correct' it by re-assigning the child and making the necessary physical changes. Almost all attempts of this sort made after the age of about three are unsuccessful, in that the individual either retains her/his original gender identity or becomes extremely confused and ambivalent. (p. 10).

By about the age of 3, then, we have learned the rules associated with competent presentation of self as male or female, and it is difficult if not impossible to unlearn these rules and to learn the rules appropriate to the alternate gender. This difficulty is presumably exacerbated by the fact that part of the definition of maleness, in particular, is 'not-femaleness'.

Thus gender is central to each person's identity (cf. Thompson, 1975) and each child is faced with the task of discovering how maleness and femaleness is elaborated in the everyday world, and of accomplishing for themselves their 'genderedness'. This accomplishment enables them to be perceived by others as 'normal', competent members of the social scenes in which they are engaged.

In what follows I will use children's responses to liberating stories (Zipes, 1982) to show the ways in which small children deal with the differences between the world as it is being socially constructed and understood by them, and the liberating messages which are *potentially* available in their play and in their stories.

The central problem that children face in understanding and accepting non-traditional messages, is to know how a person (real or mythical) who acts *outside* of what is commonly understood as appropriate for their gender, can be *recognized* as expanding what is positively available to other like-gendered people. It is not enough that the model be there — i.e. that the non-conventional action be engaged in by a known person or known hero. It is essential that there is, as well, a conceptual framework which allows that person to be located not only as a positive member of his/her gender but to be seen to be behaving *appropriately* for that gender.

The study reported here is part of a larger study of pre-school children and gender. In this chapter I will analyze the responses of seven children with whom I worked individually and intensively over a period of several months. Each child chose the stories they wanted to hear from a selection of ten stories. Each story was read to the child individually and the reading and the surrounding talk were audio-recorded. They could hear each story as often as they liked. Following each story some of the children were invited, wherever this was possible, to recreate the story by making the characters out of plasticine and play-acting the story as they remembered it. For the purpose of this chapter I will discuss the responses of the seven children who chose *The Paper Bag Princess* (Munsch and Martchenko, 1980), and the six who chose *Oliver Button is a Sissy* (de Paolo, 1981).

Since the first two of these stories are referred to in detail it is necessary to 'tell' each of the stories before proceeding with the data.

Oliver Button is a boy who likes to do 'girls' things'. His father finds this distressing. However, Oliver persists and his parents eventually decide to send him to dancing school. Oliver is teased mercilessly by the boys at his normal school but he keeps dancing. The boys write 'Oliver Button is a sissy' on the school wall. Oliver goes in a talent quest and dances well but does not come first. When he goes to school the next day the boys have crossed out 'sissy' and written 'star'.

The Paper Big Princess is about the beautiful Princess Elizabeth who plans to marry Prince Ronald. She lives in her castle and has expensive princess clothes. A dragon smashes Elizabeth's castle, burns all her clothes and carries off Prince Ronald. Elizabeth decides to chase the dragon and save Ronald. She finds a paper bag to wear and sets off after the dragon. She comes to the dragon's cave and, despite the dragon's resistance, gains his attention by asking him if it is true that he is 'the smartest and fiercest dragon in the whole world'. He claims he is and so she is able to persuade him to go on demonstrating his fantastic powers until he is exhausted and falls into a deep sleep. She then walks over the dragon and opens the door of the dragon's cave where Ronald is imprisoned. But Prince Ronald doesn't like the way Elizabeth looks. He says 'Elizabeth, you are a mess! You smell like ashes, your hair is all tangled and you are wearing a dirty old paper bag. Come back when you are dressed like a real princess'. Elizabeth replies 'Ronald, your clothes are really pretty and your hair is very neat. You look like a real prince, but you are a bum.' Elizabeth and Ronald don't get married and Elizabeth skips off into the sunset.

The children were: Anika, aged 5 years; Rebecca, aged 5 years 4 months; Katy, aged 4 years 11 months; Sebastian, aged 4 years 10 months; Robbie, aged 5 years 4 months; Mark, aged 5 years; and Leo, aged 5 years 1 month.

Although the children's responses varied considerably, as I will show in what follows, a persistent theme in their talk involved getting their genderedness right. They vary in the extent to which they see male and female behaviours as overlapping or as mutually exclusive, but they are all concerned that one's boyness and girlness should be clearly displayed. The distress that Oliver Button's dad feels when Oliver Button engages in what his dad takes to be girl behaviours, is seen by the children as understandable 'because he thinks he's pretending to be a girl' or 'because everyone'll think he's a girl'. This sympathy is felt even by the children who think Oliver Button should be free to do what he likes to do. Four of the six children who chose *Oliver Button is a Sissy* thought he should not have continued with his dancing, or if he did, he *should be teased*. These children are clearly aware that Oliver Button is unhappy doing boy things and unhappy to be teased, but they do not question the teasing — Oliver Button should know, or should be told, that he is not 'getting it right'. In this way these children reveal their adherence to a central construct of children's culture, that of *reciprocity*, or the 'active reflecting back to the other of the other's self' (Davies, 1982, p. 76). In this case, the children believe that it is correct to call Oliver Button a sissy because that is what he is. It is also interesting to note in this and later transcripts that I am providing the children through my questions and responses, with an interactional other who makes theoretically possible the extension of maleness and femaleness to include non-traditional behaviour. My requests that they explain and justify adherence to traditional stereotypes are met with the required explanations, not with a reassessment of the answer, even when such a reassessment is clearly being invited.

Robbie:	(*Oliver Button is a Sissy*)
BD	So why doesn't Oliver Button like to play 'boys' games'?
R	Because he likes girls' things.
BD	Because he likes girls' things. Mm. (Reads about Oliver Button going to dancing school.) So all the others are little girls, aren't they? (Looking at picture.)
R	That's wrong.
BD	It's wrong, is it? So you wouldn't like Oliver to go? If you were Oliver and you hated all the boys' things and you wanted to do girls' things would you want to go to dancing school?
R	(Shakes head.)
BD	Even if you loved to dance you wouldn't want to go to dancing school?
R	No.
BD	(Reads about the boys teasing Oliver.) So what sort of boys are they?
R	Big, they ...
BD	Big boys, and should they say that to Oliver Button?
R	Yes.
BD	They should? (surprised) ... (Read about boys writing 'Oliver Button is a sissy' on the school wall.) How does Oliver feel?
R	Sad.
BD	He's very sad, isn't he? So should the boys have written that on the wall?
R	(Nods).
BD	They should? (surprised) Why should they have written that on the wall?
R	Because he, because he is a sissy doing tap dancing.
BD	(Reads about Oliver practising his dancing.) So why do you suppose he keeps going even though everybody keeps giving him a hard time?
R	Because he just wants to.
BD	He just wants to and should you keep doing what you want to do even though everybody keeps giving you a hard time?
R	(Nods).
BD	Uh huh. (Reads story.) So his dad doesn't mind any more, does he, that he's a tap dancer. Why do you suppose that is?
R	Because he was good on stage.
BD	Uh huh. So if you keep doing something that you're not supposed to do if you're a boy and you get to be good at it then it's quite all right?

R	(Nods).
BD	Uh huh.

Robbie believes it is wrong for Oliver to go to the dancing school. What seems logical to me — that if you hate 'boys' things' and love dancing, you should dance — does not follow at all for Robbie unless you are able to develop a high level of competence at dancing. But correct genderedness for himself is far more important than what he might like or dislike. Similarly for Katy and for Sebastian, Oliver was behaving inappropriately — he should have done what he was told and played with the boys. Sebastian explains that he personally would do as his Dad says because his Dad can show him how to be a boy. The story of Oliver Button creates an obvious discomfort for many of the children who listen to it. For boys, it seems, gender is not fixed, it is not immutable, and there are clear risks in engaging in girl behaviour, even to the extent in some children's minds that you could become a girl. Maleness in our society is defined in a large part in terms of one's capacity not to behave like a girl and is thus construed by some boys as something that has to be ongoingly achieved. Females, in contrast, are not seen as at risk of becoming males. Some non-traditional female behaviours can be engaged in with impunity, though this may not change one's thinking about what females generally do, as is shown in the following transcript, nor, as is shown in a later transcript, does it change one's capacity to engage in behaviours labelled exclusively male.

Anika	(*The Paper Bag Princess*)
BD	If you were Princess Elizabeth would you be chasing the dragon? Would you be that brave?
A	(Nods).
BD	If I was Princess Elizabeth would I be that brave do you think?
A	(Shakes head).
BD	No? What about if mummy were Princess Elizabeth, would she be that brave?
A	(Shakes head).
BD	No? Who do you know that would be that brave?
A	Daddy.
BD	Daddy would be that brave, would he?
A	(Nods).
BD	And who else.
A	David (brother).
BD	Anybody else that you know?
A	(Shakes head).

Thus Anika, along with her father and brother, can be brave like Princess Elizabeth while other famales are still limited to the traditional stereotypes.

The delight for adults in *The Paper Bag Princess* lies in Elizabeth's capacity to turn the tables on Ronald and skip happily off into the sunset. But for children this is a puzzling and not altogether satisfactory ending. It takes several readings of the story to get them used to the ending, but generally the girls still preferred Elizabeth at the beginning rather than at the end of the story. In the following talk around the plasticine reconstruction of *The Paper Bag Princess*, I explore the ending with Anika, discovering to my surprise that not only does she not share my definition of the ending, but nor does she share my definition of Ronald. As with the older children of my earlier study, these 4 and 5-year-old children showed a belief in the existential or plastic quality of people (1982, p. 77) — if Ronald is nice tomorrow, even though he was 'a bum' today, it will be alright to marry him. Thus the traditional ending of getting married and living happily ever after is not out of keeping with Anika's idea of who Elizabeth and Ronald are.

Anika (*The Paper Bag Princess.* Plasticine reconstruction)
BD And so then what happens? Are you putting some mess on her face?
A Mmmm, that was soot.
BD Right, and so Prince Ronald tells her that she 'looks really like a pig' (using Anika's words.)
A Mmmm.
BD And then what does she say?
A Oh, Prince Ronald, you are a bum!
BD Right, and then what happens?
A They don't get married after all.
BD And what's happening in this very last picture here?
A The paper bag princess is going off into the sunset....
BD What do you think she'll do after she skips off into the sunset?
A Go home.
BD To her burnt down castle?
A No.
BD Where will she go?
A Um, to rent a house.
BD Uh huh.
A Until someone's built a house for her.
BD Until she's got a new castle?
A Mmm.
BD And what will be the first thing that she does when she gets back to her rented house?
A Clean up the place.
BD Clean up what? The new flat? Or where the castle got burnt down?
A Mmm, where the castle got burnt down.

BD	And what about cleaning herself up? Will that be important?
A	Yes.
BD	And will she buy new clothes?
A	Yes.
BD	Tell me what sort of new clothes she'll buy.
A	Princess ones.
BD	Princess ones? Like right back at the beginning? (surprised tone of voice)
A	Mmmm.
BD	(Points) Like that?
A	Mmmm.
BD	Uh huh, and will she grow her hair all pretty again?
A	Yes.
BD	And what will happen when she sees Prince Ronald in a few days after she's got all dressed up and Prince Ronald comes to visit her?
A	I don't know.
BD	What would you like her to say?
A	Hello.
BD	Mmm? (surprised)
A	Hello.
BD	Hello, and what will he say? What would happen here? Here's Prince Ronald, he's come to visit. She's all dressed up and pretty again and she says, 'Hello Prince Ronald'. Ronald says, 'Hello Elizabeth. How are you?' What does she say?
A	'Good'.
BD	She says, 'I'm good'. And he says, 'Well, you look like a real princess now!' And what does she say?
A	I don't remember.
BD	Remember? We're making this up!
A	I know.
BD	Um, what if she says, um, 'Yes, I do look like a real princess now'. And he says, 'Well then we can get married'. And what does she say?
A	'Yes, we will get married'.
BD	So, she doesn't think he's a bum anymore? (surprised tone of voice)
A	(Shakes head).
BD	Why doesn't she think he's a bum anymore?
A	I don't know.
BD	Don't know?
A	No.
BD	She just thinks he's being nice now, does she?
A	Yes.
BD	Right. OK, shall we do another story?
A	Yes.

The salience in *The Paper Bag Princess* for Anika lies, therefore, not in Elizabeth's capacity to walk away. She says elsewhere that she really likes the story because Elizabeth calls Ronald a bum, just as she calls her brother a bum if he is mean to her. But just as she gets over her fights with David, so she presumes must Elizabeth get over her fight with Ronald.

In the following transcript, Anika carefully elaborates her beliefs that males and females should be free to step outside traditional gender roles. She does this by creating a *third gender* which she labels 'tomboy'. Anika knows a girl who is called a 'tomboy' and who is accepted as such. She extends this knowledge to create a category to which males and females can belong though is careful to explain elsewhere that she is not a tomboy. Her description of the personal difficulties she encounters in engaging in male behaviour is fascinating and illustrates that the use of the third gender category is in part a device for maintaining a clear definition of the other two gender categories.

Anika	(*Oliver Button is a Sissy*)
BD	(Reads: 'Oliver Button was called a sissy. He didn't like to do the things that boys are supposed to do') What are boys supposed to do?
A	Be very rough.
BD	And what's, what's Oliver doing?
A	He's being like a girl.
BD	Is he? Why is that like a girl?
A	Because he's picking flowers.
BD	Uh huh.
A	And that's sort of, that's mainly girls'.
BD	And is that an all right thing for boys to do?
A	Mmmm. But it's just not a boy's thing.
BD	Right.
A	So I think he should be called a tomboy.
BD	Right.
A	Not a sissy.
BD	Right.
A	A tomboy.

(Discussion as to whether her brother does what Oliver Button does.)

BD	So sometimes he'll do those things but mostly he doesn't.
A	Except he really *doesn't* skip. He *never* skips.
BD	Right. Righto, would you like it if he did?
A	(Nods.)
BD	Yep.
A	But I can't skip.
BD	Right. But if he could skip he might teach you how, mightn't he?

A He *can* skip.

BD Can he?

A Yep, but he just doesn't like to do it.

BD (Reads — 'Oliver, said his dad, don't be such a sissy!') Why did he say that?

A Because he's pretending he's a girl.

BD Right. (Reads 'Go out and play baseball or football or basket ball, *any* kind of ball!') Why did his dad say that?

A 'Cause he's doing girls' things.

BD Mmm, and does it, does that matter? Is that a problem?

A Yeah.

BD Do you think his dad thinks it's a problem?

A (Nods).

BD Why do you think his dad thinks that?

A Cause he, I think his dad um thinks he wants to be a tomboy.

BD Do you think his dad might be unhappy if he wants to be a tomboy?

A Mmm, cause he just wants a boy called Oliver Button.

BD (Reads about Oliver Button going to dancing school.) And what would you think if David got some tap shoes and had dancing lessons. Would you like that, or would you hate it?

A No, I think, I'd laugh at him.

BD Would you? Why would you do that?

A Because it's a tomboy thing.

BD Is it?

A And David's got no friends that are tomboys.

BD Would it be all right if he had friends who are tomboys?

A Mmmm.

BD So why would you laugh at him?

A Because it's sort of a girl's thing.

BD Right, and you would feel funny about him doing a girl's thing?

A Mmm, I feel, you know, funny.

BD Feel.

A Feel funny.

BD Yeah.

A And when people, when people, when the wrong kind of human being does that, I get a (pause) tickle in my brain.

BD Do you? When.

A Mmmm.

BD If a boy does a girl thing you get a tickling feeling in your brain?

A Mmmm.

BD And what about if a girl does a boy thing?

A I get (pause) the same thing.

BD It makes you feel really funny?

A Mmm, and it makes me laugh.

BD   Does it?

A   Mmm, and it's like a little man is in my brain, tickling my brain.

BD   Does it feel horrible or funny?

A   Funny.

BD   Funny.

A   Like, it's like a piece of string like this tickling from side to side. (Motions as if drawing string back and forth through her brain.)

BD   And that tickling makes you laugh?

A   Mmmm.

BD   Does it make you feel unhappy at all?

A   No.

BD   So, if you were to do a boy thing and that made you laugh, but you *really* wanted to do it and it started making you tickle and laugh would you keep on doing it?

A   Oh, no.

BD   No? Is the tickling enough to make you stop?

A   Yeah, because I'd only do it when I was practising and no girl or boy is around, no one because they might laugh at me.

BD   And if you were just practising it alone, and um say like what, what would be a boy thing that you'd really like to do?

A   (Pause) Um, fly a racing, fly an aeroplane.

BD   And if you were flying that aeroplane and you were practising it all by yourself where nobody could watch you, um, would you get tickling in your brain then?

A   Yeah.

BD   You would, but you wouldn't care?

A   No.

BD   If your mum or your dad was watching you would that matter?

A   Ooh, if I got a ticklish thing I wouldn't laugh.

BD   You wouldn't.

A   Because they might hear me.

BD   So you'd just go on playing the plane, flying the plane, if they were there but you wouldn't if there were other boys or girls there?

A   Mmm. I mean if there were boys and girls there I still wouldn't laugh because you know I, you know (pause). Let's just get on with the story.

BD   Right, OK. It's hard to explain isn't it?

A   Mmm, very.

For Anika the correct behaviour for girls and boys is relatively flexible. Activities are not solely the province of one or the other — they are just what that group 'mainly' does. It is not a problem, in fact it can be quite pleasant, if people step outside of their gender appropriate behaviours, as her brother does, occasionally. However, some behaviours such as tap dancing, are problematic and lead to 'a tickle in the brain'. This can be overcome by a group of people taking up the behaviour in question so they are all doing it together, or by practising the skill alone, presumably so that one can be accepted as Oliver Button eventually is through being good at it.

This should not be taken to indicate that acquiescence to the traditional roles is easy or straightforward. Rebecca revealed quite unexpectedly for instance in the plasticine play following the reading of Oliver Button that she felt very negatively towards the boys who had pressured Oliver Button towards 'normal' behaviour even though she had stated that acquiescence was an appropraite response.

Rebecca   (Oliver Button — plasticine reconstruction)
(R constructs Oliver and BD constructs the boys. They play out the story to the point where the boys are teasing Oliver.)

BD	He feels sad doesn't he?
R	(Giggles).
BD	He tries not to cry and then, what's he doing? What are you making him do? Jump on the boys, is that what he should have done? (R makes Oliver jump on the boys and angrily pounds them into little bits.)

While Rebecca could not put her anger toward the boys into words, she could demonstrate it. Mark is able to go one step further than Rebecca. He is quite clear in his mind that the socializing power of the boys must be actively counteracted, although he did not know how this might be done. When the tape was finished he said at first that he might talk to them. When encouraged to think of what he would say he said he could think of nothing. In a second reading of the story he said it would be more effective to throw sticks at them though adults would say it was better to just ask them not to. Mark is accompanied by a 3-year-old girl, Kim, in this particular episode.

Mark and Kim	*(Oliver Button is a Sissy)*
BD	Is he nearly going to cry?
M	Yes.
BD	He doesn't like being called a sissy does he?
M	(Shakes head).
BD	Would you call somebody a sissy if they went to dancing lessons? (Interruption).
BD	Right. If those big boys were your friends Kim, and they wanted to tease Oliver would you tease him too and call him a sissy?
K	(Nods).
BD	You would? Um, and if you saw him looking sad like that how would you feel?

K	I'd still tease him.
BD	You'd still tease him, and why would you do that? (Silence). If those big boys were your friends ... and what about you Mark if those big boys were your friends and they were teasing Oliver would you tease him too?
M	No.
BD	What would you do?
M	I would, I would stop them.
BD	Would you? What would you say to them?
M	I dunno.
BD	You don't know. You'd just manage to stop them somehow?
M	Mmmm.
BD	(Reads 'Almost every day the boys teased Oliver Button') Mmm, how does he look?
M	Sad.
BD	(Reads about how Oliver went to dancing school and practised and practised.) Is that the right thing for him to do keep on going to the school?
M and K	Yes (Simultaneously).
BD	Why was it the right thing to do?
M	Because he couldn't dance himself.
BD	Because he couldn't what?
M	Because he couldn't dance himself.
BD	Because he couldn't dance he had to go to Miss Leah to learn how?
M	Yes.
BD	And if you'd been Oliver Button would you have kept going to the dancing school, Mark?
M	Um, yes.
BD	Even though the boys teased you?
M	Mmmm.
BD	What about you Kim? Would you keep going to the school even though the boys teased you?
K	(Shakes head).

But Mark was an exception. The other children either thought it correct to adhere (and to ensure that others adhered) to traditional roles. Where they thought it correct to be able to be liberated from traditional roles, the power of what was taken to be normative strongly influence what they chose to do.

So what do these episodes tell us about what facilitates the transition from being bound within traditional gender roles to being able to both see and act outside of them? Anika describes the possibility of occasionally stepping outside. She alludes, on several occasions, to the liberating effect that friends can have if they choose, to allow more consistent stepping outside simply by being friends or by engaging in the behaviour with you. Success at the non-traditional behaviour is fairly consistently seen as a means of legitimating that behaviour. Generally, however, the power of what is taken to be normal for a girl or a boy was taken to be unquestionable. It was acceptable for Oliver Button's dad to 'just want a boy called Oliver Button' even though this made life hard for Oliver Button. Similarly, parents were included with peers in the class of people in front of whom non-traditional behaviours could not be practised.

In analyzing the children's responses to *The Paper Bag Princess* I have found an intriguing difference between those who understand the story as it is intended, and those who do not. Of the girls Anika and Rebecca and Katy all identify with the princess. They see her as nice, beautiful etc. All three understand her plan. All three see Ronald as not very nice, though Katy believes he is reasonable and that Elizabeth should have done as he asked, cleaned herself up and then they could have got married.

Of the boys Sebastian and Robbie have little interest in the character of Elizabeth though are able to understand her plan. They both appreciate that she is cross and angry. Both identify with the clever prince. To see Ronald as clever is a considerable accomplishment. In order to create and sustain Ronald as a hero these boys had to attend to minute details in the picture, to successfully accomplish male genderedness, as they understood it, for Ronald. Neither Sebastian nor Robbie sees any problem in Elizabeth's rejection of Ronald, Sebastian because he presumes Ronald will find someone else and Robbie because he believed that Ronald didn't like Elizabeth in the first place. Leo and Mark both see Prince Ronald as not nice, though Leo would like to be like him. Both are aware of Elizabeth's plan to save Ronald. Both are aware of her dirtiness. Thus three of the four boys identify with Ronald and turn him into the central character. Only Mark sees Ronald as unacceptable and identifies with the dragon (who is, after all, 'the smartest and fiercest dragon in the whole world').

Apart from this strong and predictable trend that the girls identify with the princess and the boys with the prince, other differences one might have predicted are not there. For example the amount of detail perceived in the individual characters and in the relationship between the characters varies within gender as much as between gender. Both Anika and Robbie give a great deal of insightful comment on the characters and relationship (albeit from the perspective of the character they identify with). However it is possible to gain a more subtle insight into the individual children's understanding of the story, if the children are divided not according to gender, but according to whether they understand that Elizabeth is the hero and that Ronald is not at all nice. Anika, Rebecca, Mark and Leo are focussed on Elizabeth as the hero and on her plan to save Ronald. In contrast Katy, Sebastian and Robbie turn Ronald into a nice person or even the hero. For these three, Elizabeth's action is seen in terms of re-establishing her coupled state (getting her prince back) and all three think Ronald is reasonable in his request that Elizabeth clean herself up. Interestingly, the four who understand the story as it is intended with Elizabeth as hero have mothers who engage in paid work outside the home and two of them have fathers who have taken a substantial share of nurturing and domestic activity. The three children who are unable to appreciate Elizabeth as hero have full-time mothers. There seems therefore to be an interesting connection between having a mother in paid work and the capacity to imagine women as active agents in the world, as powerful people, and to see men as other than central in action outside the home. The essential *liberating* message of the story is available to these children as a way of conceptualizing the world, while the others must distort the story in order to understand it. This is not to say that the other children fully understood the story. Two of the children of working mothers saw Princess Elizabeth as 'nice', which is not an appropriate description for Elizabeth and is also an imposition of stereotypical constructions of gender on the story (cf. Ullian, 1984). And as noted earlier Anika quite readily went on to bring about a traditional 'happy ending' when prompted in that direction.

The link between having a mother who works and the capacity to accept Oliver Button's right to dance is not so clear. Sebastian, Robbie and Katy, whose mothers do not work, all thought that Oliver should do boy things and Sebastian and Katy believe he should do as his father tells him whether he likes it or not. Anika, Rebecca and Mark, whose mothers do work, thought Oliver should continue to dance (as did Robbie) but Anika and Rebecca were ambivalent about whether they would tease him or not, even though they quite clearly believed he should be free to do as he wanted. Mark is the clearest about Oliver's rights and refers to his own experience of 'girl's' things to justify this. He says 'I do lots of things that girls do and lots of things that boys do. Like my dad bought me a She Ra, and I like skipping and stuff and also I'd like to get the castle that She Ra lives in and stuff like that . . . I feel happy doing girl things, and after all I do go to dance.'

This link between the capacity to understand (at least partially) the liberating message of the stories and having a mother who works outside the home has emerged in other research. Urburg (1982) has shown that girls are 'less sex-typed in their concepts than boys, *particularly girls whose mothers worked also* (p. 668). As well, Zuckerman and Sayre (1982) have shown that 'the sons of the full-time home-makers (i.e. mothers) tend to refuse to consider opposite sex career choices, which suggests that the role-model of the home-maker mother has a negative impact on boys' perceptions of women or women's role options' (pp. 860–1). This pattern has an interesting correlation, too, with the work of Lunneborg (1982) who found that having a working mother was the most salient feature in the backgrounds of women with non-traditional careers. Kessler, Ashendon, Connell and Dowsett (1982) also point to the increase in the number of married women who work as the most significant development in families in relation to changes in adolescents' conceptions of sex-roles.

Conclusion

What I have shown through children's responses to liberating stories is that the accomplishment of genderedness is a central and complex task necessary in the elaboration of oneself as a normal and competent member of society. Some children are locked into traditional conceptions of gender while others are able to move partially towards a more liberated view of gender, where their social environment includes women who are active agents in the world, where there are men who have undertaken a significant proportion of the nurturing and traditionally female roles, *and* where they have been free to practice non-traditional behaviours in an environment where this is taken to be a normal thing to do.

I have shown that it is not enough to believe that one might be or ought to be liberated from traditional roles nor is it enough to engage in isolated interactions with liberated others, particularly if those liberated others are merely assigned to a third gender catagory thus removing any necessity to generalize from their non-traditional behaviour about what males or females are capable of doing. It is necessary to know *how* one might be liberated *and* to have the interactional and conceptual others to turn liberated ideals into possible realities. Just as some of the children could not hear or see that Elizabeth was a hero and Ronald a fool, so the people with whom a child interacts must be able to hear and see the child's actions as normal for their gender, in order for the child to proceed comfortably with those actions.

Teachers working with children must be aware of the fact that currently our society is divided into male and female categories and that children are required to accomplish not only their distinct maleness or femaleness, but if they are male they have also to achieve their not-femaleness and vice versa. The categories are taken in our society to be mutually exclusive — one cannot be both, and one cannot be roughly one or the other. It is therefore inappropriate to merely assert that it is alright for boys to do what girls do and for girls to do what boys do. For children that must be a fairly empty statement and in fact the assertion itself still maintains as given the distinction between 'girls things' and 'boys things'. What a boy *is* and what a girl *is* must be extended in such a way that liberated behaviours are seen as 'normal' behaviours which will not lead to a misreading of the gender of the actor. The extension must be both conceptual and interactional. As Evans (1982) has shown, it is all too easy for teachers to espouse liberated ideals without actually translating these into their interactions with the children.

Children must be encouraged to find ways of clearly signalling their maleness and their femaleness without limiting or constricting their potential. Most children will need a great deal of support and reassurance in this extension of themselves into liberated forms of activity, though the more they are surrounded by books which depict liberated behaviours as normal and by people who engage in liberated behaviours as if that is normal, the more secure they will feel in stepping outside of the traditional bounds and the less anxious they will feel that such stepping out compromises the accomplishment of their genderedness.

References

DAVIES, B. (1982) *Life in the Classroom and Playground: The Accounts of Primary School Children*, London, Routledge and Kegan Paul.

DE PAOLO, T. (1981) *Oliver button is a Sissy*, London, Methuen.

EVANS, T. (1982) 'Being and becoming: Teachers' perceptions of sex-roles and actions towards their male and female pupils', *British Journal of Sociology of Education*, 3.

KESSLER, S., ASHENDON, D. CONNELL, B. and DOWSETT, G. (1982) *Ockers and Disco-maniacs*, Stanmore, Inner City Education Centre.

KESSLER, S. and MCKENNA, W. (1985) *Gender: An Ethnomethodolgoical Approach*, Chicago, University of Chicago Press.

LUNNEBORG, P. (1982) 'Role model influences of non-traditional professional women', *Journal of Vocational Behaviour*, 20.

MUNSCH, R.N. and MARTCHENKO, M. (1980) *The Paper Bag Princess*. Toronto, Annick Press Ltd.

THOMPSON, S. (1975) 'Gender labels and early sex role development', *Child Development*, 46.

ULLIAN, D. (1984) 'Why girls are good: A constructivist view', *American Journal of Orthopsychiatry*, 54.

URBURG, K. (1982) 'The development of the concepts of masculinity and femininity in young children', *Sex Roles*, 8.

ZIPES, J. (1982) 'The potential of liberating fairy tales for children', *New Literary History*.

ZUCKERMAN, D. and SAYRE, D. (1982) 'Cultural sex-role expectations and children's sex role concepts', *Sex Roles*, 8.

4   The Time of Their Lives: Bureaucracy and the Nursery School

David Hartley

Introduction

In their stimulating analysis of the relationship between technology, modernity and consciousness, Berger *et al.* (1973), note the emergence of what they term a 'bureaucratic cognitive style' (p. 50). That is to say, as the technical productive process becomes increasingly complex and interdependent, so too is there an attendant division of labour along bureaucratic lines, all of this being in the interests of maximizing efficiency, regardless of the ownership of production. Through exposure to techno-bureaucratic structures, everyday consciousness may tacitly acquire bureaucratically-engendered 'traits'. This furthers bureaucracy (and its variants) as the prevalent organizational form (DiMaggio and Powell, 1983), and the bureaucratic cognitive style as the prevalent mode of consciousness. Associated with this bureaucratic cognitive style are the following tendencies: to focus on parts, not wholes; to standardize, homogenize and to rationalize procedures; to categorize in the form of lists, tables and taxonomies; to be orderly; to be concerned with predictability, not creativity; to monitor, test and evaluate in an as objective a manner as possible. Historical analyses of the transition from agriculture to factory-based entrepreneurial capitalism illustrate how a new psychology had its beginnings in the factory. It was there that the worker should come to regard the bureaucratization of time, space and demeanour as 'second nature' (Pollard, 1965; Thompson, 1967). So apparently successful was this bureaucratization of the mind that Weber (1975) has argued, somewhat pessimistically, that bureaucratic rationality constitutes an 'iron cage' which is virtually 'escape-proof (p. 1401), a view echoed by C. Wright Mills (1967, p. 238). Since Weber made that assertion, however, the bureaucratic form, commonly associated with Taylor's 'scientific management' theory in the 1920s, has been 'loosened' (Bidwell, 1965) by human relations management theory which has called for the recognition and satiation of workers' 'needs', but only insofar as they can be subsumed under those of management. This structural looseness should not suggest that the extent of bureaucratic rationality has diminished — on the contrary, it now encompasses much more of social life than hitherto. What it does suggest is that bureaucratic control has become less obvious. Its parameters have widened and its form has loosened, but the control which it 'exerts' remains. Weber argued that we are so 'enmeshed' in the bureaucratic form that we cannot, so to say, get outside of it and see it. But this socialization into bureaucratic rationality is lengthy. For some, it begins in the nursery school.

What is distinctive about the nursery school is that it instrumentalizes the expressive: that is, the formal goal of the school tends to be less academic (or instrumental) and more affective (or expressive) in its emphasis. This is why, in the nursery school, there does not appear to be a formal curriculum which is transmitted by an obviously didactic teaching style. All that one can see, so to say, is the hidden curriculum, for there does not appear to be any teaching going on. The children are said to be learning through play. Moreover, the nursery school is often the first formal organization to which the child is exposed for any length of time. Given that the dominant organizational form in society is bureaucratic, it is likely that there will be elements of that form in the nursery school, despite 'child-centred' rhetoric to the contrary. The concern here is with this interrelationship between, on the one hand, bureaucracy as the dominant organizational form in the wider society, and, on the other hand, child-centred education within the nursery school. More specifically, how are children's concepts of time and space structured along bureaucratic lines through the hidden curriculum of the nursery school?

Sociological research on this matter is very lacking. The seminal research is Kanter's (1972) study of an American Midwest nursery school in 1965 in which she typified the child as an 'organization child'. More recently, Lubeck (1985) has compared the ways in which time and space were structured in two nursery schools in the USA: one in a black, working class area; the other in a white, middle class area. She concludes that, in the former, time and space were more bureaucratized than in the latter, a finding which lends some support to Bernstein's (1975) thesis on the relationship between pedagogy and social class in the nursery school and infant school.

The Nursery Units

The research here centres on two nursery schools, or units, which are located in an urban area in Scotland. The facts about the two units are as follows. Both schools are non-denominational. Fieldhouse Nursery Unit (hereafter referred to as Fieldhouse) is located in a largely middle class, owner-occupied suburb. The housing is post-war. The nursery unit is a detached, purpose-built structure with its own garden and playground. The garden is very spacious and contains a small area cultivated by the children. The nursery itself consists of two large areas, which can be partitioned if required, and which have washing facilities. Attached to one area is a staffroom, which itself adjoins a small, so-called 'quiet' room. Attached to the other area are the children's toilet and cloakroom facilities. The two large 'teaching' areas have windows facing west, east and south. There is one nursery teacher, who is under the authority of the assistant headteacher of the infants' section in the adjoining primary school, and three nursery nurses.

Like Fieldhouse, the second nursery unit, referred to here as Nelson, is organizationally part of a primary school, but in a detached building, though not purpose-built for nursery use. (It had previously been used as primary school classrooms.) It consists of two bright classrooms linked by a cloakroom, toilet and entrance area. There is no staffroom. Storage space is confined to a walk-in area about nine feet by four. The north-east windows overlook a wooded area adjoining a road; the south-west windows front the infant school's playground. There is one nursery teacher, previously a primary school teacher, who reports to the assistant headteacher of the infant school, and two nursery nurses. The school and its nursery draw upon a mainly middle class catchment area, the architecture of which varies from Victorian to modern.

Both schools have separate 'morning' and 'afternoon' children, but Fieldhouse has 'all-day' children as well. Table 1 shows the social class (as defined by the Registrar General's *Classification of Occupations*) of the children's parents (i.e. the main wage-earner), as defined occupationally from the school records. In obtaining the latter, I was given only the list of occupations, not the corresponding names of the parents.

Table 1: *Fieldhouse and Nelson: Social Class of Parents (figures given are percentages)*

	I	II	IIIN	IIIM	IV	V	U/E
Nelson (n = 59)	8.5	33.9	22.0	30.5	1.7		5.4
Fieldhouse (n = 68)	14.7	30.9	14.7	30.9	5.9		2.9

The enrolment and social class composition of the two units, therefore, is similar, though Fieldhouse has a greater proportion of social class I parents. In both units, the research focuses upon three related aspects of bureaucracy: first, how is a bureaucratized sense of place and space tacitly acquired by the pre-school child; second, how is the child's notion of routine and clock-time structured; and third, but less importantly, how

are the children monitored? These questions are posed in the two research settings just defined, thereby allowing comparison between two
school whose size, social composition and architecture are similar.

Methodology

Ethnographic researchers often claim to have generated 'grounded theory'
(Glaser and Strauss, 1967) whereby they purport to suspend their conventional conceptual framework when selecting and interpreting their data. I
have not done this. Instead, I have drawn upon both the conceptual
insights and the sociological methodology of Weber (1974 and 1978). That
is, first, I have operationalized Weber's concept of bureaucracy as central
to the structuring of the data, particularly by considering both temporal
and spatial expressions of bureaucracy in the two schools, thereby responding to Stimson's (1986) call for ethnography to go beyond its normal
emphasis upon the spoken word. From time to time, I took photographs
of the spatial arrangements, not only to compare the two units, but to
compare these arrangements within units over a period of time. As to
temporal representations of bureaucracy, I noted the regularity and sequencing of events in the two nursery units. In addition to drawing upon
Weber's conceptual framework, I also employed his method known as
verstehen. That is, I sought to impute the meanings which actions had for
those who carried them out. I also tried to verify them by discussion with
others, and by analyzing written sources, such as newsletters and notices.
At Nelson I tape-recorded a semi-structured interview with the staff; in
both schools I chatted informally with them at break-time. The fieldwork
was carried out between September 1985 and May 1986. In reporting the
findings, I shall consider the concepts of space, time and assessment in
that order, drawing comparisons between the two nurseries as I do so.

Space: 'No Templates Please'

Buildings are expressions of ideologies. The modern office block purports
to be a physical manifestation of the social relations of bureaucracy. It is
meant to be efficient, but it may not be, simply because those who work
in it may interpret its architecture in unintended ways, thereby subverting the very functions it was designed to facilitate — the user, therefore,
assigns his own meanings to architecture (Broadbent *et al.* 1980, pp. 119–
20). In a school, spatial and physical arrangements comprise part of the
hidden curriculum, and in that sense may be experienced unconsciously.
There are exceptions to this: for example, if staff and children were to be
moved from a closed classroom school to an open-plan school, then they
would have to make sense of their new setting. But that, once done,

would become routine, thereby rendering it beyond further consideration. However, the sociological analysis of space and place in primary schools has been given little attention. An exception is Evans (1979) who reports:

> I found in my research study that, although practice had been diverse and idiosyncratic within the closed classrooms of the old school, the move to an open-plan building produced the introduction of a timetable, subject specialization at the top of the school, and a considerable amount of *streaming*.

The educational effects of the new architecture were the opposite of what had been intended. That is, although the teachers could do little about the open-plan architecture, nevertheless they superimposed on it their bureaucratic preferences for the management of knowledge (subject specialism) and the hierarchical ordering of specific groups (streaming).

To return to the study at hand, the architecture of the two nursery units is similar, as indicated earlier. That said, how are these spatial 'givens' interpreted and restructured? Consider, first, the arrangement of objects and allocation of space *within* nursery units. The initial impression on entering Fieldhouse is that of a cornucopia of colour whose arrangement seems, at first glance, random. Even the windows of the staff room and outside walls have been used as the surface for coloured finger-paintings, some of which 'run on' to paintings on the walls. For example, one part of a wall had green reeds and rushes painted beneath the window, and the reeds extended onto the window itself. Later in the year, this part of the wall had been converted to an indoor 'greenhouse', with a translucent sheet enclosing both a window pane and a table where plants grew. Paintings, all the children's own work, were displayed, not in symmetrical style, but as clustered themes. For example, one wall had a 'jungle' theme, another a 'sea' theme, another a 'transport' theme; and so on. The children were allowed to climb the step-ladders (under supervision) and attach their art work to the background. Mobiles comprising other theme-related art-work hung from the ceiling, not at adult height, but just above the children's heads. A visitor to the nursery was reported to have said,

> This would give me a nervous breakdown. All these mobiles hanging around!

All this is not to say that there was no structure: it is to suggest that the structure was not readily apparent to visitors. The *staff* perceived activities as being carefully organized. On their duty roster there was a four-fold classification of 'activity areas': (i) sand, water, floor games, music; (ii) dough, book corner, large equipment, baking; (iii) art and craft; (iv) puzzles, table toys, games, construction. Staff would spend a day on one set of activities and then move to the next; and so on. It is noteworthy, too, that there were no formal staff meetings — ideas were 'bounced off each other at break-time. This informally-produced structure was thought necessary. The maxim was:

> *Nursery Teacher*: To be structured so they (the children) can be unstructured.

The impression on entering Nelson was different, though the declared philosophy was similar:

> *Nursery Teacher*: The freedom to control themselves.

There was a greater sense of space, orderliness and quiet. For example, I could see, proportionately, far more of the floors, walls and ceiling than at Fieldhouse. There were, however, similar 'activity centres': the house music corner, art table, easels, jigsaw puzzles, water table, sand trays, story mat and corner, and piano. Nelson, however, had a separate dressing table and full-length mirror. At Fieldhouse, dress-up was located within the 'house'. The Fieldhouse philosophy of 'no templates, please' (as stated by the nursery teacher) was not evident at Nelson. For example, on one wall was a tiered row of identically-shaped, mass-produced Christmas artefacts: a templated face of Father Christmas, above a mass-produced Christmas cracker, above a Christmas card. The objects were arranged vertically, in sets, one per child. A similar standardization of art forms and symmetry of display was evident at other times in the year. It was as if the serried ranks of desks had been replaced by serried ranks of mass-produced 'art'. The declared reason for this was that, first, it allowed ease of collection by the parent; and second, it enabled the parent to see that their child 'had not been neglected' in the activity:

> *Nursery Teacher*: All the children do the same thing otherwise the mothers think their child's neglected.

Nelson, like Fieldhouse, also had mobiles, but fewer of them, and nearer the ceiling than at Fieldhouse. Those I saw were mainly based on templated shapes.

At Nelson, areas and groups of children had labels. There was the 'art' room (formerly the 'quiet' room), and the 'play' room (formerly the 'noisy' room). The children were in either the 'red' group or the 'yellow' group. The staff's duties were highly formalized. For example, the list below defines the tasks for the nursery nurses before and after the children are in the nursery:

> 8.45 ART ROOM — fill water, uncover sand, prepare art easel, put newspaper on floor, paper, paints, put out plasticine and playdough (except baking clay), paper and crayons and sharpened pencils on drawing table.
>
> 12.45 — check all areas and make inviting, fresh and tidy as possible. Sweep floor if necessary/ sand, snacks and baking/ tidy

sand tray, tidy and sweep hall, check toilet for paper towels, litter,
wet seats, wet floor, any toilet needing flushing and take appropriate action.

11.40–12.00 weekly: change table toys, replace used books in
cupboard in correct place. As required: refill paint containers
under sink; repair books and toys; shopping; children's monthly
progress chart.

Whereas at Fieldhouse there were no formal staff meetings, a formal
meeting was held weekly at Nelson.

Consider a further example of the structuring of space. In the two
nurseries, there were different levels of demarcation between and 'inside'
and an 'outside' activity. At Fieldhouse, the 'outdoors' and nature were
'brought in'. There was, for example, 'Nippy' the guinea pig, whom the
children took it in turns to care for at weekends. Frogspawn could be
observed developing in a glass bowl next to fast-growing tubs of watercress
which the children were later to eat. The inside 'greenhouse' has already
been mentioned. There were more house-plants at Fieldhouse. (In a
headteacher's newsletter to parents, the latter were asked to bring in
unwanted house-plants to 'enhance the environment of the classrooms'.)
The children were permitted to ride around on trikes and scooters in the
confines of the indoor reception area. No restrictions were placed on the
ringing of bicycle bells. By contrast, Nelson had fewer plants, no indoor
riding and no pets.

A further consideration is the extent of demarcation between home
and school, particularly the admission of parent-helpers. The attitude to
parents was similar in both schools. First, the position at Nelson:

DH: Now, when you come into a new job, some things
jell and some things grate. What kinds of things
did you want to change when you came here?

Nursery teacher: Yes. Well, I took it very carefully to begin with,
because the headteacher liked things done in the
way they'd always been done, but one of the
things I wanted to change was the fact that the
parents seemed to take over — when they arrived
with their children; when they arrived to collect
their children, more — there was a lengthy collection period from 11.45 until 12.15 at that time — it
was longer in the morning — was the time for
collecting the children, and they would come in,
meet all their friends, have a sort of chat with their
friends in the nursery room. And it was just chaos,
and I couldn't stand that, so I had to get that

> sorted out, so that I really wanted parents coming in, collecting their children, and going out. And if they wanted to chat with their friends, have it in the little cloakroom area.

The parents were, however, allowed into the nursery, but on the teacher's terms:

> Sometimes we have specific things (for them to do). Other times, it's just, 'Well, would you help any child who looks as though he's needing help, standing around looking lost, not knowing what to do, help him with puzzles, read him a story, play with the water, just help in general.' So the parents are welcome to come in. Sometimes they are a great help, sometimes they're an absolute nuisance, like the one we had yesterday, who walked around all the time with her child in her arms, and this just makes me want to tear my hair out, because I don't think it's good for the child or for the other children, and eventually I separated the pair of them and said to the children in general: 'Now when your mummies come in it's to help the ladies (in both nursery schools, the nursery nurses were referred to publicly by the nursery teachers as "the ladies") with all of the children, not just to be with you all the time'.

At Fieldhouse, parents were less in evidence. Most parents, however, were regarded as being 'good': their children attended well ('over 95 per cent attendance'), brought in odds and ends when asked, and were already 'capable'. In the mornings, the parents ushered in their children to the teacher who ticked off their names on a register at a desk near the entrance. At Nelson, the parents removed the child's outdoor clothes in the cloakroom which separated the 'art room' from the 'playroom'. The children were then escorted just inside one of the rooms. Registration was done informally later.

To summarize thus far: the standardisation and definition of activities and areas is central to the notion of bureaucracy. The old adage 'A place for everything and everything in its place' was evident, to varying degrees, in both nursery units. Spaces were demarcated; children and activities were labelled; duties and routines were specified. The limits of endeavour were thus prescribed. There is, however, a further manifestation of bureaucracy in the nursery school. In a complex industrial society, social and technical coordination requires not only a formal structuring of space, but also of time. It is to this temporal consideration, as well as to that of sequence, that we now turn. A central question is: does the pre-school engender the beginnings of bureaucratized time — that is, clock time and routine?

Time: 'The Time of Their Lives ...'

Before I undertook the detailed fieldwork at Nelson and Fieldhouse, I had visited a number of other nurseries in the area. In one of them, I was able to observe the child's first experience of a school. It had all the characteristics of 'clocking-in'. That is, on entering the nursery, each child hung up his coat on a hook beside his name-plate. Moving into the main area, the child was then confronted by four coloured sets of wall-mounted arrays of slots, each slot containing a flat lollypop stick with a name written on it. The child had to go to the array which represented his colour-group, withdraw his identity-stick from the top row of the array, and place it in the corresponding slot in the bottom row. If the stick was in the bottom row, then staff knew the child was 'in'. The child then proceeded to collect his colour-coded badge (bearing his name) and to pin it to his clothing, with the help of his parent. This elaborate procedure was reversed when the child left the nursery. Gradually, the procedure would become routine for the child, a standard practice beyond his reflection. So it was with other procedures which tacitly structured a sense of 'school' time in the consciousness of the child. These are now considered.

As far as I could ascertain, no child could tell the time from the nursery clocks. They did, however, know the *sequence* of nursery activities, which they called 'times'. At Nelson, the 'time' sequence was: cloakroom, choosing (from the 'non-directed' activities arrayed before them), tidy-up time, toilet time, snack time (and its sub-routines, more of which shortly), choosing time, tidy-up time, story/singing or other grouped and 'directed' activity, going home time. (Snack time and directed activities were all staff-controlled.) At Fieldhouse the sequence of 'times' was: arrival and registration, cloakroom, tidy-up time, snack time and story/drama/singing/news time, free time (outside, weather permitting). The sequencing, therefore, was similar in both settings, but the formality was stronger at Nelson. To illustrate this, consider 'snack time' in each nursery. My focus on snack time arose out of my puzzlement at the accuracy with which children seemed to sense that snack time was imminent. To give a flavour of this activity in both nurseries, some relevant interview and field notes are provided below, beginning with Nelson.

> *Nursery nurse*: It's a bit different this year — well, the system (for snack time) has changed this year. We do different things compared to what we used to do. It used to just be story time — well, like — how can I explain? The red group had their snack in the art room, and the yellow group had their snack in the back room; and before, they would have been the groups that went to the story corner at story time, but now the red group's in one room one week, and

	they're in the other room the other week. And that's the only way that they would get confused — you know, they would just automatically go to their corner.
DH:	I would get confused!
Nursery nurse:	Yes! But it's amazing how quickly they pick it up, and you just say to them, 'Right. The red group is in the play room', and they all just troop through, and the yellow group just goes to the other room.
DH:	What else have they got to remember other than that?
Nursery nurse:	Well, they've got to remember where their snack group is. They've got to remember that their snack group's not necessarily the same group as where they have their story, and they've got to — I don't know, I just find it's really ...

Consider now the actual routine for snack time at Nelson:

9.55: a nursery nurse goes across to the infant school staff-room for coffee break. 9.56 (to a child) 'Just stay here as it's almost snack time'. 'Right boys and girls, tidy up for snack time'. Shortly after, all the children sit down on the floor among their tables: 'Right, James. Stand up; Paul, stand — right, go and get ready for snacks' (i.e. go in twos to the toilet).

On returning from the toilet, the children take a chair and contribute it to the formation of an arc of chairs in front of the nursery nurse. A reminder to Jane: 'Jane ... just walk. If you run you might hurt yourself.' To Alan: 'Keep your feet still Alan, please'. To all: 'Hands together please (for a little prayer). Not over your face!'

'James. Come and get your milk'. (James gets up, walks to the nursery nurse's table in full view of his friends, takes his milk in a blue, stackable plastic mug, and takes it back to his seat.)

'Susi. Come and get your milk'. And so on, one by one.

When the children are finished, they walk out, singly, and stack their mugs ('Don't pile them up too high'.) They then receive a biscuit and fruit and return to their seat in the arc.

10.15 (the children still in the arc formation) The children force some exaggerated coughs: 'Don't be silly'. They then return, on cue from the teacher, in twos, not running, and carrying the chair they have been sitting on back to a table.

This arrangement varied slightly across the three staff. The general procedure, however, was similar.

At Fieldhouse, pre-snack 'tidy-time' was at 9.55 a.m. This meant that the children swept up, mopped floors and put away everything that had been on the tables and floor. The children then assembled in the two large areas, and the partition was drawn, separating one snack group from the other. In both areas the tables (two of them) were brought together, the children sat down, and one of them would be assigned to walk round the tables counting the number of children. Sometimes, they would all count together:

> *Nursery nurse*:   Let's count together ... how many on that table? Eight. On this one, six, but here comes Alice, so there's ... seven!

The exchange continues:

> *Nursery nurse*:   Excuse me. Someone is trying to tell me a story. Did you eat your breakfast? What have you got in your pocket? CARS! and BUSES! (She holds up the toy bus) Is it a special one? Yes, it's the one that goes to the airport. What about this? What colour is it? RED! How many wheels on it? You ARE clever this morning.

The 'bus-cake' was then brought in as part of the transport theme (at Fieldhouse, snack-time and the group activity which immediately succeeded it were usually linked to the 'theme' of the day):

> *Nursery nurse*:   How many windows?
> *Children*:   Three ...
> *Nursery nurse*:   What did we use?
> *Children*:   Eggs ... flour ... apples ... butter ... sugar.
> *Nursery nurse*:   Now, someone who's very strong ... (The children raise their hands) (Jim hands out the cake and slice of apple.)
>
>   I think we'll have our snack, and then we'll have news time. If you cough, blow or sneeze, use a hanky if you please!!
>
>   The people on this table are nearly finished ... I'm looking for someone to wash up ... Peter ... who's sitting nicely. Peter, choose someone to dry, and don't leave bubbles in the bottom of the cup. (The children then move to the story mat to sing a song 'about a bus', thereby integrating it with the 'transport' theme.)

The differences in the arrangements for snack time may be summarized: At Fieldhouse there was no pre-snack, two-by-two toilet ritual; at

Fieldhouse, the children sat with the teacher around a table, and were served by a child, from a tray, in marked contrast to the Nelson practice whereby the children had to wait to go up to the teacher's table, one by one; at Fieldhouse, there was no prayer ritual; at Nelson, the snack tended not to be related to the wider, on-going 'theme' or to a subsequent group activity, like singing or drama; the 'trooping-out' ceremony at the end of Nelson's snack time was not evident at Fieldhouse; there was a greater group emphasis at Fieldhouse: that is, they counted themselves, noted who was 'missing from the group', and sang or played together; and at Nelson, children were 'paraded' in a set routine.

So far, we have considered two representations of bureaucracy in the nursery school: one spatial, the other temporal. At Fieldhouse, notions of time and space were less formal than at Nelson. Again at Fieldhouse, there was greater self-control and choice, less ritual (itself a form of control), and more discretion for the children. Nevertheless, the broad parameters were carefully defined by the nursery teacher. Within those spatial and temporal limits, the child had discretion. Finally, we turn to a third element of bureaucracy, that of monitoring and performance criteria.

How Are They Doing?

In the earlier reference to Berger *et al.*'s (1973) analysis, it was indicated that part of the 'bureaucratic cognitive style' was a tendency to test and evaluate in an as objective a manner as possible. In this respect, the two schools differed, as the following extracts from their respective prospectuses suggest. First, Nelson:

Assessment

Continuous assessment of the young child is carried out in the form of check-lists which include headings such as social development, language development, play, tactile-skills, motor control, creativity, physical development, visual and auditory development, concentration and speech. The nursery staff observe the children and note progress throughout the term. This is the only effective way to achieve a real conclusion.

Now, Fieldhouse:

Assessment

A child's progress is continuously being monitored by the staff and

69

this is reported to his parents in an informal way.

Both 'assessment' sections proceed to stress that, wherever a difficulty is suspected, parents and appropriate support agencies will be notified. At Nelson, the teacher felt that the checklist which she had inherited was too general. It had fifteen decisions to be taken each month on each child. The range of response options on each item varied from two per item to ten per item. Space for comments was provided. Her intended replacement schedule would be different:

> The things that I'm assessing are more specific things. But I would like to get a better way of assessing them, that's not terribly time-consuming, because with sixty children it is time-consuming.
>
> *Her reasons for the assessment were*: . . . to help me decide what I should do next with the children.

As to their reliability, there were doubts voiced by a nursery nurse:

DH:	Do you assess the children?
Nursery nurse:	Well, just in . . .
DH:	Those checklists?
Nursery nurse:	Yes.
DH:	Yes, and you yourself do that, do you?
Nursery nurse:	Yes, we do fifteen every month, and this had (inaudible) as thirty.
DH:	I see. And does there arise a situation where you and another, say . . ., would rate the same child . . .
Nursery nurse:	Differently?
DH:	Yes.
Nursery nurse:	Oh yes!

In neither nursery was I able to see actual reports on the chidren. That, however, is not the point at issue. At issue is the way in which the children were assessed, and the formality of that procedure at Nelson. At Fieldhouse, assessment was far less formal than at Nelson. There were no checklists, although the staff could discuss a child's development informally if asked.

Conclusion

The broad concern of this study has been with the interrelationship between bureaucracy, as an organizational form, and childhood, as defined in the pre-school. A comparative methodology has been applied to two settings of similar enrolment, catchment area and architecture. Given the limitations of the case-study, appropriate caution in applying the findings to other contexts is warranted, particularly when it is kept in mind that this is a Scottish study. In both nursery units, the declared ethos was that the children should be given structured freedom, not licence. The implementation of this ethos differed markedly in the two schools. The differentiation and specificity of time, space and assessment was greater at Nelson, both for children and, especially, for nursery nurses. In both settings, however, parents tended to be kept at the margin. In both settings, too, the sequencing of events and the structuring of space was teacher-directed: the children 'chose' from the range of activites on offer. Within those temporal and spatial limits, the children had varying degrees of freedom — more at Fieldhouse, less at Nelson.

How may these events be explained? What the data here suggests is that the principles and practices of the pre-school are the expression of the interaction of a number of considerations: the pervasiveness of an increasingly 'soft' form of bureaucracy, best typified by human relations management theory; the idealism of 'child-centred' educational philosophy and its expression in the Hadow and Plowden Reports (Ministry of Education, 1933; CACE, 1967) in England and in the Primary Memorandum in Scotland (SED, 1965); the cultural and historical roots of pre-school education; and, finally, the biographies and professional socialization of practitioners. These are now discussed.

Berger *et al.* (1973) expect more and more domains of social life to become bureaucratized. The prevailing 'cognitive style' will be 'bureaucratic', as defined earlier. But, following Bidwell (1965), we can envisage a loosening of Weber's pure form of bureaucracy to take account of the increasing emergence of human relations management styles, particularly in the service-sector of the economy. This may result in a greater tendency in educational organizations, including the pre-school, for 'loose' bureaucracies wherein social control will be less overt, and where spatial, temporal and social relationships will be more 'open' within the broad parameters of the bureaucratic structure (Hartley, 1986). In many respects, however, the nursery school may also have been influenced by eighteenth and nineteenth century continental, child-centred educational philosophy (Deasey, 1978). That is, it is to be doubted that Bernstein's (1975) 'invisible pedagogy' in the nursery and infant school is the consequence *only* of a shift towards less hierarchical and bureaucratic forms of control in industry. Rather, this pedagogy and educational philosophy *pre-dates* modern industrial production and its organizational arrangements. In a similar vein, King (1979, p. 450) has cited the historical work of Aries, who has traced the roots of child-centredness to a period *before* modern industrialism. Thus the association between 'child-centred', 'invisible' pedagogy in the nursery school and the emerging human relations management style in the workplace is arguably no more than an affinity, not a cause and effect relationship. Current practice in nursery schools, therefore, may reveal this interaction between, on the one hand, the bureaucratic tendency (in its pure and soft forms), and, on the other hand, the idealism of child-centred educational philosophy. The former requires *standards* of time, space, content and assessment; the latter calls for notions of *individual* growth, choice and assessment. It is to be suspected, however, that the teacher is less aware of the bureaucratic 'imperative' than of the child-centred 'imperative': that is, she might more readily assert that she is doing this or that because it accords with the principle of child-centred education, not with the need to bureaucratise the mind of the child so that he will 'fit in' to society's dominant form of organization She might be completely unaware of why she structures time and space along bureaucratic lines: for her, it is the 'way things are'. Put another way, the hidden curriculum which the teacher constructs and transmits may, ironically, be hidden from her consciousness.

There are two further considerations which may be part of the explanation. The first is historical. Those who are familiar with nursery school practice in England may regard the practice of 'snack time' to be very formal, particularly as it occurred at Nelson nursery school. Scottish practice may be partly explained by Roberts' (1972) argument, as follows:

> It must be concluded that, despite the efforts of our well-remembered makers of Scottish education, infant education put down no roots in this northern soil. The traditional parish school did not welcome children who were too young for the real education of learning to read, write and count, and parents held a similar view of what schooling was for and how long it should last — perhaps three years of irregular and seasonal attendance — which they took with them into the crowded city slum. (p. 44)

Thus the reduced emphasis in Scottish pre-school education on play may be a cultural residue of the intellectualism and formalism to which Roberts alludes. There may be a related reason, particularly in respect of Nelson nursery school. The headteacher had originally been trained as a primary school teacher, and had taught as such before assuming a position in the nursery school, after which she had trained as a nursery teacher. Her greater emphasis on formality of method and assessment may reflect this. From all of these considerations, therefore, a mono-causal and determinist theory of the organizational form of the nursery school would be unwarranted. Explanations must include reference to the meanings which those in schools assign to their situation and to their actions. This, though interesting, is not enough: in addition, reference must also be made to the wider cultural, political and historical contexts in which the school and its members are located. What *is* warranted is a more diverse sociological and philosophical analysis of the pre-school, one which complements the rather one-sided psychological perspective which has hitherto prevailed.

References

BERGER, P.L., BERGER, B. and KELLNER, H. (1973) *The Homeless Mind*. Harmondsworth, Penguin.

BERNSTEIN, B. (1975) 'Class and pedagogies: visible and invisible', *Educational Studies*, 1, 1, pp. 23–41.

BIDWELL, C.E. (1965) 'The school as a formal organisation', in MARCH, J.G. (Ed.) *A Handbook of Organisations*, New York, Rand McNally.

BROADBENT, G. BUNT, R. and JENCKS, C. (1980) *Signs, Symbols and Architecture*, Chichester, John Wiley.

CENTRAL ADVISORY COUNCIL ON EDUCATION (CACE) (1967) *Children and their Primary Schools, Vols I and II*. (The Plowden Report) London. HMSO.

DEASEY, D. (1978) *Education Under Six*, London, Croom Helm.

DIMAGGIO, P.J. and POWELL, W.W. (1983) 'The iron cage revisited: institutional isomorphism and collective rationality in organisational fields', *American Sociological Review*, 48, pp. 147–60.

EVANS, K. (1979) 'The physical form of the school', *British Journal of Educational Studies*, XXVII, 1, pp. 29–41.

GLASER, B. and STRAUSS, A. (1967) *The Discovery of Grounded Theory: Strategies for Qualitative Research*, Chicago, Aldine.

HARTLEY, D. (1986) 'Structural isomorphism and the management of consent in education', *Journal of Educaton Policy*, 1, 3, pp. 229–37.

KANTER, R.M. (1972) 'The organization child: Experience management in a nursery school'. *Sociology of Education*, 45, 2, pp. 186–212.

KING, R. (1979) 'In search of the invisible pedagogy', *Sociology*, 13, pp. 445–58.

LUBECK, S. (1985) *Sandbox Society*, Lewes, Falmer Press.

MINISTRY OF EDUCATION (1933) *Report of the Consultative Committee in Infant and Nursery Schools*, (The Hadow Report) London, HMSO.

POLLARD, S. (1965) *The Genesis of Modern Management*, London, Arnold.

ROBERTS, A.F.B. (1972) 'Scotland and infant education in the nineteenth century' *Scottish Educational Studies*, May, pp. 39–45.

SCOTTISH EDUCATION DEPARTMENT (SED) (1965) *Primary Education in Scotland* (The Primary Memorandum). Edinburgh, HMSO.

STIMSON, G.V. (1986) 'Viewpoint: Place and space in sociological fieldwork', *Sociological Review*, 34, 3, pp. 641–56.

THOMPSON, E.P. (1967) '*Time, work-discipline, and industrial capitalism*', *Past and Present*, 38, pp. 56–97.

WEBER, M. (1949) *The Methodology of the Social Sciences*, translated by SHILS, E.A. and FISHER, H.A. Glencoe, The Free Press.

WEBER, M. (1978, original 1922) *Economy and Society* edited by ROTH, C. and WITTICH, C. Berkeley, CA, University of California Press.

WRIGHT MILLS, C. (1967) *Power, Politics and People* Oxford, Oxford University Press.

5   Making Sense of School

Margaret Jackson

Introduction

When starting school young children enter an environment very different from anything which they have previously known. King (1978) described infant classrooms as an 'educational casbah' full of a rich variety of furniture, displays, materials, games, etc. These rooms are constantly changing spheres of activity, reflecting not only the children's work but also the aspirations and ideals of the teachers' ideologies. In addition, classrooms can be seen as communities where roles and rules become defined and social groups are formed and maintained, challenged and reformed. In this chapter I will argue that children's academic performance in school is closely related to their competence within the social organization of the classroom.

Willes's work (1983) suggested that, for a young child entering school, the organization routines of classrooms have a crucial vitality and importance. These routines form a large part of the patten for each child's time in school and place the control of activity firmly in the hand of the teacher. It seems then that for young children, an important aspect of starting school is concerned with becoming familiar with the rules and routines of daily classroom life. It is about the development of a level of social competence which allows access to the learning patterns of the classroom. It must also be remembered that learning experiences at school are very different from typical learning experiences at home — a difference which Cashdan (1980) describes as being similar to that between an *a la carte* menu and a *table d'hote* menu. I would argue that an important part of making sense of school is being able to use previous experiences and adapt them to the different ways of learning.

The classrooms in which I carried out my study bear many similarities to those described by King and Willes and indeed they can be said to bear many characteristics of that which King describes as 'the recognizable social world of the infant school', where the teachers' typification of the children in the class influenced the reality of everyday life in the class-rooms. I spent a term working with the three teachers in two reception classrooms. I had previously taught in the school and so was familiar with the organization and routine and I felt readily accepted by both staff and children.

The school was a modern semi open-plan building on a new estate built to cater for overspill from the inner area of a major metropolitan city. Many of the families had been moved from tightly-knit communities and returned 'home' each weekend and so there was little sense of community on the estate. An urban-aid project was just one of the ways of providing extra help for the social problems of the estate.

There were over 400 pupils aged 5–8 in the school, divided into twelve classes with fourteen full-time teachers, two full-time nursery nurses and one part-time ancillary plus the head. A full-time teacher and nursery nurse worked in the attached nursery class. Apart from the deputy headteacher all the staff were female and for many of them it was their first appointment.

I worked in the two adjacent reception classes, which opened onto a wide corridor used for art and craft activities. Although organized as two separate classes they frequently worked together and shared resources. Three teachers worked in these classrooms; one, a temporary scale 1, withdrew groups from both classes and the others, a scale 1 teacher and the scale 3 language consultant, were each responsible for one class.

The two classrooms were similar in many ways. Both were fully carpeted and the hessian covered walls were covered with displays mostly of children's work. The teachers had brought in objects to personalize the rooms: one had large pieces of driftwood and logs to sit on and the other had some child-sized cane table and chairs. In each class the children were organized into groups based on ability as perceived by the teacher and work was arranged on an integrated basis. In general the activities were teacher-directed and occasionally most of the class were given a simple activity to enable the teacher to work with individual children.

At the same time as myself, a group of young children entered these classrooms for the first time and for them it could have seemed a strange world and might well have been alien from much of their previous experiences. I wanted to tell the story of the reception class from the perspective of the children and attempt to uncover new levels of meaning. Thinking reflectively about what is already familiar is one way of getting below the surface and in focussing on children's perceptions one would expect to be helped towards a closer matching of classroom activities and children's understandings. As a researcher I felt that I was adopting similar sense-making strategies to the children, in forming, testing and reformulating hypotheses.

I used various and several techniques for collecting data. Each of these shed new light on the classroom situation and also revealed the differing perspectives of child, teacher and researcher. In this way I aimed to provide triangulated data and to broaden in detail the description of the children's responses. In summary, the data-collecting methods used were :

1 The Linguistic Awareness in Reading Readiness Test, (Downing, Ayers and Schaefer, 1983).
2 Participant observation of each child during two normal days' activities.
3 Audio-recording of each child telling a story.
4 Video-recording of each child in the book corner, followed by focussed interviews about the recording with each child.
5 Interviews with each child about the nature of story.
6 Examination of the teachers' record of work and the school language policy.

I hoped that the combination of the different techniques used and the different perspectives gained would serve to provide a rich description of what was going on in the classroom.

Making Sense

In considering how young children make sense of school, it is necessary to spend some time considering how they have previously made sense of the world around them and of the extent to which language plays a part in this process. A young child who is beginning formal education comes to school already possessing considerable knowledge about the world. Almost from birth children are making sense of their environment and the sense-making process is an active one, involving previous experiences and encounters in learning about the new.

A young child starting school can show well developed thinking skills and throughout life may have been engaged in creating hypotheses and then testing and reformulating them in the context of the social and physical environment. Effective early teaching is likely to take into account the characteristics of children's thinking and the social nature of the learning process. Language is a vital component of this process and has been used to learn about the world, to control behaviour and to establish roles. Halliday (1978) defined language as 'meaning potential' and so included the social environment of the child as an important factor in the learning process. It is difficult to separate general learning about the world from learning about language at these early stages. The language we use to talk about the environment gives meaning and definition to our experience and activity. As Wells and Nicholls (1985) says,

... just as children learn the language system through experience of using it as a resource, so in increasing their control of the resources of language, they also increase their understanding of the experiences that are encoded by those resources. (p. 35)

Language can thus be seen as a functional resource and so the emphasis is placed on shared responsibility for learning within the social context. It then becomes apparent that within this model, the adult is seen as collaborator and facilitator rather than instructor.

One way in which an adult can facilitate learning is by providing an environment conducive to active learning, which allows children to test and reformulate the hypotheses formed from past experiences. In school, children progressively need to be able to turn language and thought in upon themselves; in Donaldson's terms (1978) to cope with disembedded language. Play is one way in which children are able to do this and to make new discoveries about the environment. In imaginative play children take themselves into new and exciting worlds and their knowledge of spoken language serves as a means for creating story, exploring new situations, developing relationships and acquiring new knowledge. It is this excitement of exploration which needs to be extended and providing opportunities for play can be one way of leading children into new worlds beyond the immediate and allowing them to be involved in their own learning.

As children actively interact with the environment their past experiences exert a strong influence on the learning process, as is illustrated by some current research in early literacy learning. The work of Fox (1983) showed that the beginnings of future literacy competencies can be found within the child's existing narrative competencies. Young children are able to use the literary conventions of story-telling and to demonstrate a range of understandings clearly related to the organization of text. In many different ways children are able to use their literary experience for their own narrative purposes. Dombey (1983) related the experience of being read to aloud to the experience of learning to read. She showed how the child learns relationship with the author, creation of meaning through written text alone, syntactic patterns to help prediction, pleasure from the experience and taking an active role in gaining meaning from the texts.

Sense-making can thus be seen as a continuum of learning and making sense of school becomes part of the continuum. New experiences build upon old as children test and reformulate hypotheses they have created. The question then arises of the extent to which children's past experiences are exploited in school and also of how appropriate the ways in which children use past experiences are to classroom activities.

My study was relevant to this issue and showed how some children make the connection between past and present learning while others do not tap into their own learning resources. Examples from the experiences of Kevin and Lee illustrate the point.

Kevin and Lee

Kevin was observed in the book corner with three other children. They had been told that they could do whatever they liked: read alone, read to each other or just talk about the books. They were video-recorded. Kevin ignored the camera, selected a book, sat down and immediately became engrossed in it. The book was an annual and for twelve whole minutes Kevin intently looked at this one book, paying hardly any attention to the other children. He handled the book carefully, turning the pages from right to left. When he dropped the book he turned through the pages until he found the page at which he had been looking. He studied each page at length, sometimes holding the book closer to get a better look and occasionally tracing the puzzles with his finger. Sometimes he was so long looking at one page and sat so still, that, apart from eye movements, one might have thought he had fallen asleep!

Later that day Kevin and I watched the video together and I recorded his comments. He was able to tell me exactly what was on each page, knew just what the book was about, what he had been doing and which pages he had enjoyed most and why. He seemed to have been lost in the world of the book and had brought and gained meaning from his interaction with the text. He had not been a passive receiver but had actively involved himself with the book and had had strong reactions and responses which he was able to talk about and share with another person.

MJ: Why did you choose that book?
Kevin: Cos I wanted to read it.
MJ: Can you remember what was in the book?
Kevin: It was animals ... a monkey.
MJ: What was the monkey doing?
Kevin: He was eating ... eating his food.
MJ: Why did it take you so long to look at that page?
Kevin: I couldn't see them all. They were all hiding and you had to find them.
MJ: And did you find them all?
Kevin: Only a few ... but I didn't want to find all of them ... I was looking at it. I missed something that I wanted to see.
MJ: What are you doing there with your finger?
Kevin: Your finger has to go round and round.
MJ: Like a puzzle was it, like a maze. And did you do it?
Kevin: Yea.
MJ: You found your way to the middle did you?
Kevin: Yea.
MJ: You found your way to the middle did you?
Kevin: No — to the bottom.

Kevin was clearly reading for meaning in this situation and although he was, as yet, unable to decode the words, he was behaving very much as a reader. He brought expectations to the text and became actively involved with it; he was aware throughout that he was able to manipulate the text and the situation for his own purposes and wishes within the constraints which had been stipulated.

Kevin had exploited this time in the book corner to the full. He knew what was expected of him in the situation and this can be attributed to a great extent to the influence of past experience. In another interview Kevin talked about his experience with books at home.

MJ: Can you read?
Kevin: Sometimes I can.
MJ: Could you read before you came to school?
Kevin: Yes.
MJ: When did you learn to read?
Kevin: My brother teached me how to read.
MJ: Can you remember how he taught you to read?
Kevin: Cos he reads better than me.
MJ: How do you know?
Kevin: Cos he reads me a story when he's at David's and Diane's when it's bedtime. I just listened to the story and I watched the pictures.

That is just one example of Kevin talking about reading a book with an adult at home. He had had opportunities for sharing and was able to use that past experience to make sense of the classroom activity.

The influence of past experiences on present situations was apparent with other children also but not always to such positive effect. Lee spent a similar time in the book corner but in contrast to Kevin, he did anything but look at a book. He climbed on the furniture, examined a vase on the shelf, talked to the other children and looked at the pictures on the display board. Why was there such a difference in the way these two children behaved in the same activity? I have already suggested that Kevin's past experiences equipped him with the strategies for making the most of the school activity and it seems that Lee lacked those strategies. On several occasions he was definite in his assertions that he could not read, had come to school to learn how to do so and saw no point in looking at books until he had learned to read.

MJ: Can you read?
Lee: (Shakes head)
MJ: Are you learning to read?
Lee: Mmm. I'm learning now.
MJ: What sort of things are you doing to help you to read?
Lee: Um. Getting books and take them home to read them.

MJ: What do you do with the books when you take them home?
Lee: My mum will say the word and then you have to say it.

It seemed that Lee's experience of books had not been so pleasurable as Kevin's. He had not shared a book with an adult for enjoyment's sake and did not know how to bring his own understandings to the text and use them to enable him to interact with the text to gain meaning. Lee was waiting until he could 'crack the code'.

On another occasion Lee was sitting next to two girls who were looking at a book together. One was 'reading' to the other when Lee intervened:

Lee: No. You don't do it like that.
Gill: But she's only pretending.
Lee: But the words don't really say that.

Lee must have had some knowledge of the language of books or of matching sound to symbol to know that the girl was not correctly decoding. However, he did not realize that his knowledge of spoken language could be helpful to him when dealing with written language. He did not make the connection between what he already knew and what was required of him in school. He did not possess the strategies for exploiting the activity in ways which are traditionally valued by school. Lee was using his past experience to make sense of school, as was Kevin, but with very different results.

In these examples both children were using their past experience to make sense of classroom activities. The connection Lee had made between his reading experience at home and the activity in the classroom denied him certain strategies and knowledge which would have helped him to gain more from the classroom activity. He seemed to regard school learning as something which would be 'done to him' and not requiring his own active participation. Kevin did not seem to perceive such a difference between home and school learning and expected to be an active participator in the situation. Thus he used sense-making strategies which enabled him to exploit the activity more fully.

Classroom activity is by its very nature problematic; the teacher controls the activity in that she decides on the resources and the aims but the children bring to bear their own understandings on the learning process. Teacher and children bring different meanings to the situation. To children the aims of the activity may not always be immediately apparent and they will use their own understandings to make sense of the situation. It may be that often the transition between home and school learning is so great that children perceive it as two distinct 'methods' rather than a gradual development and thus they do not see that their past experiences have an important bearing on their learning in school. Lee saw school as being the place to learn to read and did not use his extensive knowledge of spoken language to help him to deal with written language. Kevin was most able to make the connection between what had gone on at home and his new experience at school and he was the one identified by the teacher as being the most successful in the classroom.

Social Competence

One way of analyzing data such as that which I have reported above is to consider the process of making sense of school as a process of developing social competence. Children need to become aware of the expectations and demands of the school situation so that their own learning will become appropriate to the constraints of the situation in the classroom. Evidence from the data which I collected showed that some of the children were not aware of the classroom expectations. These children were not regarded by the teacher as being successful because the product of their learning process did not match the product which was expected.

We can consider the children's developing social competence in three main areas:

(i)   in procedural and organizational routines;
(ii)   in interpersonal relations;
(iii) in learning 'how to be taught'.

Procedural and Organizational Routines

The organization of the classroom environment, both in management of time and materials, is an important part of life in a reception class. Hamilton's account (1977) of first days in school show how, during this time, much of the teacher's concern is with procedure. These procedural routines are an integral part of the transition from being an individual at home to being one of a large group at school. A young child's capacity to grasp the organizational procedures of the classroom has an influence on the learning process. As Cook-Gumperz (1986) says,

> ... familiarity with the subtleties of classroom social organisation is a pre-condition for gaining access to learning opportunities. (p. 60)

The following incident showed how one child missed learning opportunities because of her unfamiliarity with the procedural routines of the classroom.

Donna

The whole class was told to get out writing books, pencils and namecards, sit at a table and practise writing their names. In her record of work the teacher said that this was to serve both as practice in letter formation and also as a help in learning how to write their names. Donna spent a long time looking for a pencil, sharping it and then finding a space in which to sit. When she was finally settled she did not start writing but began comparing her namecard with that of her neighbour. She counted the letters, pointed out those which were the same, got up and found both names on the drawers and named each letter. After five minutes the teacher came and told Donna off for not getting on with her work.

In this short time Donna showed a great deal of knowledge about written language: she could identify letters and showed good visual discrimination in matching; she showed awareness of different combinations of letters to form words; she knew that the names on the drawers signified to whom each drawer belonged. She did not actually practise any letter formation but paid great attention to each letter and how the particular combination of letters made up her name. In fact, Donna displayed considerable metalinguistic knowledge.

One cannot criticise the teacher for feeling that Donna had not 'done her work'. Although there was nothing concrete to show for it, Donna had probably gone a long way to achieving the teacher's original aims. With a class of over thirty children it is difficult for a teacher to be aware of all the learning that is going on and it is easy to see why she felt that Donna was 'wasting her time'.

In this small incident Donna made sense of the activity by making it her own and becoming actively involved in her own learning. She used her current knowledge based on past experience as a basis for her present learning; she made, tested and reformulated hypotheses; she used language functionally within a social context. Language plays a central role in the child's coming to terms with the environment. Before starting school a child has already achieved considerable understanding of languge as a system. Experience of language has been used to construct a system of rules and the overgenerallization of these rules that frequently occurs in the spoken language of young children reflects the strategies they use to construct and modify their own 'grammar'. Learning language, however, is more than learning a system and as they learn the rules of form children also learn rules of use; they learn how to use language as a resource for communicating with other people within a variety of contexts. Donna was using her knowledge of written language as a resource for her own learning. In fact, Donna's knowledge was greater than that which was required for the given activity. She used that knowledge to make the activity her own, to bring meaning to the task, to make learning the personal and active process she had known it to be in the past.

However, in the classroom, the ultimate power rests with the teacher. Thus a child has to conform to the organizational norms of the classroom to exploit the full learning potential of the situation. Donna did not do this and despite her sophisticated manipulation of the text she was perceived by the teacher as not fulfilling the demands of the required task and as causing a disruption within the classroom. It seems then, that for a child, active learning and relevant use of past experience and knowledge are not enough in the classroom. Conformation to expected behaviour patterns is what is also required by busy teachers.

Interpersonal Relations

A classroom can be seen as a social community and the relationships which are formed in that community have influence on the learning which takes place. A model of collaborative learning requires children to use language for negotiation, questioning, identifying issues, planning actions and establishing learning relationships and making sense of school demands a social competence within this interpersonal context. It involves forming understandings, not only of the physical but also of the social environment. Children are required to collaborate with each other and with adults and to recognize and respond to different roles in different situations. The range of social relationships with an adult is just one illustration of the complexity of social understanding required. Being in the school assembly, working in a small group with the teacher and sharing an activity on an individual basis are all very different social contexts and require different responses. The child whose past experience does not include using language in these ways or for whom the school experience is so strange could find this difficult. Tina, in the following incident, made sense of the physical context of the classroom environment before she felt able to enter into the social context.

Detailed observation was made of Tina during two full days. The first of these was after she had been in school for exactly one week and the strongest impression of this first day's observation was of the isolation she experienced. She watched and listened to all that was going on but resisted any attempt to make her join in, either by the teacher or another child. Tina spent a long time in the home corner and when the other child playing there tried to include Tina in a game, Tina just silently walked away. She walked round and round the home corner, exploring and trying out all the things in it. When the teacher came and talked to Tina about what she was doing, there was again no response and as soon as the teacher left Tina started to do something else. It seemed that at that stage Tina just wanted to absorb and watch all that was going on in the classroom for herself. Extracts from the field notes describing just two minutes, show Tina's intense investigation of the physical environment:

> *11.19*: Tina goes back to the phone. She puts the receiver which was dangling down, back on the phone. Sits down on the end of the bed. Stands up again immediately. Walks back

> to till. Picks up and looks at it from all sides. Tries to look inside. Takes money out of till drawer and puts it back in. Picks up money from floor and from box of spare money and puts in till drawer.
>
> *11.20:* Walks along, opening all cupboards, looks in each one then closes door. Looks inside saucepans on stove. Closes till.
>
> *11.20:* Walks to edge of home corner and looks around classrooms. Goes to bed, sits down, stands up. Walks to number table, watches children working. Walks round edge of classrooms.

The second day's observation of Tina took place two months later and again she spent considerable time in the home corner. It is interesting to make comparisons between the two occasions. On the second day Tina was playing with the other child, engaging in dramatic play and talking about what she was doing. She provided an almost continuous running commentary on her activites, sometimes addressed to me, sometimes to the other child and sometimes to herself. Generally she was labelling objects and actions but sometimes she provided an interpretation of what was going on. She also discussed and planned with the other child what they were going to do. The field notes show Tina's increased verbalization:

> *9.34:* Tries to put up ironing board — puts it up upside down. Turns it round the right way. 'I don't know where the iron is now.'
>
> Sits on the high chair. 'I'm the baby. I'm sitting in the high chair.'
>
> *9.35:* Takes plate and spoon out of cupboard — sits back. 'I'm a baby.' Sucks a skittle.
>
> Tells another boy to sit on the bed but he refuses. 'I'm having a bottle.

Tina, during these first two months in school, had made sense of the situation to the extent that she was now able to contribute to and attempt to control the social context of the play. At the early stages of Tina's school life the teacher identified Tina as likely to have problems because she felt that Tina was not playing an active enough role in classroom activities for effective learning to take place. It could well be that the expectations of the teacher were too great. Tina's sense-making strategies may not have fitted in with the school expectations but they enabled her to come to terms with the vast array of new experiences. She began by exploring, observing and investigating and later she used her newly-acquired knowledge to express herself and the issues that were currently important to her. Just before Tina started school her mother had had a new baby but it was not until Tina felt familiar and confident with the new classroom environment that she felt able to use her new understanding to explore the new situation at home. She needed to make sense of school before she could relate it to the rest of her life and use it for active learning. For Tina that process involved observation and assimilation before participation.

Learning in the reception class is very much about collaboration with others and a lot of interaction with others is expected and encouraged. Lee had spent a long time building an elaborate model with Cuisenaire rods but was unwilling to discuss it with the teacher. Tina was unwilling to discuss her dramatic play with the teacher or other children. It seems that until young children are able to use language as a resource for negotiation with others and as a means for establishing collaborative learning relationships, the pattern of learning in the classroom remains inaccessible.

Learning 'How to be Taught'

Children come to school as active learners. They have probably had experience of investigating their own environment and learning through real and important problem-solving. Frequently they have had the sole attention of a concerned adult who has been learning alongside the child. Learning has been 'embedded' in concrete situations of everyday life.

In school children are required to conform to the pattern of learning of their classroom and this may not be the same as their previous active learning. Donna adapted the prescribed classroom activity, creating her own problem-solving situation and collaborating with another child. However, in doing this, she was rejecting the specific demands of the teacher and it is rare that children are given the power to do this in the classroom. An important part of 'making sense of school' is learning to confine active learning to the constraints of the situation.

School learning rarely expects children to be completely passive and frequently there are clear patterns of participation. Tina did not follow these patterns and 'made sense of school' in her own way. Lee did not participate in the learning situation, either in the book corner or after he had made his model, but waited to be instructed. Both these children were classified by their teachers as likely to have problems because their sense-making processes were not as expected.

I would thus argue that social competence in learning 'how to be taught' requires discernment of and compliance with the accepted learning patterns of the classroom.

Conclusions

I began by describing the 'recognizable social world' of the classroom and suggested that any description or analysis of classroom action must take into account the social elements of that classroom. 'Making sense of school' involves an increasing awareness of the social environment and an increasing ability to participate effectively in that social environment. Children, as active learners, bring to bear their past experiences and their own understandings and perceptions of the situation. These perceptions may not necessarily match the perceptions of the teacher, for learning in school can be a very different thing from learning at home. As children begin to make sense of school so they become aware of the perceptions and expectations of the teacher and frequently adapt their own behaviour to comply. As Stebbins (1981) says.

> Effective classroom participants have the requisite skill and knowledge to interpret the speech and behaviour of other participants there and to respond sensibly. (p. 258)

I have considered how children as active learners begin to make sense of school, how they begin to adapt and refine their learning strategies to comply with the expectations of the school and also how they adapt and refine the classroom activities to comply with their own understandings and past experiences. Thus they become effective classroom participants. I would argue that this sense-making is an essentially social process and is centered on the development of social competence within the classroom. The young child comes to an understanding of the different relationships and roles which exist within the classroom, of the expectations that the teacher holds, including those behaviours which are valued and those which are discouraged, and of the value and relevance of past experience. These understandings are reached within the social context as children interact with other participants and, at the same time, social competence is assessed by their behaviour within the classroom in response to the social and learning environment.

I would want to go on to argue that the same criteria for effective classroom participation should and do also apply to teachers. They also need the ability to interpret the behaviour of others and respond accordingly. Adopting this way of seeing and reflecting on classroom activity could be one way of enabling teachers to modify their behaviour in the classroom to take account of the child's perspective and thus ensure that classroom action is fully effective. It is because teachers have the power to control children and structure the classroom situation to which the children must respond that this sensitivity to the perceptions of the children is so vital. An awareness of the messages about learning and the curriculum which are conveyed through the social context of the classroom can only help teachers to help children to become more effective classroom participants.

References

ARMSTRONG, M. (1980) *Closely Observed Children*, London, Writers and Readers.

BRUNER, J. (1984) 'Language, mind and reading', in GOELMAN, H., OBERG, A. and SMITH, F. (Eds), *Awakening To Literacy*, Victoria, Heinemann Educational Books.

CASHDAN, A. (1980) 'Teaching language and reading in the early years', in BRAY, G. and HUGH, A.G. (Eds) *The Reading Connection*, London, Ward Lock.

COOK-GUMPERZ, J. (1986) *The Social Construction Of Literacy. Studies in Interactional Sociolinguistics 3*, Cambridge, Cambridge University Press.

DOMBEY, H. (1983) 'Learning the language of books', in MEEK, M. (Ed.) *Opening Moves* Bedford Way Paper 17, London, University of London.

DONALDSON, M. (1978) *Children's Minds*, London, Fontana.

FOX, C. (1983) 'Talking like a book: Young children's oral monologues', in MEEK, M. (Ed.) *Opening Moves*, Bedford Way Paper 17, London, University of London.

HALLIDAY, M.A.K. (1978) *Language as Social Semiotic*, London, E.J. ARNOLD.

HAMILTON, D. (1977) *In Search Of Structure*, London, Hodder and Stoughton.

KING, R. (1978) *All Things Bright and Beautiful? A Sociological Study of Infant Classrooms*, Chichester, Wiley.

ROWLAND, S. (1984) *The Enquiring Classroom*, Lewes, Falmer Press.

STEBBINS, R. (1981) 'Classroom ethnography and the definition of the situation', in BARTON, L. and WALKER, S. (Eds) *Schools, Teachers and Teaching*, Lewes, Falmer Press.

WELLS, G. and NICHOLLS, J. (Eds) (1985) *Language and Learning: an Interactional Perspective*, Lewes, Falmer Press.

WILLES, M.J. (1983) *Children into Pupils: A Study of Language in Early Schooling*, London, Routledge and Kegan Paul.

6 Letting Them Get On With it: A Study of Unsupervised Group Talk in an Infant School

Thea Prisk

The Questions

The language of young children has been the subject of many studies (Halliday, 1973; Crystal, 1976; Richmond, 1982). Common to these is the assumption that communicative language is a tool which aids the development of intellectual growth. But what happens in the unsupervised group? Can teachers assume that valuable learning processes actually take place in that noisy corner where six children are discussing a collection of slugs? This chapter describes a study of young children's talk undertaken in an infant school and was designed to address these issues:

(i)   Does unsupervised talk have educational value?
(ii) Can young children make progress in problem-solving without an adult being present to steer them towards successful solutions?
(iii) Can access to data collected from unsupervised groups help teachers to understand their pupils' needs?

The Context

In the school where this research took place we were aware of the importance of speech, believing that classroom organization should include opportunities for children to discuss problems, think aloud, and work together in groups. Our language policy placed considerable emphasis on the value of discussion; we believed that talking to, and with, children was a way of evaluating their understanding. However, as headteacher, I was worried that the emphasis on adult-led group talks and the involvement of parents in the implementation of the policies, decreased the opportunities available to the children for experimentation on their own. In discussing this the teachers felt that, if it was intended to extend opportunities for unsupervised talk, they needed to have more knowledge of its educational value in order to feel justified in encouraging it. We felt that the only way to evaluate what was actually happening was to study the problem-solving talk that took place in our own school. Studying the language of discussions undertaken by children we knew might enable us to make more accurate judgments about the educational outcomes.

Minns (1976) believed that teachers can understand more effectively the way children learn if they study the talk of groups where no teacher is present. Although data collected from teacherless groups may reveal a mass of irrelevancies, inconsistencies and even incorrect solutions, we need to know what is happening in terms of interactive processes in order to judge the value of the activity. An opportunity to follow these issues was provided when I undertook a part-time course (MA in Applied Research in Education) at Cambridge Institute of Education. The advantage of part-time study is that it enables the student to get to grips with an existing problem in their own educational establishment, providing both motivation and support throughout the process, and so I was able to focus on unsupervised group talk.

Starting Points

My first problem was how to study a discussion without being present when it occurred. Tape recording appeared to be the obvious method. I tried to take recordings in a normal classroom but the material was largely untranscribable; I therefore decided to withdraw the children to a quieter room. I had intended to record children tackling a variety of tasks, some involving texts and some where materials had to be manipulated in response to certain predetermined rules. During a trial period I found that, when children were manipulating concrete materials, much of their questioning, answering and expression of understanding was non-verbal. The possibility of explaining the process without affecting this by being an observer was unlikely; I therefore decided to concentrate on tasks in which the children were dealing with written material. Four types of activity were selected because they appeared to yield interesting and analyzable data:

(i)   Discussion of short stories.
(ii) Reading and discussing poems.
(iii) Reading an extract from a story and predicting what might happen next.
(iv) Discussing an extract from reference material.

Initially I was uncertain whether children of infant school age could tackle tasks of this nature unsupervised. Would they be able to collaborate, would the discussion have any educational value? Torbe and Medway (1981) felt that teachers could be put off by listening to tapes of children working alone and stated that the results might be discouraging. Teachers may be faced with:

> ... a shapeless, clumsy, incoherent mass of irrelevancies, incorrectnesses and ignorance. Is this what we are supposed to see as evidence of learning? Our feelings may be confirmed that our pupils will get best value out of us from what we can give them, not from our allowing them to get in a mess for themselves. (p. 41)

Young children tend to look to teachers for confirmation of their ideas. How would they cope with no authority to whom they could appeal in moments of doubt? It was inevitable that they would sometimes come to wrong conclusions but this did not constitute a valid reason for rejecting unsupervised group learning. It happens anyway in playground, classrooms and home.

The children selected, three girls and three boys, came from two parallel classes of 6-7-year-olds. They were given a simple explanation about the reasons for the project. I told them that I wanted to find out how children coped with various activities when the teacher was not there. The data was then gradually collected during a period of two months. It was at this point that my enthusiasm for the project was almost quenched by the size of the task. There were twenty-eight recorded discussions varying in duration from fifteen to twenty minutes and the transcription process was both difficult and time-consuming. Astonishment kept me going for again and again exchanges between children appeared to reveal linguistic skills more usually attributed by language researchers to children more than twice the age of those I had recorded.

A form of categorization system was developed and used to avoid making false assumptions (Prisk, 1983). Subjecting the material to an analytical process should, I hoped, prevent the findings from being affected by opinions formed prior to the commencement of the project. However, the act of categorizing also seemed to be a way of delving deeper into the meaning in a systematic way. As Schatzmann and Strauss (1973) put it:

> ... analyzing data involves thinking that is self conscious, systematic, organized, and instrumental. It is thinking objectified and operationalized. Above all it is extremely active — better still, an interactive process between the researcher and his experience or data — and it is sustained rather than intermittent or casual, as ordinary thinking. (p. 109)

The methods chosen to record and stimulate group talk had effects upon the pupils' discussion. Although they worked without supervision for considerable periods, they had an audience, they had been told that the recordings would be transcribed and there were examples in the collected material which showed they were aware of this. Sometimes they attempted to clarify points which would be unclear to anyone unable to observe their paralinguistic behaviour. In many studies of talk, researchers have pointed out that the presence of a tape recorder has acted as a stimulus to the participants. Barnes and Todd (1977), Richmond (1982) and the Schools Council (1979) all commented that the use of this instrument appeared to reduce the 'off task' behaviour and, at the same time, encouraged the children to express themselves clearly. I found evidence of the children using the tape recorder to keep their friends in order if they felt that their co-participants were behaving badly or not cooperating in the solving of the set task. The tape recorder became the group's conscience.

During the project the tasks were presented in various ways. Some were formally structured, the groups being asked to discuss written questions. This appeared to limit responses; the children did not explore possibilities but accepted the first response tendered by a participant. It was as if the provision of set questions limited their search for meaning. Variations in the structure of tasks provided evidence which indicated that, if a range of suggestions is to be provided by pupils, and if they are to be encouraged to produce tentative solutions and explore ideas, then the structure should not lead children to believe that 'right answers' are all that is expected of them. Much class work demands explicit responses which can be evaluated as right or wrong. In group discussion there can be little opportunity for the exploration of half-formulated theories and half-understood ideas if the task is too structured.

It was thus difficult to arrive at a successful format for the presentation. When the task was completely open the children frequently experienced difficulties in structuring their discussion. Sometimes they couldn't start and would appeal to me, stating that they could not find anything to discuss. When this happened I would suggest a few avenues to explore and leave them to continue. This appeared to be a successful strategy. Because the questions were not written down they could forget or ignore them. The reassurance provided by having been given a starting point gave them courage, they were then able to continue on their own. When the structure provided was tight they tackled the problem as if speed and brevity were essential ingredients for success.

Coping Alone

In classroom discourse it is usually teachers who select which speaker shall contribute. They structure the discourse by deciding what will be discussed, how long will be devoted to each section and when conclusions should be drawn. One of the facts which emerged from the analysis was that, when I was present, the children did not use their organizational skills. I identified the problems, selected the order in which they were tackled, provided the boundaries, indicated when a new topic should be introduced and signalled when the task was satisfactorily completed. I was in fact responsible for over 80 per cent of all the structuring moves. Teachers tend to dominate groups by providing all the boundaries, rarely allowing the children time for the type of reflective consideration which reinforces learning.

Barnes (1976) feels that the language used to organize experience for others incorporates the same strategies used in organizing experience for oneself. The skills necessary in social negotiation appear to be similar to those which aid the understanding of alternative viewpoints. Teacher-dominated talk, although necessary and valuable, cannot help pupils to acquire all the social and communicative skill important for their future educational development. Sharing responsibility in a group for methods of tackling a problem appears to give practice in skills important for future success in learning. If teachers do not provide opportunities for the children to structure their own thinking the pupils, by becoming over-reliant on externally imposed structure, may find it progressively more difficult to monitor and evaluate their own strategies.

Analysis of the collected material revealed that the children were all capable of structuring discussions and using a variety of questioning techniques. As soon as I joined the group their behaviour changed and they appeared to hand over control of the discussion. If pupils do not fully exercise their problem-posing skills in the presence of teachers, it would appear to be worthwhile to structure their learning in a way which allows them to practise this art.

Working Together

I attempted, in the early stages of the analysis of the transcripts, to separate the social language from the cognitive language in order to find out how much talk was devoted to problem-solving and how much to maintaining relationships within the group. This proved impossible. Conversation is fluid and one speech act could often be described as fulfilling both functions. It became clear however that social skills had an effect upon the children's ability to profit from learning.

There was little evidence of children attempting to dominate the group in which they were working by taking for themselves an unfair proportion of the time; the contribution level was fairly even. The recordings showed that self-selection was the most frequent precursor of speech moves, although there were occasions when the children nominated others. Sometimes they seemed to be aware of the fact that one member of the group was not being given much chance to contribute; sometimes their motive appeared to be an attempt to involve a member of the group whose behaviour was beginning to jeopardize the success of the discussion.

In the following example three boys (Ben, Matthew and Christopher) were making a story together.

> *Matthew*: Well, what happens after that? I know — the roof fell off! How did — how could she get away?
> *Ben*: With great difficulty. Come on, Christopher you haven't said much in this bit have you?

It was difficult to be sure whether Ben was genuinely trying to involve Christopher; he could have been trying to avoid contributing himself. Matthew, on the other hand, had frequently tried to enlist the contributions of the others.

In the following extract the children (Ben, Victoria and Sally) had been discussing a poem. At the start of the session I had suggested that, if there was time at the end, they could discuss their own reminiscences. Both Victoria and Sally had volunteered several recalled experiences. Ben had been less forthcoming.

> *Sally*: I didn't see this wasp, I put my hand on the — no — oh — oh, yes — I put my hand on the wasp and it really, really stung. That's the fourth time I've been stung by a wasp.
> *Ben*: I've only been stung once.
> *Sally*: I've been stung four times.
> *Ben*: Right on the ear.
> *Sally*: Coo — I've been stung there, there — or there, and somewhere over there on my hand.
> *Victoria*: So what — I haven't been stung anywhere, 'cept by stinging nettles and I've been stung there, there, one on my hand and all over the place. I've even had one on my back there. Have you any more memories, Ben?
> *Ben*: Oh yes — I remember one — I remember in America (tells another lengthy reminiscence).
>   (I entered at this point)
> *TP*: How's it gone? Do you think you've got as much out of it as you want to?
> *Sally*: Yes.
> *Ben*: I have thought of one thing.
> *Victoria*: 'Twas a really good thing though.
> *Ben*: Yes, I was going with my grandad to a safari park ...

In this discussion Victoria showed that she was aware of the need to equalize the opportunities for contribution available to participants.

Of course, studying the conversational skills of six children cannot reveal generalizations applicable to other cases for the results may be attributable to their particular personalities. However, the transcripts clearly showed that some of the children who took part did possess skills which enabled them to structure the discussions in a way which facilitated the participation of all members.

My interest in collaboration was not limited to the social aspect. If pupils were engaged solely in negotiating relationships there would be little learning taking place. I was looking for evidence of ability to use the ideas offered by co-participants. Could these young children evaluate suggestions, provide evidence to support theories and, by discussion, arrive at group consensus? The example which follows (from Matthew, Victoria and Christopher) shows that they could.

Matthew:	Alright, what is the first thing to discuss?
Victoria:	Think of anything. Pick something easy first. Who stole the acorns?
Matthew:	Acorns? — Apples!
Victoria:	I know that.
Christopher:	Who?
Victoria:	Gordon.
Matthew:	How do you know?
Victoria:	If you look further back in the book you can see an apple fall from his pocket. And so it must have been.
Matthew:	And the trail of apples led to him. Yes — the trail of apples came to him.
Christopher:	Where's that where he ran into the field?
Matthew:	Look, yea. 'Cos they're following the trail of apples.
Victoria:	It leads to the wood where he is. There's the hedge.
Christopher:	Where? Where?
Matthew:	He's in the wood, he's in the wood though. Look, 'cos Gordon's in the wood.
Christopher:	So he's already ahead of them. He *must* have dropped the apples.
Victoria:	Yes.
Matthew:	So he was the one that . . .
Victoria:	I think we've solved that.

The discussion started with Victoria as the only participant who had solved the problem. The text of the story did not answer the question and the boys appeared to have missed the clues in the illustrations. Both boys sounded excited as they accepted and built upon Victoria's suggestion. Initially Christopher was doubtful but the evidence convinced him and he provided more corroborative clues. As soon as Victoria was sure of their agreement she closed that section of the dialogue and selected a new topic. The above extract illustrates collaboration in a task where there was a correct and verifiable solution. Collaboration in open-ended discussions presented different problems. Two of the set tasks involved group story-making. In these children could not evaluate contributions as right or wrong. In order to work together it was important that they used the contributions of all group members. They sometimes showed considerable skill. The dialogue in the example which follows (from Victoria, Caroline, and Sally) was fast; it appeared sometimes that the children were anticipating utterances before they were verbalized.

Caroline:	He came from a junk yard, 'cos people — perhaps he was made by somebody who bought things from a junk yard.
Sally:	Perhaps his head ...
Caroline:	Use those car lights as ears or eyes ...
Victoria:	... seems a bit funny to him ... (unclear) but he could be made in the junk yard and then controlled and sort of got out of control. He looks very sad.
Caroline:	Yes. He's probably lost his master.
Sally:	Aaah.
Victoria:	I think he might have been made underground though. You know, those sort of mines.
Sally:	Iron, like.
Victoria:	Yes, sort of like that. That could have been wired up and people — and somehow he might of suddenly he was made — he might of been made a long time ago and they might have buried him over like — um — the Mary Rose. That might have kept ...
Sally:	Kept him.
Victoria:	And suddenly this sort of ...
Sally:	Water ...
Victoria:	Earthquake — or water ...
Sally:	Pushed the ...
Victoria:	Pushed all the mud away and suddenly he sort of ...
Sally:	And then ...
Victoria:	Came to ...
Sally:	Something must have turned his controls at the back.

In the preceding extract the speed of delivery increased as the children became involved with the task. After Victoria suggested that the robot had been preserved in the same way as the *Mary Rose* they built on each other's suggestions with speed and excitement. The children did not appear to be fighting for the floor; they were creating a single story together.

The clearest examples of children working together to achieve deeper understanding of the material were demonstrated when Ben, Sally and Victoria were discussing poetry. Victoria showed considerable ability both in internalizing the poet's message and in communicating this to other members of the group.

1	*Ben:*	Then Mrs. Prisk said — you had to find out what this poem is all about.
2	*Sally:*	It's about animals.
3	*Ben:*	It's all about animals.
4	*Sally:*	It's about a lady — when she lives in a flat and they're not allowed animals and she so longs for them.
5	*Victoria:*	It's sort of loving and a feeling about animals and how she feels about them. It's sort of trying to prove it to other people that animals are good for loving and things and need care.
6	*Sally:*	Mmm.
7	*Ben:*	Yes.
8	*Victoria:*	And why should they abandon them from flats — from flats and things when they ...
9	*Sally:*	It wakes people up — it wakes people up and things doesn't it?
10	*Victoria:*	Yes, well they have got a right to keep a cat or dog if they're going to feed them and made them — home comfortable and things.
11	*Ben:*	'Cept it would be no fun for the animals having to be locked up in a flat all the time.
12	*Sally:*	Yes but — if they — if the — this lady ...
13	*Victoria:*	Ben's got a point there.
14	*Sally:*	If the — um — person — um — would treat them well, not to bark — not to wake up the neighbours and things.
15	*Ben:*	How'd you stop it though?

In the above discussion the children showed that they were capable of entertaining more than one hypothesis and of evaluating conflicting opinions. Ben and Sally (2 and 3) gave a summary of the poem's surface meaning. Victoria (5) goes deeper and attempts a re-verbalization of the emotional message. At 8 she takes the viewpoint expressed by the poet. Sally 9 considers the feelings of other flat-dwellers; Ben 11 points out that the animals too have rights. At 13 Victoria demonstrates that she can consider views which conflict with her own. The children were constructing their understanding together by sharing their perceptions in a way which deepened and extended their understanding:

The following extract also evidences their ability to probe the meaning of a poem.

Victoria:	I think I know what she means — know how she feels. If you're an adult and you've grown up and remember that what would you feel like?
Sally:	Upset that it isn't there any more.
Victoria:	An adult?

Sally: Mmm.
Victoria: Sort of remem ... you'd sort of remember the very faint
              taste of the bilberries and cream sometimes.
Sally: Mmmmm — yes.
Victoria: And you'd remember it. And then perhaps suddenly do
              something that reminds you and then forget about it.
Sally: Mmmm.
Victoria: And then do it again and it reminds you — when you go to
              bed. You really, *really* wish it was back like that.

Victoria was able to understand and express the poem's message. Ben and Sally appeared to appreciate her point, there was a noticeable pause before the children resumed their discussion. Their experience of the type of nostalgia described by the poet was necessarily limited. To savour an old woman's recollections of childhood would have been difficult for them. A teacher might not have expected them to appreciate this aspect of the poem, or might have felt it necessary to direct them towards it. Without help or direction Victoria was not only able to empathize with the poet, she also led the others towards a deeper understanding. This extract illustrates another important benefit to be gained from group talk. Victoria focussed on the central message and used considerable skill to enable others to share her perception. She selected a collection of communicative behaviours appropriate to the task. The change in intonation coupled with the slowness of her delivery reinforced her meaning.

It thus appears that unsupervised small group discussion can afford opportunities for children to:

(i)   identify problems and solve them without adult intervention;
(ii)   search for solutions unaided, therefore gaining experience in
       selecting relevant information;
(iii) collaborate with others both socially and in order to deepen
       their own understanding;
(iv)   structure discussions effectively;
(v)   discuss and evaluate conflicting hypotheses;
(vi)   improve their skill in communicating personal insights to
       others.

So far I have concentrated mainly on the children's successes. During the project examples of children failing to meet the set demands did occur. It would be impossible to list reasons for these failures in a way which would enable other teachers to avoid the same pitfalls but identifying some of the problems I encountered could perhaps suggest general areas of difficulty.

The composition of the group appeared to have great importance. After some of the less successful discussions recorded, children stated that they had not been able to work well with another child. After one particularly fruitless discussion they asked if they could work with the children they knew well because they felt they made more progress. Studying the collected data revealed that all-male groups were less successful than those in which the sexes were mixed. This was probably due to the personalities of those involved but it nevertheless seems wise to consult children about their preferences when working together in this way.

Individuals in the groups had differing views about the main aims of some of the discussions. Difficulties were encountered when members were in conflict about aims. Problems of this nature were sometimes exacerbated by the choice of task. Group discussion with such young children appeared to work best when the material was of an intellectual level which presented some difficulty, but not too much. When the tasks were easy, or the children thought they were, they treated them lightly and did not search for deeper meaning. Teachers planning work of this nature need therefore to be aware of the intellectual capabilities of their pupils.

Another difficulty encountered was failure to progress through a task. The children would get stuck at some point, and, dissatisfied with an outcome, lacked the confidence to leave the problem and continue with a further section. This problem occurred several times and highlighted again the importance of choosing material which fell within the intellectual capabilities of the group.

Sometimes the children appeared unable, or unwilling, to give their reasons for disagreeing with another's contribution. It was as if they were uneasy about criticizing each other in case they damaged the harmony of the group. It appeared that consensus and calmness in social relationships were maintained by participants on occasions when arguments might have better served the cognitive demands of the task. I was conscious several times that children were trying to hide their disagreements from me as if they felt I would be displeased by these exchanges. It could be that children who have only recently acquired the skill of maintaining social relationships will need also to acquire the skill of maintaining these through intellectual disagreements in order that they can freely exchange points of view in a way which will aid their cognitive development. A sensitive teacher, aware of this need, could do much to facilitate this by showing that she values disagreement when it is the product of a thoughtful approach. It is possible that the maintenance of a 'happy atmosphere' so entrenched in the ideology of infant teachers may retard the development of those skills which enable individuals to question and reject fallacious statements. There are many adults who react, when their views are questioned, as if they have been personally insulted. I believe that young children could be shown that thoughtful questioning of another's point of view can take place in an atmosphere of reciprocity and need not damage social relationships.

One of the most obvious failures which occurred was when the children could not reach a correct conclusion without a teacher or other authority to provide the information needed. As the material presented for the tasks was in written form, the failure was usually either inability to find the correct meaning for a word, or misinterpretation of a literary convention. Frequently the combined knowledge of the group enabled them to solve such problems successfully, sometimes they failed. It could be argued that these failures illustrate the need for adult participation in the group work of such young children. On the other hand there is no doubt that they were practising search skills while attempting to find answers. Diana Hutchinson (1981) felt that it is vital for children to develop a questioning attitude. It is possible that this cannot be effectively fostered in a situation where uncertainty is forestalled.

> It is vital for teachers to encourage children to form the habit of asking questions, especially during the early years in school. Children will then develop a 'set for curiosity', which is an essential motivating force in learning situations and also a factor in developing the ability to concentrate for long periods. (p. 24)

I have identified five of the types of failure which were evidenced when children were working without adult intervention. Participants sometimes failed to collaborate effectively; they did not share each other's perceptions of the task; they were unable to make progress; they failed in attempts to communicate their understanding and they sometimes reached incorrect conclusions. This list of difficulties looks like a fairly comprehensive reason for not including group work in a school's language policy. Teachers encountering these aspects of unsupervised talk could feel justified in thinking that allowing such activities would only increase the difficulties faced by their pupils. Nevertheless, each failure contained within it potentially valuable learning experiences. Errors can be seen as avoidable; they can also be more positively evaluated. Learning to accept the truth is one process; teachers can lead pupils towards successful outcomes but children also need to struggle with difficulties, formulate their own hypotheses, to evaluate conflicting opinions and to search for answers by themselves. Children given the opportunity to play with alternatives are, at the same time, learning to recognize the truth.

Conclusion

When the research described here was undertaken the aims and possible outcomes were unclear. As a staff we felt that we needed to know more about an activity which we instinctively felt had value. I believe that the process illuminated some of the educational benefits which result from including small unsupervised group talk in an infant school language policy. For instance:

1   Teachers granting autonomy to pupils by allowing time for the activity are also giving children valuable experience in identifying problems and the opportunity to indulge in the type of tentative talk which permits new meanings to be fully understood. Understanding arrived at by search, evaluation and the rejection of inadequate solutions is more likely to be remembered and re-used than knowledge which has been acquired second-hand through the teacher.

2   Studying group talk enables teachers to evaluate their own performance. If the activity is seen as a method of encouraging children to organize and structure their own discussion the teachers need to be aware of the effect of their intervention. As an experienced teacher of infants I had not envisaged that the study would reveal aspects of my behaviour which hindered the process I believed I was encouraging. The children studied did not appear to monitor their own progress or structure their discussion effectively unless they saw themselves as being totally responsible for the outcomes; when an adult was present they did not assume this responsibility.

3   Observing and studying dialogue can provide valuable insights into the skills and abilities of the participants. Although the results of such study are not generalizable to other situations, teachers who undertake the activity are more likely to evaluate their pupils' language skills accurately and will therefore be able to plan learning activities which stimulate and extend children more effectively. Indulging in a study of the type described here takes considerable time and effort. The rewards of increased understanding make the process worthwhile. Insights acquired during the project illuminate other dialogues. Links between social and intellectual skills are revealed; connections between children's ability to structure their thinking and their competence in ordering their own and others' problem-solving talk become apparent.

4   Teachers in busy classrooms may be tempted to intervene too frequently in group work because they overhear remarks which appear irrelevant. Listening to recordings of children talking increases awareness of the circumlocutory nature of discourse. Confidence about the likelihood of worthwhile outcomes may enable teachers to grant autonomy to pupil groups for longer periods. Increased opportunity to talk through problems is likely to give learners more confidence in their ability to tackle problems effectively. They may also become more efficient at identifying the questions which must be posed in order that difficulties can be resolved.

The most fascinating outcome of the project was an unanswered question. Barnes and Todd (1977) noted that some young adolescents appeared to be capable of a skill which they called 'reflexivity', describing this as the ability to monitor behaviour which enables the actor to evaluate and be aware of both his own and others' strategies. They saw this ability as an indication that the 13-14-year-olds they studied were moving towards the 'formal operational' stage of development identified by Piaget. Frequently, when transcribing the collected discussions, I was amazed by the abilities evidenced by the children. It is possible that the participants were functioning at a level in advance of their peers. Many of the characteristics which Barnes and Todd include in their definition of reflexivity were evidenced in the data collected. Examples of children entertaining alternative hypotheses, evaluating their own and others' contributions and showing awareness of the needs of the audience were all there. On the basis of the limited material collected it was not possible to do more than raise questions. Are these skills examples of hypothetico-deductive thinking? Should we expect to find them in the talk of 6-7-year-old children?

Questions of this nature can only be answered by considerable further research into the problem-solving talk which can be undertaken by children in infant schools. There is no doubt that the project had beneficial outcomes for the school. The discussions which arose from the implications of the results had considerable effect on staff perceptions. What had started as an attempt to evaluate a small part of the language curriculum had effect upon all areas of the school's activity. Classrooms were reorganized to facilitate group work; group problem-solving was seen as a valuable method of tackling mathematical, scientific and creative topics.

Research of this nature is extremely difficult for class teachers to undertake. The time involved is hard to find. But, when undertaken in the school, and involving children from the school, it appears to have more impact than the reported findings of unknown researchers.

References

BARNES, D. (1976) *From Communication to Curriculum*, London, Penguin Education.
BARNES, D. and TODD, F. (1977) *Communication and Learning in Small Groups*, London, Routledge and Kegan Paul.
CRYSTAL, D. (1976) *Child Language, Learning and Linguistics*, London, Edward Arnold.
HALLIDAY, M.A.K. (1973) *Explorations in the Functions of Language*, London, Edward Arnold.
HUTCHINSON, D. (Ed.) (1981) *Making Language Work*, London, McGraw-Hill.
MINNS, H. (1966) 'Children talking — teacher learning', in TORBE, M. and PROTHEROUGH, R. (Eds) (1976).
PRISK, D.M. (1983) 'Group talk in an infant school', unpublished MA dissertation, Cambridge Institute of Education.
RICHMOND, J. (1982) *The Resources of Classroom Language*, London, Edward Arnold.
SCHATZMAN, L. and STRAUSS, A. (1973) *Field Research: Strategies for a Natural Sociology*, Englewood Cliffs, NJ, Prentice-Hall.

Schools Council (1979) *Learning Through Talking 11–16*, London, Evans/Methuen Educational.

Torbe, M. and Medway, P. (1981) *The Climate for Learning*, London, Ward Lock Educational.

Torbe, M. and Protherough, R. (Eds.) (1976) *Classroom Encounters: Language and English Teaching*, London, Ward Lock.

7 Becoming a Junior: Pupil Development Following Transfer from Infants

Peter Woods

I'm a dingle dangle scarecrow with a flippy floppy hat (Music Time)

The age of 7 in our school system is a critical one for many children. Like those of 5, 11/12 and 16, it represents a major transition in the pupil's career, in this case from infant to junior. Yet we know little about how this transition is accomplished (see Bennett *et al*, 1984) or what it means to the pupils concerned.

In this chapter, I want to consider some aspects of pupil development among 7-year-olds following transfer, as manifested during an eighteen-month association with an urban, multi-ethnic junior school. The school is in a largely working-class area, and had some 200 pupils in total, 44 per cent of whom at the time were white English, 56 per cent from ethnic minority groups — mainly Asians (Hindus, mostly Gujarati, but with some Pakistani and Bengali Muslims, and Sikhs), and a few of Afro-Caribbean, Italian and Chinese background. Most of the ethnic minority children were first generation English, though some were second, and some had been born in other countries. There were well established and thriving Hindu and Muslim communities in the town.

In the course of my eighteen months at the school, beginning in the summer term of 1985, I spent one day (sometimes half-a-day) a week mainly with class 1. This was then, actually two successive classes — the last term of the 1984 intake, and the whole year of the September 1985 intake (a class of some twenty-two 7-year-olds). There were two intake classes at the school, and occasionally, I looked at the contemporary groups. I draw on here my studies of all four groups, but mainly that of the 1985/86 class 1. Methods were ethnographic, in this case largely observation (unavoidably 'participant'since I was unable to resist getting drawn in to the activities of the class) unstructured, naturalistic conversations, and study of documents (mainly the children's writing and art work).

Transfer

I was interested to compare this 7+ transition with the 12+ of some previous research (Measor and Woods, 1984). The latter was found to consist of three status passages (Glaser and Strauss, 1977) compounded into one, and operating at two levels to do with (i) the more immediate physical and emotional effects of the change of schools; and (ii) the longer-term changes following transfer, worked out over the ensuing year. The former were attended by considerable anxiety, which the pupils handled to some extent with the use of myths. The 7+ transfer also takes place on two levels but is not attended by the same kind of developments as in puberty (as is the 12+), nor the fragmentation involved in moving as only part of a cohort to a large, sectionalized, specialist institution. The younger pupils' anxieties, therefore, on the first level are on the whole more immediate, and more localized and more susceptible to conventional treatment. They are, however, keenly felt and there are shades of certain aspects of the later experience in the following accounts, written by the pupils towards the end of their first year in the juniors. In the interests of confidentiality, all names used are pseudonyms. The accounts focus largely on the teacher who will be at the centre of their school lives over the next year. Despite several visits paid to the infant school the previous term, she was not only unknown, but she could quite possibly be completely inhuman.

For instance, Daniel told me 'I was very frightened when I stepped inside the classroom. I was thinking that if Mrs Brown saw my behaviour she would just take (me) to the headmaster and get me a smacked bottom'. Dipak was told by his cousin that 'the teachers are bad and if we do a bit wrong we get smacks with a slipper. When I came in the classroom I was shaking but my cousin tell me lies ...'. Sarah was also 'shaking', but received different advice which helped modify the concern: '... my sister said don't because Mrs Brown is nice she tells you jokes. So when I came in I was still a bit scared ... but not shaking'. According to her teacher, Sarah was 'a terribly nervous child, who had stomach aches all the first week and burst into tears one day when she thought her sister had gone home without her'. Caroline on her first day actually 'started to cry because I thought I might get hit ... but I haven't' Kaushik was also worried when he first came because he 'thought that Mrs Brown would hit me. Afterwards she said she only shot people's heads off. I thought she really meant it so when it was dinner time I said to my Dad don't tat me to that school. I forgot how to say take. He said he won't tat me to school but take me ... so then I went school someone had done something wrong and Mrs Brown said she's going to shoot his head off. I didn't look but when I opened my eyes his head was still on so I wasn't scared any more...'. It is within the bounds of belief therefore that your teacher can legitimately take the ultimate disciplinary measure! At 7 your new teacher can seem as strange as 'a creature from Mars and come down in a space ship' (David).

Things were a little strange. The school was 'big', the whistle deafened Hemang. He had also been very worried about the older boys in the school. But these problems were quickly overcome. He found that on the second day 'I felt a bit better but on the third I felt alright because I got used to all the boys and I started having great fun playing football and lots of other things....'.

Older pupils were quickly seen as a resource rather than a threat. They offered a broader base of friends on which to draw. The size of the new school also was not a big problem. It was almost impossible for example to get lost. And their teacher was discovered to be human, and quite an asset, as we shall see later.

These first order problems, therefore, though acutely felt at the time, seemed to be fairly rapidly resolved. One might argue that the anxieties associated with transfer, as long as not too great and prolonged, act as a catalyst for the deeper changes that are to come. Robail (1985) argues that such anxiety 'is a necessary emotion of learning about life, and perhaps a desirable emotion to provoke that will provide a landmark of growing-up' (p. 5). This, then, is the connection with the second order changes involving the infant school child becoming the junior which took longer to accomplish and involved a status shift equally, if not more, profound than that at 11+ or 12+.

Personal Development

One more step along the world I go
One more step along the world I go
From the old things to the new
Keep me travelling along with you. (*Assembly Hymn*)

New Skills

Over the year as a whole pupils acquired new skills and knowledge, new behaviours and attitudes to learning, and promoted formulating identities in significant ways. This was not so much a result of linear progress as the pupil career unfolds, but rather of quantum leaps that both cause and reflect a profound shift in status, and provide a new platform from which to reach new heights of learning.

Taylor (1986) argues that 'literacy should become the stock in trade of primary education (and) must increasingly be recognized as essential to the development of thresholds of thought, feeling and action in many subject areas, not only of intellectual endeavour but also of social and moral insight in children' (p. 120–1). Taylor sees literacy as including understanding story and play, which 'involves rules, teaches self-distance' (p. 121), allows the objectification of action — all elements involved in the shift from the egocentricity of infancy towards what Piaget has termed 'formal operations'. The tools for the acquisition of this literacy are fashioned, arguably, during this first year.

Capacities increased almost from the first day of term. Thus when Dipak did his news he 'almost filled up the whole page'. Gita used to do '1 or 2 pages and now I do 3, 4, 5 or 6'. James 'remember when I could not read when I came to this school. But I can read and write now with a pencil *or* a pen' (my emphasis). Looking back, Rajesh could see that they had been '"infants" in the other school . . . doing baby work . . . (but) . . . at this school we do some hard work'.

For Hemang 'the thing that I've learnt very well is my hand writing because in the infants I used to write like this

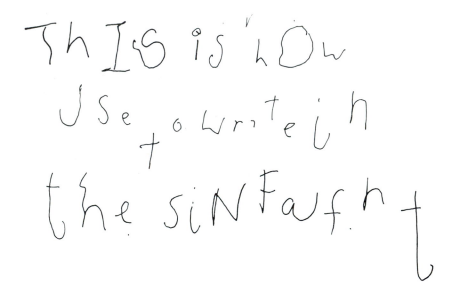

Amina liked it 'when we were learning joined up writing' — a prominent symbol of having progressed to a new stage in learning. Like the second set of teeth (which most of these pupils were to acquire during the year), there is no advance beyond 'joined-up writing' — it is the ultimate. Daniel (a British Afro-Caribbean) claimed that within two months he had more than doubled his vocabulary and gained new fluency:

Before I was eight which was in November I learned how to spell and read in fact when it was my birthday I knew about more words than I knew when i was at the infants school.

Daniel's new found skills are illustrated in the following graphic poem:

HALLOWEEN is the spookiest date in the world
All the wiches come out to do spells and wicked things
Lots of ghosts and skeletons come out to scare people
Lots of wicked people turn from wiches to ghosts I hate them
Owls fly in the midnight hour they dont talk just hoot
Wizards and witches Ghosts and Skeletons come out and do tricks
Every ghostly thing scares people even some people are awake
Every wicked person trys to see a black cat to help her with her
    spell
Near Halloween so get ready to stay up till midnight.

Daniel was aided in the structuring of this poem by it being an acrostic — the first letter of each line spelling out 'HALLOWEEN'. However, if anything, he over-indulged his new talent, being much given to long disjointed stories, full of non-sequiturs, devoid of shape, simply following his thoughts as they jumped now here, now there. Perhaps this is what he meant when he told me 'I may be stupid but I've got a clever brain'. He had ideas, fuelled by his new literacy, but just strung them together in a line — all beginning, no development, no middle, no end. By the end of the year, however, in response to structured and planned activities, Daniel's writing was showing another significant development that had taken much longer — mastery of form. He had learned the discipline of economy and structure. Together with his extended vocabulary, this makes a powerful springboard for the kind of development Taylor speaks of.

    Here then is an illustration of his writing towards the end of the year (there is no space for an earlier one!):

Our Move from Town to the Country

Long long ago in a town there lived a family of witches and wizards who hated living in towns. Townies were so noisy not even their major powers could stop the noise. So one day the Chief Wizard said it is time to leave the town. So all the wizards and witches packed up, put their things in their car and drove it to the country. They had some adventures while they were on there way. It was 75 minutes after they had left their house when they all saw something very strange it looked like a cloud of yellow. When they got nearer they stopped and went out of the car and thought. It took them a long time to think soon they decided what to do. They went right through the yellow cloud. No sooner had they found themselves in space this yellow cloud had vanished, so they looked in their spell book. It was on page 708 but they just didn't look on that page. So they first drove in space waiting if they could think of a bright idea. Then they had a great idea. They called upon the God of Wisdom. We want to have the wisdom to know how to find ourselves in the country. No sooner had they said this they found themselves in the country. Then the chief of witches said What a relief!

Daniel's was the most obvious case to illustrate this achievement. It was one that others reached to varying degrees at various points throughout the year. Hemang showed early mastery of form (he told me a splendid story about 'Gnasher', which he invented on the spot and which grew in carefully cadenced evil to a grand finish where 'Gnasher' over-reached himself — a neat illustration of how these skills help the moral to be internalized). For much of the first term Dipak could not sort and order his thoughts, and his teacher was feeling quite 'demented because he had potential, but was not progressing'. However, after sustained work with pictures, muddled-up sentences, role-play etc, Dipak made a significant breakthrough as late as the summer term. Others had not quite arrived there, or showed signs of it in some respects and on some occasions, but not at others.

Some of these young children occasionally made rapid advances almost in an instant. Invariably, something seemed 'to click' leading to a new level of understanding or unlocking of new skills. Steven, for example, according to his teacher 'had improved no end since open day when his parents came in, and his teacher told his mother how improved he was. Since then he has not looked back'. Rewards, as others have noticed (for example, Jackson, 1968; Pollard 1985), played their part. Sarah had been delighted when she got her first piece of 'news' back to find 'it had a star and it said good try'. I was reminded by Sheela 'If you think I've done it all right you can give me a star!'.

For Daniel 'something happened that never happened in my life before. My behaviour thanks to Mrs Brown herself changed. I felt like a new boy ready to work ... its just like being a man in prison with a bad teacher ...' Daniel thus felt liberated. He had been encouraged to develop the predisposition that facilitated the extension of vocabulary and writing skills mentioned earlier.

There were many such examples. Another form it took was the freeing of conceptual blockages and unlocking of illogicalities. My favourite example of this is the case of Karupa and the vase. The class were asked to draw and paint a decorated vase of flowers. While the rest got on with it, Karupa was unable to start satisfactorily, wrestling with now this line with her pencil, now that, with much rubbing out. When the teacher sat next to her to talk about it, the problem was discovered to be the convex shape of the vase. All the vases Karupa had known, including the one they currently had at home, had been concave. The breakthrough came when she was encouraged to trace the lines of the vase with her finger. Her eyes opened wide and she smiled hugely as she suddenly saw what was needed. Then she was off, going into the most intricate detail on the decoration on the vase. She had some problems of technique here, the colours running together, but she soon learned that if she left one colour to dry, the running did not happen. She put in the green stems and flowers afterwards, filling up the paper, showing good skills of design, perspective and colour. It took time and she was the last to finish, but from a position of total blockage, she had produced a masterpiece, which received a special commendation from the teacher and from the rest of the class. The product could not have been more at variance with the initial approach to the task.

I came across several similar examples across the curriculum, and no doubt this is a common occurrence. Progress in these instances is not a matter of pupil training or abilities, but a case of tracking down impediments and identifying switch-mechanisms. Pupils are aided in this by what I take to be another fairly common feature of junior school work, and which certainly applied here. This involved a move toward more pupil-centred learning, and to acquiring the attitudes and dispositions needed for it to work. In this case, pupils had been taught previously largely by traditional methods. They were used to having knowledge transmitted to them, and to external forms of discipline and control. At the junior school, teaching in these classes was based on different principles. Knowledge is not defined solely by the teacher, but is reinterpreted and 'appropriated' by children as they relate it to their own concerns (Armstrong, 1980; and see Rowland in this volume). The case of Karupa and her vase illustrate the scenario and the unpredictability of learning very well. The problem was in her own limited world-view of vases, heavily influenced by the one she saw every day. How could they possibly be any other shape? The problem was overcome with the help, which did not tell her, but adopted her position and viewpoint through what Rowland (1984, p. 148) terms a 'conversational relationship'. The chef d'oeuvre was then threatened by lack of knowledge of technique which she was motivated to rectify. In this process she discovered artistic skills she had not previously demonstrated. The whole was governed by a rationality that many feel 7-year olds do not possess.

Individual development gained from taking place within a cohort undergoing transition. Moving up to the new school is a distinct mark of growing up that one does as a member of a group. It was a matter for particular note, therefore, among many in the class that one girl had forgotten to go to her new school on the first day and gone back to the infants — a clear case of regression. Warish also wrote 'In the infants I think we wasn't moving but we did move into this class I didn't know that we was changing ...' The transition is that less profound than the

12+ to the extent that some had no prior knowledge of it!

During the year it was thought remarkable that Gita 'can't even ride a bike, she still has to have a three-wheeler' and that Ann 'still has baths with her father ("I wash his back for him")'. Mind, you, Urmi's brother 'still does poos in his pants and he's 10!'. Their new status is marked in so many ways. Robail (1985) reports a subtle but emphatic change of vocabulary: 'Kirsty, the majestic, the well-behaved Kirsty, had told the teacher in a loud voice that she was so upset she needed a "pee". With her sense of the occasion the infant "wee-wee" had been promoted to a junior "pee" . . .' (p. 6).

New Attitudes

The move from infant to junior is a considerable transition for young children to make. They have experience of only a small range of teaching approaches. Their adaptability, as yet, is limited. It is not surprising that, at the beginning of their junior career when first exposed to this new approach, they were, for a time, in a kind of limbo. They had lost the stern external controls of the old (perhaps their expectations of even sterner ones were behind the views of their new teacher as a monster), without, as yet, having developed the internal ones of the new. At the beginning of the year, therefore, this class were a noisy, rather undisciplined group, its members bursting and vying with each other at times for individual attention and with very limited powers of application. During the first term their teacher said she was having to shout at them more than she would like. Basic instinct seemed particularly to prevail during that essential feature of the junior classroom — queueing up, where at times there was a great deal of pushing, thrusting, chattering. The teacher had, on occasions, to remind them of their new-found status: 'Go away! Go away! That's infant behaviour again!'

Gradually, however, in the course of the year the class 'learnt to learn' by these new methods, and internalized the rules associated with them (see Getzels, 1977). They learnt, for example, when to approach the teacher and when not; how to use their fellow pupils, books and other documents, parents and themselves as resources; how to be more cooperative and less competitive in their work (the protective 'hands round their work' syndrome gradually disappeared); how to pace themselves in their work; how to relate the more informal, casual moments with the more formal into an integrated experience, instead of separate, oppositional ones. Rowland (1984) argues with respect to the class of 9/11-year-olds he studied that 'There were interludes in the work of many of the children when they would step back from their work, "play" with it and chatter not too seriously about it. It was during such episodes that their work became more really their own, was placed in a more social and everyday context and was understood more deeply by them' (p. 95). The basis for such constructive experimentation was possibly laid in the first junior year.

Identities

As long as I live
I shall always be
Myself — and no other
Just me

> Walter de la Mare
> (on classroom wall)

This is an important year for some pupils 'coming out' and establishing an identity for themselves with which they could both cope with the demands made on them and generate and retain their self-respect and sense of personal dignity. It was an enormous advance, for example, to 'be allowed to go to school by myself', one of those unmistakable symbols of new-found independence after two or more years' subscription to the 'mothers and toddlers' club. During the year the teacher remarked on one child who seemed not to have made the personal and social advances that the others had, and whose mother still insisted on bringing her to school.

There were some remarkable gains here. Warish was very withdrawn at first, but by the middle of the year he was going to his teacher to ask for 'words' and eventually 'even getting a bit naughty'. She did not discipline him too much in case 'she put him back to square one'.

Sarah had been very tearful at first and very dependent on Ann, but by the first half-term had broken free and 'was working well on her own'. Ann herself had been rather overbearingly egocentric to begin with, but over the year came to channel her need for self-expression more into drama. Sanita also found relief in drama, but as an aid to self expression. Withdrawn, unsmiling deep into the year, overburdened with domestic responsibilities with five younger siblings, she came back from the last rehearsal of the year with delight all over her face. 'I'm a servant' she told me 'I like plays'.

A few of the Asian children, especially girls, seemed to want an exclusively westernized cultural identity. Many of them spoke their mother tongue at home and were encouraged to celebrate Asian cultures, within strong and thriving communities (especially in this case Hindu). But Yogita, for example, preferred to speak English, and found conversation in the mother tongue 'boring'. While some were keen to have their names pronounced correctly, one girl preferred her English nickname. Others played games with English derivatives. Some called Shuli 'Sugar'. 'So we're going to call her (Saneha) "Semolina". Good int it?'

One of the older girls had fought against her parents involving her in

Hindu culture, throwing out all the makeup, refusing to wear the clothes. Another girl, asked by her mother to wear a sari for the Diwali ceremony, announced that she 'was not going to wear curtains'. Amina also, in Class 1, fiercely resisted wearing any other dress than her jumpers and jeans. Another girl at the beginning of the project on 'Ourselves' described herself as having blue eyes, fair hair and white cheeks, and drew herself hiding behind her mother (although most of the Indian children coloured themselves pink). Kaushik reported that his family had told him that to go into the sun and get dark brown was bad — it was good to be pale. When asked 'why? he replied 'You know, just good'.

Others seemed to adapt to dual cultures more readily, taking a pride and delight in their Indian identity. Meena, struggling to learn to speak and write English (which she would eventually accomplish), almost became a different person when performing an Indian dance. Some conversed or spoke in their mother tongue at every opportunity clearly accepting their bilingualism as an asset. The opportunities for mother-tongue speaking were, however, restricted by, among other things, the very number of languages involved. Of the two Muslims in the class, for example, Sanita was Bengali speaking and Skakeel Urdu, and they could not speak each other's language. Dipak's description of himself led off proudly with 'I'm an Indian ...' Such identities were readily accepted, and esteemed, by others. Some white English children were delighted to have Indian friends. They took part in the Indian festivals, as they did most other things, with enthusiasm and without inhibition, taking the roles of Ram, Sita and Ravan and others, as did Chinese, Afro-Caribbean, Pakistani and Italian children. There was a similar inter-ethnic mix at other festivals, such as Christmas, and the Chinese New Year celebrations.

This account points to the conflicting pressures operating on these children. There are several factors involved. Most importantly, some argue, in its social, political and economic structure, society favours certain cultural forms (see, for example, Brah and Minhas, 1985). Some families struggling for status and/or survival see 'westernization' as a strategy, and exert pressure on their children to conform to the majority culture. The greater the struggle, the greater the pressure, and sometimes the struggle is compounded by social, geographical, religious and linguistic factors within the minority groups. Thus Amina, a Punjabi Hindu and an untouchable, did not consider herself part of the dominant Gujarati community, and reacted against it as her family saw better chances in conformity to Western styles.

Gender identities appeared to be fairly well established, and to become further consolidated over the year. Friendships and interests were gender specific. The most popular play activity amongst the boys was football, with a number of rough and risky variations (such as lining up against a wall while the one who was 'on' kicked the ball as hard as he could towards them to see if he could hit one of them). Several had become consumed by the whole football culture, their enthusiasm shown by such things as collecting insignia of the various clubs, and championing one in particular. Indian boys were among the most prominent here — Pradeep, for example. Amongst his other football enthusiasms, he had a World Football Book 1986 which had all the countries in, details of which were on stickers that you bought from the 'Sid' shop. He was proud of the fact that he knew all the countries ('I know all the countries, don't I?').

A 'craze' of the year among the boys was 'transformers' — machines or creatures which, with a few adjustments here and there, could be turned into another form, mostly in this case superhuman monsters. These toys indulged mostly in a great deal of macho posturing, and mechanical wizardry, combining within them two of the most prominent elements of Western maleness. Perhaps it was this fact that made them so popular.

Their influence was considerable. Steven, for example, over several weeks, filled a whole exercise book in his own time, with a story about Grimrock (who transforms into a Tyrannosaurus Rex), Starscreen, Shockwave, Thundercracker, Megatron and many more. Developing literacy skills and gender identity are used here to promote and consolidate each other. The same is true, of course, of other skills. Two pictures, for example during the year to rival Romanna's vase were Tony's of the Iron Man — full of detail, with teeth, patterns on the arms, aeroplane seats and passengers, wheels and tail gunner; and Steven's wolf — fierce, aggressive, eyes malevolent and fangs dripping blood.

The following two examples from essays on 'Things I like doing best' point the contrast:

> Hemang likes to 'play football because it is great fun and my best football team is Liverpool. I like riding my bike with Jignesh because we do skids and other stunts too. I like to break-dance . . .'

> Ann likes . . . 'playing with my Sindy doll. I like playing with Sarah. I like to play with my doll's pram with my baby doll . . . I like to play school as well as ball. I like going for rides in my dad's car best of all. I like to knit as well. I am knitting a blanket for my doll's pram. I have a lot of wool to knit a blanket . . .'

Television was universally popular. Boys watched programmes like *Streethawk, Airwolf, Star Wars, Masters of the Universe, The 'A'Team*. Mitesh liked playing with his train-set, Melvin his BMX, Shuli liked her doll and 'helping my mummy to do the housework'. Boys were collectors — of model cars, badges, can tabs. For Christmas, boys wanted transformers, a watch, a sledge, a BMX, a 'Commodore plus'. Grimlock, a B wing fighter, He-man figures, The 'A' Team, Superman, a computer. Girls wanted fuzzy felts, a scalectric ('for me and my dad' — Ann), games, a book, a Sindy doll, felt tips and a colouring book, a Barbie (doll), a desk with drawers, the Hart family.

Here we see gender identities becoming more firmly establshed as boys are drawn into the football culture of the school and girls develop their own kind of interests. With the development of firmer relationships, as we shall now discuss, these identities become clearer as friends reflect and cultivate interests and selves both by their own increased and deepened natures, and by their increasing differentiation from others.

Social Development

Would you walk by on the other side
When someone called for aid?
Would you walk by on the other side
And would you be afraid?
There's a child in the streets
Gives joy to all he meets
Full of life with many friends
Works and plays till daylight ends
There's a man for all the people
A man whose love is true
May the man for all the people
Help me love others too. (*Assembly Hymn*)

The first year of junior school is an important year for social development, in learning to relate to others in ways beyond the immediate, physical, rather selfish manner of early childhood. And in so doing, gaining a new conception of the self — from an interactionist viewpoint, developing a notion of the 'me' as well as the 'I', learning to see the self as others do (Mead, 1934). Friends play a crucial role here.

Psychologists argue that there are two critical stages of children's friendships, one at age 3/5 when the focus is on momentary specific physical actions and physical accessibility, and the other at 11/12 when friendships involve more psychological compatibility and longevity (Rubin, 1980). Again I would argue that the first year of junior school is crucial in the progress from one stage to the other. With the other developments already discussed and the general exposure to junior school culture with its point of centrality on an age group above them, the 7/8-year-olds are pulled towards deeper and different forms of friendship.

The junior school vastly increases the potential friendship range. Unlike the 11+ or 12+ transfer, there was no evidence here of fear of losing one's friends (or of being bullied) in the new school. They fall quickly into the swing of things. Boys very soon established their membership of the 'male club' (Lever, 1976). Hemang felt better on the third day because 'I got used to all the boys and I started having great fun playing football and lots of other things'. Another boy on the first day 'met a lot of children. But knew they were nice children and they were. Then I said to one child could I play football with you and he said you could play football he was good. But I was rubbish'. In the second term, Daniel 'made some second, third and fourth year friends. They were getting used to me'. Rajesh only knew 'one of the fourth years when he came and now I know lots of fourth years'. Girls also had more resources. Amina, 'has got more friends in this school and I like it here the best'. She has friends in class 7, 6 and 5.

Main friends were, however, within the same class. Friends spent time with each other, helped and cared about each other, were 'kind', shared and gave each other things, found each other attractive, played and had fun together. They provide physical, intellectual, emotional and moral support (see also Davies, 1982). Here we see elements of both stages mentioned earlier. Friends need to be with you, there is some emphasis on physical aspects, but also, in the caring, thoughtfulness and reciprocality, some emotional and psychological. This was, perhaps, a little more evident among the girls than the boys. Already, the classic formulation of boys being members of a group with looser connections between individuals while girls cultivated dyads with stronger ties is apparent.

Rashan's friend was 'Karen and I like her so much. Her eyes are so beautiful. She looks so nice. She is kind to people. I go to her house to call for her at dinner. I go to her house to play sometimes, we have good fun. I play with her every playtime. She has hazel eyes and gold and brown hair. Her clothes are nice. She wears lovely shoes'. Andrea's friend, Rothna, 'tells me everything, she is kind', while Rothna thought Andrea 'sometimes looks pretty and we share sweets and toys'.

The boys used different terms, but they help each other, do each other favours, are kind to each other. Physical attraction does not appear to be a factor, but participation in the football culture appears a powerful thread uniting the boys. Malcolm's friends, Surdip and Rajesh, are 'both helpful, we all like playing football I know that if I fell over they would fetch the teacher'. Rajesh remarked that sometimes Surdip 'brings his football and he lets me play and sometimes he is happy and when I don't no a word he helps me and when he doesn't no a word I sometimes help him'. Warish likes Darren 'because he does not fight with me. I give Darren lollipops and he comes to my house', while Darren thought 'Warish as good as gold'. James always lets his friend Farooq 'play with my football and he always says you can come to my party'.

A more sophisticated approach to friendship is further illustrated by the development of degrees of friendship. For Caroline, 'Sangeeta in the other class is my first friend, Sheela in this class is my second friend, and Gita is my third friend'. Gita is of lower standing because she 'breaks friends when you haven't got something she wants, and when you're playing and pretending you're strangling someone she believes it and she's nearly crying'. Gita has not yet learnt the rules of this more advanced form of friendship, is unable to reciprocate in kind, is still within the individualistic mode more typical of infants. Among most of the pupils here, there was more investment of self in the friendship and more consideration of the other. They are more able than infants to distance themselves from the relationship and to see it objectively.

Friendships were for the most part gender specific and multiracial (see also Denscombe *et al*, 1986). Penny's best friend was Shirley, an Afro-Caribbean; Rashan was friendly with Karen, James with Farooq, David with Warish, Malcolm with Surdip and Rajesh ... and so on. Mandy liked Rashan because she 'is pretty and she is indian. She is kind and helps people. We shares sweets and time together. We play with my ball we play tickie as well. Rashan has got black curly hair and brown eyes I like her. I like because she is Indian and I have never had an Indian friend before'. In some instances, therefore, inter-racial friendships were struck up as a matter of deliberate choice.

These associations were long-lasting, most of them surviving my eighteen-month period at the school, despite occasional tiffs here and there. In their general interaction in class, there also seemed a high degree of racial interrelatedness. Michelle 'needed to know how to spell everything' and Rajesh always helped her, spelling the easier words himself and pointing out others on the board. One day when Winston was reading to me, and struggling, Surdip came to his assistance, interpreting his untidy writing, making suggestions. Jonathan and Daniel held hands on an outing to the park ... and so on — there were many such examples. This illustrates also the considerable resource pupils were to each other in learning. As Karen claimed when she was sitting next to James. 'I give him words and nudge him if he is not listening'.

In the playground, football predominates for the boys, and there is no apparent racial discrimination. As Pradeep told me 'it is all against all' (boys, that is) and that is exactly what it looked like! In one of the teacher's opinions 'The children see no ethnic boundaries. It comes later from the home and the media, and prejudice builds up. At this age, they all get on together, they are quite uninhibited'. The teacher capitalized on this — indeed pupil cooperation was central to her policy. It can be seen that where relevance, reconstruction and problem recognition and solving in their own terms are considered important, pupils can be of the greatest assistance to each other. So they did a great deal of group work, paired and group reading, joint discussions etc, and were encouraged to help each other generally.

My observations of, and discussions with, pupils in general bore this out. However, there were one or two pupils who seemed outside the general pupil society and had no friends. The only thing that distinguished them from the rest as far as I could tell was that they were of a minority race or religion within the school. Kamlesh, for example, a Muslim, was an isolate, and when asked to write about her friend, could only write about her teacher. The same principles of friendship are evident, though unfortunately an adult cannot meet them all!

My friend's name is Mrs. Brown. She is very kind. She looks nice as well. She helps me with words all the time. I can not play with her because she is an adult. Well she is a teacher as well . . . she can make me laugh all the time . . . she taught me about tadpoles as well.

Surdip, in one of his confidences, said to me once 'Shall I tell you something. I said "Who likes Shakeel?" They all put their hands down. I said "Who likes Andrea?" They all put their hands up (as they did for Shirley, Karupa and Surdip himself). All of them put their hands up except for Shakeel, 'Poor old Shakeel' I said 'I like Shakeel'. 'So do I' said Surdip 'if he doesn't be silly'.

Winston, an Afro-Caribbean, went through a period of what he and his mother felt to be persecution. Sarah was laughing at him becaue she said his picture of Father Christmas was 'rubbish'. Sheela 'nicked his rubber', Jonathan kept teasing him and accusing him of calling him 'Bogglass' when 'it wasn't him but Caroline' . . . These things happened to other children, but they seemed more able to cope. Winston was reduced to tears on occasions and to complaints to the teacher. In desperation, the teacher placed him with Daniel, the only other Afro-Caribbean boy in the class, and there a kind of peace prevailed. Kulmeet, a Sikh, was also excluded, even from the list of Gita's friends which included almost the whole class. This was not through an oversight — rather she included her through oversight, then deleted her: '. . . Caroline, Sheela, Sarah, Amina, Kulmeet — I mean *not* Kulmeet . . . Wayne, Hemang, Pradeep . . . and all of those'. Kulmeet, Kamlesh, Winston and Shakeel seemed pleasant, happy, outgoing, friendly children — there was no evident reason why they should not have friends. The racial factor was one of the things that distinguished them from their peers, but exactly how it operates must be the subject of further study.

There were also, from time to time, conflicts within the class. Sometimes there were just tiffs between long-standing friends. As Karen reported, 'Sometimes we have fights but we always make up again and for ever will be . . . we sometimes change seats . . .' This sense of longevity is important, and sometimes a disagreement can bring it into question, as when Stephanie fell out with Rebecca: 'She says she's going to get her brother on to me. I'll get my cousin on to her. I said "Right! I'll not be your friend for good now!"' But they were soon friends again, as were Urmi and Andrea when they fell out (Urmi spent much of the day on the floor under desks avoiding Andrea's dreadful gaze!).

Conflict was a particular problem at one time of the year with some of the girls — Ann against Gita, Gita against Sarah, Sarah against Caroline. They were spiteful toward each other, Ann actually hitting Gita in the stomach on one occasion. The boys, too, at times had fights. After the assembly, for example, on 'good friends and loving care', two boys in class 1 were found fighting and 'calling each other silly names'. The principles of friendship are not always easy to live up to!

Pupils were encouraged to have a caring attitude towards each other, and certainly 'caring' was one of the prominent features of the school ethos. It was evident in pupil-pupil and teacher-pupil relationships. It was reflected in certain curriculum activities, in the children's reactions to visitors such as 'Baby Elizabeth', the two baby lambs, 'Welliphant' and Susan, a handicapped girl. The children were very positive about Susan, not mentioning in their reports things she could not do, ony those she could — how she ate, what she liked, how she got about, took a shower, went swimming, got cream cake ('naughty but nice') all over her face, wrote with a pencil in the mouth — all beautifully illustrated, the whole put over with affection and humour as they joined with Susan in her outlook on the world. On another occasion a relief teacher brought her 5-year-old son in with her because he had hurt his leg, and the class 'adopted' him. Ann did him a stencil of Roland Rat, Kaushik drew him a tall thin man.

Caring was celebrated too within the festivals of the major religions of children at the school. Diwali, for example, is a time for sharing in everyone's happiness, for distributing gifts as part of that festival of sharing — as is Christmas. In one typical letter to Santa Claus, Hemang generously wrote

> Would you please get something for people in Ethopia because they are very poor because they can't grow lots of vegetables. This is because it is very hot thats why so could you please at least give two sacks of grain each for one tent. All I would like is one transformer.
>
> Thank you Santa.

Love from Hemang

Winston seemed to think of everybody except himself:

> I am writing to you please can you get the ghanies a new home to live in and dont make this one burn down. And make them have some clothes and some shoes and toys could you help the Ethiopians and please get my sister a doll too.

Love from Winston

In general I would argue that there is evidence here of significant development along three crucial dimensions identified by Rubin (1980, p. 42) — taking the other's point of view, seeing people in psychological as well as physical terms, and seeing social relationships as more enduring systems. There is still much of the former 'infant' state evident, but there are signs here of the basis having been laid for the development of more complex relationships.

Conclusion

I have outlined elsewhere a conception of the pupil's career as a series of steps or stages, consisting of points inspiring pronounced change followed by comparative plateaus of consolidation and gradual development (Woods, 1980). The transition from infant to junior at 7+, especially where different institutions are concerned, is one such stage. How general the changes documented here are would be a matter for further research, as would the conditions under which they occur (for example, where infants and junior are taught in separate institutions or departments, labelled as such, taught by different methods or by different curricular schemes, have access to different materials and situations, experience different school ethos or teacher personality . . .). There would need to be comparisons ideally not only between schools and school-systems, but within schools to establish whether these processes are indeed more pronounced here than at other stages in the primary school career.

The evidence advanced here points to the possible significance of such a move. Pupil's personal concern at the time was real and keenly felt, but short-lived. At a deeper level, pupils began to undergo a profound change. Some acquired basic skills they had hitherto lacked, and/or significantly extended their knowledge. This equipped them better to shake themselves free from 'infancy and take on the role of 'juniors'. This involved, in this case, learning to take more responsibility for their own learning, recognizing the need for the acquisition of certain skills, cultivating attitudes that facilitated the reconstruction of knowledge, becoming more independent — of parents, of each other, of the teachers, forming new kinds of friendships. The new juniors became subject to the influence of older children, with whom they quickly began to form liaisons, and they began to be effected by the school in general with its ethos of work, caring, participation and fun. Friendships crossed racial boundaries. Indeed, at this age in some cases this actually promoted friendships, though not with real minorities within these classes.

In the construction of pupil identities pupils from minority racial groups adapted to the majority culture in different ways. Some actively promoted the culture of their forbears, others rejected it. No doubt there are variations in between. For these children this is a critical matter and a source of great tension as others fight for what they are to become. If, as is suggested here, the 7/8 year age group in the present social and institutional arrangements is a key one in the development of perspectives, in beginning to identify the 'me' and to acknowledge enduring systems as opposed to present practicalities, the form of their racial adaptions will also take a pronounced step toward consolidation.

So, too, will gender identities. Boys join a strong collective entity based on football culture, while girls begin to cultivate more personal and intimate friendships, both being consolidated by the further cultivation of specific matching gender interests. Rubin (1980) argues that neither boys' nor girls' development is complete where this occurs, and that they should have access to both kinds of social patterns.

Life-chances are determined or constructed for many people in the early years. The channels of their educational potential which is realized at secondary school are already formulated before they arrive there. I have argued here that the 7/8 year age group is currently a crucial one in the development of those attitudes, abilities and relationships that go to the making of educational success at that level. In this sense the transition is not only one of infant to junior. Like joined-up writing and the second set of teeth, there are other ultimates here, and they lay down the means for the next transfer to secondary, and indeed for later life.

Acknowledgement

I am grateful to Andrew Pollard and to teachers at the school for their comments on an earlier draft of this chapter.

References

ARMSTRONG, M. (1980) *Closely Observed Children*, London, Writers and Readers.

BENNETT, S.N. DESFORGES, C.W. COCKBURN, A.D. and WILKINSON, B. *The Quality of Pupil Learning*, London, Lawrence Erlbaum.

BIRCH, S. (1983) 'Shared and unshared meanings in the classroom', in WILSON, M. (Ed.) *Inside Classrooms*, Reading, Bulmershe College.

BRAH, A. and MINHAS, R. (1985) 'Structural racism or cultural difference: Schooling for Asian girls', in WEINER, G. (Ed.) *Just a Bunch of Girls*, Milton Keynes, Open University Press.

DAVIES, B. (1982) *Life in Classroom and Playground* London, Routledge and Kegan Paul.

DENSCOMBE, M., SZULC, H., PATRICK, C. and WOOD, A. (1986) 'Ethnicity and friendship: The contrast between sociometric research and fieldwork observations in primary school classrooms', *British Educational Research Journal*, 12, 3, pp. 221–35.

DONALDSON, M. (1978) *Children's Minds*, London, Fontana.

GETZELS, J.W. (1977) 'Images of the classroom and visions of the learner', in GLIDEWELL, J.D. (Ed.) *The Social Context of Learning and Development*, New York, Wiley.

GLASER, B.G. and STRAUSS, A.L. (1977) *Status Passage*, New York, Aldine.

JACKSON, P. (1968) *Life in Classrooms*. New York, Holt, Rinehart and Winston.

LEVER, J. (1976) 'Sex differences in the games children play', *Social Problems*, 23, pp. 478–87.

MEAD, G.H. (1934) *Mind, Self and Society*, Chicago, University of Chicago Press.

MEASOR, L. and WOODS, P. (1984) *Changing Schools: Pupil Perspectives on Transfer to a Comprehensive*, Milton Keynes, Open University Press.

POLLARD, A. (1985) *The Social World of the Primary School*, London, Holt, Rinehart and Winston.

ROBAIL, D. (1985) '"You haven't changed a bit, Miss": Infant-junior transition', mimeo.

ROWLAND, S. (1984) *The Enquiring Classroom*, Lewes, Falmer Press.

RUBIN, Z. (1980) *Children's Friendships*, London, Fontana.

TAYLOR, P.H. (1986) *Expertise and the Primary School Teacher*, London, NFER-Nelson.

WOODS, P. (1980) *Pupil Strategies*, London, Croom Helm.

8   Child in Control: Towards an Interpretive Model of Teaching and Learning

Stephen Rowland

My first recollection of being confronted with a class full of children on my own as a student teacher was the overriding fear: 'Would I be able to control the situation?'. My second thoughts were along the lines of 'Will the children understand what I'm getting at?'.

I suspect that most of us, except perhaps for the supremely confident or the insensitive, never fully come to terms with, or overcome, these feelings. They underly a view of learning and of the social setting of the classroom which is essentially oppressive and authoritarian for both the teacher and the taught. As we gain experience in teaching and managing a classroom, most of us discover that we can, usually, control the situation. We also gain skills which, we believe, usually enable us to make ourselves understood. But with this experience and skill there also comes a danger: the danger that we see teaching as being a matter of controlling the situations and the understandings that develop in the classroom. If the things that happen in the classroom are the things we had planned to happen, and if the learning that took place was what we intended, we think we have succeeded. Indeed, most of the very language of education objectives and of the curriculum, is based upon the assumption that the successful teacher is able to control and predetermine these situations and understandings.

In this chapter I want to question this assumption that the teacher should be in control. I want to suggest that the crucial questions for the teacher are 'Can the children control their activity?' and 'Do I understand what the children are getting at?' rather than 'Can I control the situation?' and 'Do they understand what I'm getting at?' As far as my own teaching experience is concerned, it is only by becoming absorbed in these first two questions that I can overcome my anxieties about the last two. But what I want to say is, I hope, more than merely a strategy for overcoming the fears which we first feel as student teachers. It is also an attempt to reconceive the task of teaching as being principally a task of active observation and interpretation, rather than one of performing and instilling. It might be useful to compare the point I am making with the position that has been adopted by sociologists of the primary classroom. Pollard (1985), for example, suggests that negotiation (which I understand to be an attempt to evolve a collaborative way of working together) is one of a number of 'situational strategies' which teachers may adopt in order to cope with the power which teachers and children have to threaten the interests of each other. It may be seen this way. My claim, however, is that the process of negotiation between teacher and learner is a logically necessary element of 'teaching' as I understand that term. It is based upon the assumption that learning is a process of construction or reconstruction by the learner and that therefore teaching, which is a deliberate intervention in the learning process, must be founded upon an attempt to understand the learner's present state of knowledge. This claim, which stems from an epistemological understanding rather than from analysis of the power relations in the classroom is not in conflict with the sociologist's observation that teachers use negotiation as a strategy, but asserts that such a strategy is an essential element of teaching rather than simply a means of obtaining control or of 'coping'.

I shall pursue these ideas of negotiating and attempting to understand the child in relation to a sequence of events which took place in a classroom in which I was teaching some years ago. Drawing upon these events, and my developing understanding of them, I shall then attempt to construct a model of how I understand the process of teaching and learning. But first I must say a few words about the idea of 'control' that will be central to my argument.

Teacher concerns about 'keeping control' and fears of 'losing control' in the classroom normally relate to the overt behaviour that takes place. In an authoritarian classroom the behaviour of the children will be rigidly controlled by the teacher. But such attempts to control children can always be (and often are) resisted by them. Children then 'take over' control of the situation, or events can become 'out of control'. At this level 'control' is about the power that individuals exert over each other's behaviour. Underlying the control of overt behaviour, however, is a much more intangible but powerful force for control which is exercised in the classroom. This is the kind of control which is exercised over the language, the definitions of concepts, in other words, over the very tools for thinking. It is evidenced in the ways in which teachers and children express themselves as they negotiate and pursue their activity. The danger of the authoritarian classroom lies not so much in the control which the teacher has over the behaviour of the children, but the control which is exercised over their minds. Unless children are enabled to exercise control over this, their learning is liable to be sterile, to be dependent upon the teacher and ultimately to produce conformity without thoughtfulness.

In the classroom children may be free to choose between one work package and another, and be encouraged to introduce their own interests into their work. But as long as this work is expressed in terms which are legitimated solely by the teacher, or is directed towards the development of knowledge, concepts or skills which are defined exclusively by the teacher, then the children's control will be illusory. It will amount to little more than a more pleasant, and perhaps more effective, means of producing the kind of conformity which militates against critical self-determined thinking. A superficial technical competence may be gained, but at a high cost to the imagination which surely is the source of continued learning.

How, then, can children exercise this kind of control? As teachers we want to develop their ideas and introduce them to new ones. How can children be expected to exercise control over ideas which they haven't yet 'got'?

In order to pursue this question, I need to relate my story about Dean, a 10-year-old boy who was working in a primary school classroom in which I taught and researched alongside another teacher. In this account, which I shall relate from the notes I made describing and reflecting upon the day's events in the classroom, we shall see how Dean grasps and takes control over a new concept only after I, as teacher, realized that it was fruitless to force upon him my own understanding of the concept.

At the time, several children in the class of 9-11-year-olds had recently been searching the hedgerows around the school for wildlife. Dean and a few of his friends were engaged in examining and making homes for their collections of caterpillars.

Dean was sitting at a table next to his best friend William. While William drew his caterpillars, I worked with Dean who had just completed some writing about his creatures. Before us was a jam jar full of grass with various caterpillars crawling about inside it and around the rim. My notes (Rowland, 1979) take up the account:

5th June

... we talked about species. We had not examined any reference books together and Dean did not seem concerned to find out the real names of the different varieties. Instead, he had invented his own names. A type of thin small caterpillar he called 'Mr. Diet'; the black and yellow ones were 'Arthur'; the brown furry ones 'Stannage'. He did not use these as 'pet' names but as names which referred to any caterpillar which appeared to be of that type.

But as we watched William drawing a caterpillar a problem arose. William was carefully drawing a 'Cyril' which had six 'legs' and ten 'suckers'. Dean noticed that most of the ones he had called 'Cyril' only had six 'legs' and four 'suckers'. He didn't suggest inventing a new name for this different variety of 'Cyril'. Thinking that we should clarify our criteria for classification, I suggested that we list the different varieties we had in a table in which the different columns registered the name, colour, number of 'legs', number of 'suckers' and comments relating to each variety of caterpillar.

While we were talking about my idea, Dean seemed to think it was a good one, but when he began to fill in the table, he became frustrated about the differing number of 'legs' and 'suckers' on the various 'Cyrils'. He said, 'I call all green ones like that Cyril'. I'm not bothered about how many legs they've got'. It seemed that I had imposed my own system of classification and Dead did not like it.

We then talked about how his caterpillars differed. I was now keen not to impose my own ideas and Dean decided that these should be the attributes we should look for — colour; fat, thin or medium; hairy or not hairy; where it was found or what it ate (considered normally to be identical). He made a table like this:

Colour	Fatness	Hairy	Found on	Sameness
Green	Thin	Not hairy	Hawthorn	Not the same
Yellow and Grey	Fat	Bit hairy	Hawthorn	
Brown	Fat	Hairy	Dock leaf	Not the same
Brown	Fat	Bit hairy	Hawthorn	

I asked him why he had headed another column 'sameness'. He said, 'So I can write down if they're the same or not'. My objection seemed to me to be too simple and obvious to explain. I had assumed that the purpose of such a table was a list the attributes of different *classes* of caterpillar. Dean, apparently, saw it as a way of recording the attributes of his different *individual* creatures. I did not explain my point except to say that I could not see the need for the last column. He explained that he would list all his caterpillars in pairs and say, for each pair, whether or not the caterpillars were identical. I said, 'But surely, if they are both the same, you wouldn't bother to list them both?' He said that he would and that he would show me how when I returned to school tomorrow. There seems to be quite an exercise in logic in all this.

One satisfaction of working with Dean (though at times a frustration too) is his willingness to reject or modify strategies that I suggest. In this business of classification I think that problems will be encountered by him following his own strategies which would have been glossed over had he merely followed mine. It will be interesting to see whether the problem still interests him tomorrow. He does appear so far to have wanted to work at a level of abstraction beyond what I might have expected.

7th June
Yesterday Dean *did* want to return to making his table comparison for his caterpillars. He got down to it as soon as he arrived, ten

minutes or so before the official beginning of school. He selected two caterpillars to record and wrote in the columns:

Green and black	Thin	Not hairy	Hawthorn	Not the same
Green black/white	Medium	Not hairy	Hawthorn	

Before completing the final 'sameness' column he did not look at the insects to see if they in fact were of the same appearance, but instead checked through his columns, comparing entries, to establish than the entries were different. Thus the 'sameness' column did not refer directly to the appearance of the insects or whether, on some other evidence, he thought they were of the same type, but rather was an identity relationship between the attributes which he had selected to compare. This is a subtle, but I think most important, distinction since it shows the level of abstraction at which Dean was working.

Dean then went on to show me how he would record the entries of similar caterpillars. He first selected two individuals to record. He was thus not merely going to write down the same entry twice. Each entry had to correspond with observations made of a particular caterpillar. For each he completed the attribute columns: green and white; thin; not hairy; hawthorn. 'Same' was written against the entries in the 'sameness' column. Dean then put on a perplexed and frustrated expression, saying that he needed an extra column. He said this should be a 'name' column. I asked him if he meant a column for names like 'Cyril', 'Stannage' and 'Arthur' that he had invented. He said 'No, it must be for their real names'.

Dean seemed to have discovered the need for a taxonomy. Having selected (what he considered to be) criterion attributes by which to describe the caterpillars, he saw that a class could be made of those creatures with identical attributes, and that such a class should be given a name. It was this identity of selected attributes, rather than direct appearances, which characterized Dean's conception of class and is indeed central to any such system of classification.

By this stage Dean was ready to make use of a reference book, from which he identified his last recorded caterpillar as being that of a Winter Moth.

There is little doubt that had Dean uncritically followed my original suggestion of tabulating his invented names for the caterpillars against my selection of attributes he would never have confronted problems of classification and taxonomy in such depth. His approach may seem somewhat eccentric (and therefore unpredictable) to us, but then we take for granted, or perhaps have never enquired into, the internal logic of the problem with which Dean was concerned.

Looking back on this sequence of events, what fascinates me is that the understanding which Dean arrived at actually sharpened my own understanding of what taxonomy is about. In no way could I have engineered the situation to ensure that Dean arrived at this understanding. Indeed, he arrived at it in spite of my attempts to structure his thinking in the earlier part of the activity. But this is not to say that I played no part in this emerging understanding. He invented a way of classifying, he then saw the need for a 'real' system. During this process, once I had dropped my attempts to constrain his thinking along my lines, I acted as a kind of reflective agent to his thinking.

These three ideas of inventing, discovering a need, and the teacher acting as a reflective agent are crucial elements in the learning process, whether we are talking about writing a poem or learning how to grow vegetables in the garden. I believe that they are central to the learning and teaching relationship. I shall return to them later.

So far, I have only represented those aspects of learning related to exploration. Teaching and learning also involves instruction. This may appear to contradict my earlier comments about the need for children to be in control. I think, however, that in certain contexts, it does make sense to say that a child can be in control while they are pursuing a course of instruction. Clearly, it is not practical, and perhaps it is logically impossible, to learn everything through discovery alone. Nevertheless, it is vital that the child's control is not lost. To see how this context for instruction might emerge, and the effect it might have, I shall return to take up the story of Dean. For, several days after the events reported above, Dean's work reached a new phase where he recognized a need for instruction in order to meet his own objectives.

12th June

... I suggested we weigh the caterpillar. Dean said that if we used a classroom scales 'it would weigh nothing'. I aked if he could invent a way of weighing such a small thing. After a while thinking he said, 'If you get a stick or something and balance it on something like this, then you can put the caterpillar on one end and weigh it against something on the other end'. It was lunch time by now and he said he would think about it over his meal.

On returning in the afternoon he said that his father had explained that using Dean's method he could compare the weight of the caterpillar with something else, say a feather, but could not find its actual weight.

Talking over the problem, I suggested that we could weigh the creature against centimetre wooden cubes (part of some classroom maths apparatus) using a metre rule pivoted at the centre.

We could then find out how much each cube weighed by measuring a number of them against a standard 50g weight. Dean liked the idea, so we followed this plan. Using a classroom scales 103 cubes balanced 50g. Jason, who had come to join us, said that this was near enough 100 and that then each cube must weigh ½g.

We then pivoted the metre rule to balance at the 50cm mark. On one end we placed the furry caterpillar, on the other end the cube. The caterpillar weighed more than the ½g cube. Using two cubes we saw that it weighed less than 1g. I suggested we cut a cube in half to make a ¼g weight. Using this we found it to weigh more than ½g but less than ¾g ...

... (the following day) the caterpillar was again weighed as being between ½g and ¾g. Dean suggested that we could halve the cube again to get a more accurate measurement. I agreed and added that we could even make further halvings. Thus, we soon had a cube, a half-cube, a quarter-cube and an eighth-cube weighing ½g, ¼g and ¹⁄₁₆g, respectively.

Dean has not yet come across fractions in his maths scheme. (Throughout the school children use workbooks from a graded primary mathematics scheme.) We worked together at the blackboard for a while talking out how to write and name fractions and the various relationships involving the fractions we required. He had no trouble in understanding this.

Using the new weights and the rules, Dean measured the caterpillar to weigh ½g and ¹⁄₁₆g.

We returned to the blackboard for more talk about how we might add fractions, using diagrams to help in the explanation. I led him carefully through this, asking many learning questions. In this way, Dean soon found that ½ and ¹⁄₁₆ could be combined as ⁹⁄₁₆. Thus he recorded ⁹⁄₁₆g as being today's weight for the caterpillar ...

... I then suggested that since he had appeared to grasp ideas involved in fractions so well, he might like to find some work from his maths scheme on this topic. To my surprise, he took up this idea enthusiastically.

Dean is currently on book 3 in this scheme (out of five graded books intended for use across the junior age range). He returned to me having found a book 5 with a section on fractions. With practically no help from me he soon completed several of the tasks in this section. I do not wish to go into the details of this textbook work here, but merely to note that he had little difficulty in tackling an exercise that was 'theoretically' one to two years in advance of the book he is currently working on. I do not here imply that his current book is too easy for him. On the contrary, I have seen it present him with considerable problems on several occasions. Nor do I wish to criticize this particular graded scheme, one which is in common use in may English primary schools at present. Rather, my point is that where a mathematical idea has arisen from a meaningful context and one over which the child exerted an overall control of the objectives, he was able to work at an apparently higher level than might otherwise have been expected. Furthermore, the assumption that the various 'levels' of mathematical competence are related in a rigidly determined and hierarchical fashion is strongly brought into question if a child is able to 'skip' at least a full year in a carefully graded scheme and yet have no difficulty in tackling the tasks set, so long as such tasks bear a direct and understood relationship to the activity over which the child has been able to exercise control.

This account of Dean investigating his caterpillars raises, for me, important questions about the relationship between exploration and instruction in the learning process. Educational discussion has been pervaded by arguments between those, often characterised as 'traditionalists', who emphasize the value of didactic methods of teaching, and those, characterised as 'progressive' who emphasize the value of exploration.

The value of exploration and discovery was brought to the fore and given respectability by the Plowden Report in the 1960s (CACE, 1967). By the late 1970s, however, due largely to a changing economic climate and political debate reflected in the 1977 Green Paper (DES 1977) there was more scepticism about the value of such approaches. In 1978 HMI, in its survey of primary schools (DES 1978), observed 'didactic' and 'exploratory' methods operating in classrooms and concluded that the most successful teachers used a combination of both approaches, but little light was thrown upon how the two might be combined.

Since 1978 the increasing financial pressures on education have given less opportunity for teachers to develop more innovative and child centred approaches to teaching. HMI, however, reported in 1985 (DES 1985a) that 'very few schools were good at providing opportunities for children to exercise choice or initiative' (para 6.3). In mathematics (DES 1985b) they warned that 'imposed methods ... are quickly forgotten' and that mathematics should not be seen as 'an imposed body of knowledge' (para 1.6).

Thus the debate between exploratory and didactic methods is still very much alive.

From my observations of Dean's work, and many similar instances of investigation in the primary classroom (Rowland, 1984), it seems to me that the relationship between the child's control and effective learning is of the utmost importance in this debate. For this reason, I shall now sketch out the characteristics of didactic and exploratory models for teaching in relation to the child's control. The weaknesses of both approaches, I shall argue, suggests a need for an alternative, interpretative, model which allows for the possibility of both children controlling their learning and teachers making a proper contribution to its development. I begin with the Didactic model.

The Didactic Model

CHILD

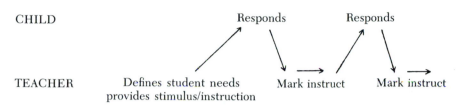

TEACHER

This model for teaching and learning is often seen as the 'traditional' approach in which the teacher has the virtually impossible task of defining exactly what each child needs and of providing appropriate instruction. The aim is to instil certain prespecified skills or knowledge in the child. The teacher imparts instruction (either directly or through programmed learning packages), the child responds; the teacher marks, and further instructions follow.

This way of working keeps children busy, but such busyness is in response to the teacher's initiatives. It is the teacher who is really active, keeping control of the children's behaviour and the substance of their learning. All the instruction and stimulus is defined by the teacher in the language of the teacher. It is the teacher's knowledge and skill which the child attempts to copy, and success is measured in terms of the match between the two. Such a basis for educating the young may be suitable as a means for conditioning the next generation to the needs of society as perceived by the teacher. But can it educate them for a future society in which they will play a critical, responsible and self-determining role?

HMI (DES 1985a, para. 7.11) and researchers, (Galton, Simon and Croll, 1980) have found that such a model for teaching and learning predominates. It is not easy to escape from this model, even where more favourable teacher/pupil ratios might seem to make a more radical approach possible.

Indeed, I have found that even in the most favourable circumstances of teaching a single child to play the piano, under no pressure of time or space, it is very difficult not to teach in a didactic manner. After all, I have the knowledge and skill. Isn't my task to transfer this knowledge and skill to the child? Am I not the one who knows best which activities will promote these abilities?

As an alternative, or as a compliment, to the rigid Didactic Model, many teachers have valued a more exploratory approach to learning.

An exploratory model

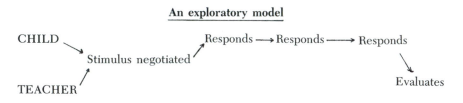

The HMI survey of 1978 (DES, 1978) characterized such an approach as one in which:

> the broad objectives of the work were discussed with the children but then they were put in a position of finding their own solutions. (para. 3)

Here, negotiation plays a key role at the beginning of the activity, with aims being agreed upon. Now the children are more active, providing their own interpretation of their work as it proceeds, making their own judgments and developing their own strategies. Once the work is under way, the teacher takes a back seat, only to come forward again when it is time to evaluate the work done.

Such a way of working is essentially individual. The teacher's role is often seen as being more of a provider of a stimulating environment than as an instructor. Here the learner has much more control over both the language and the concepts which develop as a result of the activity, although this control may be no more than an illusion if the evaluation of the activity is solely the responsibility of the teacher.

Such an approach to teaching children has been an important part of the work in a number of primary schools where 'play' and 'open-ended' activities have been encouraged. While the sense of freedom and responsibility that an exploratory model offers the learning is to be welcomed, the idea that learning takes place when individuals are 'put in a position of finding their own solutions' may fail to recognize the essentially social nature of learning. Left on their own during activity, with only their own resources to call upon, children may rely only upon that knowledge and those strategies with which they are familiar. Anyone trying to learn on their own easily becomes stuck into their own ways of thinking. Such ways of thinking may be expressions of a particular ideology of which, on one's own, it is difficult to gain any critical awareness. Without teachers or peers with whom to interact during the process of learning, children are liable to become more entrenched in their present position. This problem arises whether the subject matter is a mathematical investigation which may requrie new insights, or a social enquiry which demands a new perspective on issues of racism. The danger is that an exploratory model of learning, while intending to be a radical alternative which empowers the learner with greater autonomy, may actually have the opposite effect by protecting the learner from the challenge of social interaction. Confidence may be gained, but the opportunity for growth lost.

The limitations of both the didactic model and the exploratory model are, I think, apparent. To advise, as the HMI report appeared to, that we should therefore combine both strategies might seem strange. Might this not merely ensure that the children received the worst of both models? What we need is a model which helps us to decide when and how exploration or didactic instruction are appropriate. For this purpose I tentatively propose an alternative model, which I shall call the interpretive model, because, at its heart lies the idea of the interaction between teachers and learners as essentially an attempt by each party to interpret the expressions of the other.

The interpretive model

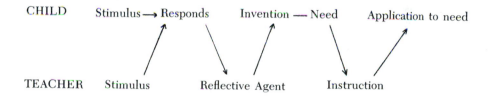

In this model, the initial stimulus for activity may come from the child or from the teacher. In either case, it is vital that it is the child's interpretation of that stimulus which motivates the activity. Only then can the child's control be assured. She is not trying to guess what's in the teacher's mind in responding to the teacher's resources, but formulates her own ideas. Once the activity is under way, the teacher's role is then to act as a reflective agent, aiming to help the child identify concerns and needs, and also to provide positive yet critical feedback to the student. The child, in turn, critically responds to the teacher's contributions. Neither is 'right' or 'wrong'. As Radley (1980) puts it: 'Both student and teacher are engaged in a two way process of expressing what it is they are trying to formulate and grasping those things which the other person is indicating' (p. 42) In the course of tackling problems, children will invent. Such invention, even where not successful, is a powerful means for increasing awareness of what skills and knowledge are needed. Once the child recognizes this need, their control of the activity can be temporarily handed over to the teacher, or indeed to another child, for a period of instruction. This instruction does not have the purpose of developing skills in isolation, but of empowering children to meet the goals which they have set for themselves. In this model, unlike the didactic model, instruction is an enabler of the children's control rather than a mechanism for concentrating the teacher's control.

Returning now to Dean and his caterpillars, it is interesting to see how his activity followed the path suggested by the interpretive model. My initial interventions for classifying the caterpillars were rejected by Dean thereby ensuring that his response was indeed *his* rather than my response to the initial idea. My conversation with him as a reflective agent were my attempts to understand his procedures and respond to them. His somewhat idiosyncratic inventions here led *him* to see the need for a taxonomy which eventually led him to make use of a textbook in order to find out the 'real' names of his caterpillars. Again, in the caterpillar weighing part of the activity, he invented the system for weighing in collaboration with his friends — which led him to a problem (the adding of fractions) which, in order to solve, required my instruction. This instruction was not performed, in the first instance, in order to teach Dean 'how to do fractions' but in order that he could meet his own goal, or need, of plotting the growth of his caterpillar.

The implications of such a model are far reaching. For now the distinction between learners and teachers becomes less clear cut. Learners can become teachers, and teachers become learners. Since the children have a controlling influence upon the language and the concepts with which they grapple, they therefore exert a controlling influence upon their curriculum. We can mediate in this, and indeed we must, by presenting continual challenges and a widening of horizons, but, in the final analysis, it is the children who 'own' their curriculum. It is not our curriculum which is given to them.

References

CENTRAL ADVISORY COUNCIL FOR EDUCATION (1967) *Children and Their Primary Schools* (The Plowden Report), London, HMSO.

DEPARTMENT OF EDUCATION AND SCIENCE (1977) *Education in Schools: A Consultative Document*, London, HMSO.

DEPARTMENT OF EDUCATION AND SCIENCE (1978) *Primary Education in England*, London, HMSO.

DEPARTMENT OF EDUCATION AND SCIENCE (1985a) *Education 8 to 12 in Combined and Middle Schools*, London, HMSO.

DEPARTMENT OF EDUCATION AND SCIENCE (1985b) *Mathematics from 5 to 16*, London, HMSO.

GALTON, M., SIMON, B. and CROLL, P. (1980) *Inside the Primary Classroom*, London, Routledge and Kegan Paul.

POLLARD, A. (1985) *The Social World of the Primary School*, New York, Holt, Rinehart and Wilson.

RADLEY, A. (1980) 'Student learning as social practice' in SALMON, P. (Ed.) *Coming to Know*, London, Routledge and Kegan Paul.

ROWLAND, S. (1979) 'How to intervene: clues from the work of a ten year old', *Forum for the discussion of New Trends in Education*, 23, 2.

ROWLAND, S. (1984) *The Enquiring Classroom*, Lewes, Falmer Press.

9   Classroom Task Organization and Children's Friendships

Steven Bossert

Editor's Note

This chapter is drawn from parts of 'Tasks and Social Relationships in Classrooms' by Steven Bossert (1979). Bossert studied the consequences of the organization of classroom instruction at Harper School — a university-operated private school serving upper-middle class families in the USA. Two classes of 9-year-olds, taught by Ms Hunt and Mr Stone, were studied for three to four hours each week over a period of six months. The classes were mixed at the end of the year for organizational reasons and Bossert was able to study the same children in the classes of Ms Field and Ms Park.

   Some key features of each teacher's approach to teaching and class organization are described below:

Ms Hunt	(3rd grade) retained tight control of her class. Teacher led question and answer sessions — recitations — were the key instructional strategy used.
Mr Stone	(3rd grade) expected children to be self-directed. He used small-group projects extensively and there was considerable flexibility in the activities in which the children engaged.
Ms Field	(4th grade) was very much like Ms Hunt favouring tight control and predominantly using recitation and whole-class assignments. Seat places were fixed by Ms Field.
Ms Park	(4th grade) gave the children considerable choice. She introduced individual and small-group projects with a very varied curriculum.

Thus, whilst Mr Stone and Ms Park used a multi-task form of classroom organization and allowed the children considerable choice and control, Ms Hunt and Ms Field favoured recitation and whole-class tasks with tight control. Bossert's research is essentially concerned with the consequences of these forms of organization for the friendships and social relationships which children develop.

Introduction

In Harper School a variety of factors influenced pupils' selection of play- and workmates. As tables 1, 2, 3, and 4 indicate, the children usually formed into friendship and work groups with seatmates of the same sex. Children who had the same teacher during the previous year associated frequently at the beginning of the year, but once regular task activities began, differing patterns of peer relations emerged. As the school year progressed, the children in both Field's and Hunt's classrooms associated increasingly with children performing at similar levels. In Park's and Stone's classrooms, however, achievement level did not affect friendship and work group choices. To what extent did differences in these classrooms' activity structures affect the patterns of peer association that emerged?

Recitation-organized Classrooms

In the recitation-organized classrooms, the emergence of academically homogeneous peer grouping paralleled the formation of academic elites. In Field's room, just as old friendships began to weaken, the math honor guard was created. Field encouraged its members to work together on math problems, and they soon began eating and playing together during lunch and free time. In the fourth week of school, Carl, David, Michael, and Eric asked to have their desks moved together in the back of the room, forming a new row for the math honor guard. This allowed the boys to work together and talk without having to obtain Field's permission to use the back room. The move was one of the first in which pupils from different third-grade classes formed into a friendship group: Eric and David were friends in Hunt's room, and Carl and Michael were classmates in Stone's room.

Table 1. *Weekly summary of peer group composition: Ms. Field's classroom*

Week[a]	Number of			Percent of groups homogeneous by					
	Groups	Changes	Children not in groups	Sex	Race[b]	Neighborhood[c]	Classmates last year	Seatmates	Achievement level[d]
1	8	–	2	100	63	50	63	100	38
2	8	1	2	100	63	50	63	100	38
3									
4	7	5	3	100	71	58	43	85	58
5	6	2	4	100	67	50	17	83	67
6									
7	7	1	2	100	43	43	14	85	85
8	7	2	3	100	58	43	14	100	100
9									
10									
11									
12	7	3	3	100	43	58	29	100	71
13									
14	7	3	3	100	43	58	29	85	71
15									
16									
17									
18									
19									
20	7	3	3	100	58	58	14	100	85
21									

Note: Peer groups include those children who worked and played together.
[a] Only weeks in which groups changed are noted. In a week where there were two changes, both are listed (see table 4).
[b] Race was defined by visual inspection. The categories were Caucasian, black, and Oriental.
[c] Neighborhoods were indicated by the official, community named areas. The children lived primarily in two non-adjacent neighborhoods, Lakeside and Parkwood.
[d] Achievement level was defined by teacher ratings of each of their pupils. These occurred twice during the observation period.

Table 2. Weekly summary of peer group composition: Ms. Hunt's classroom

	Number of			Percent of groups homogeneous by					
Week[a]	Groups	Changes	Children not in groups	Sex	Race[b]	Neighborhood[c]	Classmates last year	Seatmates	Achievement level[d]
1	9	–	0	100	67	34	78	100	11
2									
3	9	5	3	100	45	45	33	100	33
4									
5									
6									
7									
8									
9									
10	10	4	1	100	50	50	30	90	60
11									
12	7	5	4	100	29	43	14	100	71
13									
14	7	1	5	100	29	43	14	100	71
15									
16									
17									
18									
19									
20									
21									

Notes: See table 1.

Table 3. Weekly summary of peer group composition: Mr. Stone's classroom

Week[a]	Number of			Percent of groups homogeneous by					
	Groups	Changes	Children not in groups	Sex	Race[b]	Neighborhood[c]	Classmates last year	Seatmates	Achievement level[d]
1	7	—	4	100	29	43	86	100	29
2	7	4	2	100	29	43	58	100	29
3	8	6	3	100	50	75	50	87	25
4									
5									
6	8	6	4	100	63	75	38	100	38
7									
8	8	4	6	100	38	63	38	100	38
9	8	2	5	100	38	63	38	100	38
10	8	1	4	100	38	63	38	100	38
11									
12	7	8	5	100	43	71	29	100	29
13									
14	7	2	6	100	43	71	29	100	29
15									
16	9	7	3	100	33	78	22	100	44
17									
18									
19	7	2	4	86	58	71	29	100	29
20	9	4	3	100	67	78	44	100	33
21									

Notes: See table 1.

137

Table 4. *Weekly summary of peer group composition: Ms. Park's classroom*

| | Number of | | | Percent of groups homogeneous by | | | | | |
Week[a]	Groups	Changes	Children not in groups	Sex	Race[b]	Neighborhood[c]	Classmates last year	Seatmates	Achievement level[d]
1	7	–	2	100	58	29	71	100	14
1	5	6	1	100	20	20	0	100	0
2									
3	8	5	1	100	25	50	38	100	25
4	7	3	1	100	29	58	43	100	14
5									
6	6	3	1	100	50	33	17	100	0
7	7	4	0	100	43	14	50	100	29
8									
9									
10	5	6	4	100	40	40	20	100	20
11									
12	7	3	3	100	58	58	43	100	14
13									
14	7	2	2	86	58	43	14	100	43
15									
16	7	2	3	100	58	58	43	100	14
17									
18									
19	7	3	1	100	29	58	43	100	14
20	7	3	1	100	71	58	43	100	14
21									

Notes: See table 1.

During the fifth week of school, two other friendship groups emerged, mixing children from different third-grade classrooms. At the suggestion of Field, the two top performers on the independent reading laboratory (SRA) moved their desks together in the back of the room, away from the rest of the class.

Don:	(as he walks by to pencil sharpener) Tom and I are going to move our desks over here after lunch. Ms. Field wants us to.
Researcher:	Why are you moving?
Don:	Well, you see we're the two best on SRA. I skipped over to green and so did Tom, so Ms. Field wants us to work together on some of the exercises. Nobody else is that far. We can help time each other and correct them.

These two pupils occasionally played together before they moved their desks; however, *after* the move, they began to work and play together exclusively. Even when one of the boys wanted to play a game that the other did not like, the latter deferred in order to remain with his friend.

[Ms. Field tells the class that they can have a 15 minute break.]	
Don:	Let's go play checkers.
Tom:	Naw, I don't want to.
Mike:	(turning around in his seat) I'll play checkers.
Don:	I want to talk to Tom.
(Tom and Don get up and look out the back windows, talking.)	

Also during this week, three girls on the castle committee asked if they could move their seats together. Field approved because 'they are good girls — they're sharp and they get their work done, not gab all the time'.

By the end of the fifth week, then, nine of the ten top-achieving pupils had formed into three exclusive friendship groups. The only other performance-homogeneous group consisted of two 'average achieving' boys who had been best friends in Stone's room and who remained together throughout this year. In part, Field encouraged groupings among the top-performing pupils; they were the only ones who were allowed to work together while the rest of the class worked alone or with Field. These work group associations soon generalized: the pupils worked and played together during all activities within Field's class and in special classes as well. Gym was a notable exception for the boys. When the children were allowed to choose teams, the top boy athletes usually chose to play together regardless of academic performance level. After gym, however, the performance-homogeneous groups reformed.

During this period, the other pupils also began forming friendship groups based on academic performance. Because the top-performing pupils had already segregated themselves from others (sometimes physically by moving their seats away from the rest of the class), only the 'average' and 'poor' performing pupils remained free to interact. However, when Field did allow group work, she also encouraged the others to work with children performing at their own level. As with the top-performing pupils, this resulted in an increasing homogeneity of groups with respect to academic performance. For example, Frank, who had associated with David and Eric until they joined the other math honor guard boys, began eating, playing, and working with Fred and Patrick: All three were characterized by Field as 'bright, but not consistent workers'.

Play groupings were affected. For example, the split between Karen and Alice over Alice's joining two other friends stemmed from Karen's need to finish assignments while the other girls played. Rather than continually fight to gain acceptance in an ongoing game, Karen withdrew from her long association with Alice and later began playing with Robert and Terry, who also had to spend much of their free time finishing assignments. But, after the seventh week of school, Karen never consistently worked with any group.

By the eighth week of the second year, all seven groups of children who normally worked, ate lunch, and played together consisted only of pupils achieving at the same level. Furthermore, these friendship groupings remained fairly constant throughout the remaining thirteen weeks of observations in this classroom. Although there were three changes, these did not alter significantly the acheivement level composition of the groupings (see table 1).

The emergence of friendship groups in Ms. Hunt's classroom was very similar to the patterns that developed in Ms. Field's. As the year progressed, the children began associating with others performing at the same level. By the end of the tenth week of school, six of ten friendship groups consisted only of academic 'equals' (see table 2). One of the crucial events influencing the emergence of academically based peer relations in this classroom was math grouping. In the seventh week, after Hunt separated the class into two groups for math instruction, several friendships dissolved. Friends who were placed in different math groups began associating more often with the children in their own math group than with their former friends. Anne, for example, who had been 'best friends' with Karen since the beginning of second grade, soon began associating with Ellen after the two former friends were placed in different math groups. In all, three of four friendship groups that contained academic 'unequals' separated during the three-week period after the class had been grouped for math instruction.

Two characteristics of this classroom seemed to heighten the impact that math grouping had on friendship patterns. When Hunt split the class into math groups, she changed the seating arrangements so that children sat next to others in the same math group. This was done to 'minimize the moving around to get settled for math'. Because there were few occasions for the children to interact freely in this class, most peer associations occurred between seatmates. By organizing the seating arrangement by math group, Hunt caused new patterns of association to develop among children achieving at the same level. Furthermore, because math was one of the few subjects during which children were allowed to work together, work groupings naturally formed only among children who had the same assignment. Children in different math groups could not work together. As in Field's room, these work associations usually developed into play associations, causing the increase in friendship groups based on academic performance level during the three weeks following math grouping.

Like Field, Hunt tended to allow only the top-performing pupils to work together on class assignments or special chores while the other pupils worked alone. When all the children were allowed to work together, Hunt usually selected the work groups so that children who were performing at the same level worked together.

> *Hunt:* OK. You all can start work on this assignment. Remember to do page 106 first (in math book). And, who knows what you do? OK, Michael.
>
> *Mike:* You head up a new sheet with title and name.
>
> *Hunt:* Good. Now, you can work in pairs if you're quiet. OK, now. (Children split up into pairs, some do work alone.)
>
> *Hunt:* Announcement. I see that some of you are going to work with someone in another math group. Well that isn't too good. So please pick your partners from your own group. Amy and Laurie. [Girls in different math groups — they separate and find new partners as do the remaining children.]

Lynn and Erica, for example, became 'best friends' while working on a mural for their social studies project: Both were the top performers in the class.

The emergence of friendship groups based on academic performance in the recitation-organized classrooms seemed to reflect the importance that achievement played in these classrooms. As a task activity, recitation makes pupils' performances public and comparable. Because the entire class, or at least a large portion of it, works together during a recitation, each child's performance is visible to both the teacher and fellow pupils. If a child answers correctly, everyone knows because the teacher usually praises the answer. However, if an answer is incorrect, the recitation continues until someone produces the correct response. As Jackson (1968) has pointed out, a pupil's self-esteem is constantly challenged during recitation. When a child answers incorrectly, he may receive both the disapproval of his teacher and the ridicule of his peers. In a recitation class, the children know which of their peers are the most capable just by their participation in the task.

In addition, demonstrations of performance often depend on others' performances. During recitation, a pupil's ability to demonstrate his knowledge and receive praise depends on others' answers. When another pupil gives the correct answer, a child cannot show that he also knew the answer for that question. In these classrooms, children often tried actively to get the teacher to call on them; they raised their hands high, sat up in their seats, and said aloud that they knew the answer.

[Work sheet correction]
Hunt: Now who wants to answer question 3?
        (Raised hands)
        Ok, Kim.
Kim: It's ...
Hunt: (interrupting) Read the whole sentence Kim.
Kim: A principal highway is marked by a single red line (several of the kids jump up and down in their seats, raising their hands and saying, 'no, no').
Hunt: There seems to be some disagreement. OK, Martin. (Martin is just about standing behind his desk with his hand raised.)
Martin: Phew! It's a red and black line.
Hunt: Read the whole sentence Martin.
Martin: A principal highway is marked by a red and black line.
Hunt: Good. Kim look at your map again and see. OK.

Task performance, therefore, depended in part on fellow pupil's performances and one's ability to answer the teacher's questions during recitation. In this way, recitation creates a competitive situation.

Rather than compete against every other pupil in the class, though, the top-performing pupils formed support groups that helped each other on assignments. As one of Field's pupils said, 'You need smart friends in the fourth grade. The work is harder than in the third, and you have to count on someone to help.' These groupings were reinforced by Hunt and Field because only the top performers were allowed to work together at the first of the year.

[Social studies recitation]
Hunt: Well, Erica and Lynn you've just really understood this reading well. Why don't you two go back and work on the board [bulletin board] in the back room. Let me help you get started. [Hunt shows the girls where the paper and alphabet stencils are and spends about 3 minutes helping them start. Meanwhile the rest of the class is talking.] OK now class. Let's cut the talking, we still have work to do.

When the rest of the children were allowed to work together, they also formed into academically homogeneous groups. Following the top performers, the average pupils began working and playing together, leaving the poorer pupils to work alone or among themselves.

[Conversation, eighth week]

Frank: Look at those guys. [Robert and Terry are wrestling on the rug. Everyone else is working in groups on math assignments.] They're stupid.

Researcher: I thought you liked Robert. [After David and Eric formed a friendship group with Michael and Carl, Frank joined Robert, Terry, and Andrew.]

Frank: I did, but they goof off too much. Look at them. Pat and Fred are better friends. We can all work together — on SRA and stuff.

Because many of the special privileges in Field's and Hunt's classrooms were allocated on the basis of task performance, it became important for most of the children to finish their assignments on time and do their best work. The formation of academically homogeneous groups allowed the children to help each other, thus increasing their ability to obtain rewards. Children who associated with others achieving at lower levels often could not take advantage of their performance. For example, even though Laurie was often excused from recitations in Field's class because of her consistent high performance, she usually sat at her desk waiting for her girlfriends while the rest of the top achievers played or worked on other projects in their own groups. For most children, the rewards derived from task performance were sufficiently salient to cause them to join friendship groups that helped them perform and enjoy their rewards (such as extra free time) collectively.

During interviews with the fourth-grade children from Field's room, twelve of the twenty-three pupils specifically mentioned academic performance as a criterion for selecting friends.

As Thibaut and Kelly (1959) have indicated, status systems within a group emerge when group members are affected by the actions of others. Status systems based on competitive relations among pupils seem most likely to develop in classrooms where pupils observe and are affected by others' performances. This was the case in both Field's and Hunt's classrooms. Their extensive use of recitation and class task activities, such as tests, work sheets, and common assignments, allowed pupils to compare their task performances. The children knew their peers' achievements and constantly compared their performances. Comparisons were important because success in these classrooms depended on other pupils' performances; recognition and rewards, such as the math honor guard and castle committee, were based on a child's performance in relationship to the entire class. Rather than compete against everyone, the top-performing pupils in these classrooms tended to form friendship groups that provided academic support. These groups were encouraged because only the top performers were allowed to work together on assignments and given extra free time and assistance. Associations during task activities soon generalized to play situations as well, creating achievement-homogeneous friendship groups among most of the top performers. When the entire class was allowed to work in groups, the average pupils also began choosing to work with children achieving at their same level. In part, this was a consequence of the task structure. Because everyone progressed at a different rate through the common assignments, the children were usually at different stages in completing their work. Hence it was natural for children to work with others who progressed at the same pace: Children could not work with peers who were on a different SRA level or in another math group. The groups formed during task activities remained together during all other activities, thus creating the performance-homogeneous peer structures observed in these classrooms.

Multi-task Classrooms

Unlike group patterns in Ms. Hunt's and Ms. Field's classrooms, achievement level (as identified by the teacher) did not effect the friendship group choices of Mr. Stone's and Ms. Park's pupils.

Only three of the eight friendship groups in Stone's class during the tenth week consisted exclusively of academic equals. Because the predominant type of activity in his class was class task, the pupils knew how well their fellow classmates were performing on some tasks. Comments were often made on a child's speed or lack of it in completing a work sheet, but this seemed to produce little competition because work sheets were not graded and the children usually worked together.

> [Class working on work sheets — alone and in pairs]
> *Rick*:   (turning around to Don and Bob) I bet Tom and I can beat you. We're already on number six.
> *Bob*:   Who cares.
> *Rick*:   We're fastest.
> *Don*:   This isn't a race Rick. We're just taking our time.

Stone did not give special privileges to children who finished quickly or had the best score; but he did praise the top performance on most class tasks.

Furthermore, as the number of multi-task activities increased throughout the year, the children in this classroom became involved in tasks that were neither comparable nor public. This decreased the opportunities to make performance comparisons, because the children worked on a variety of different tasks. These multi-task activities also increased the opportunities for children to interact freely in a variety of task situations.

Rather than encouraging those performing at similar levels to work together, multi-task activities encouraged children to choose groups according to their interest in the task. It was not uncommon for children who were considered 'best friends' to do different tasks during multi-task activities, and this often led to the shifting of friendship group membership.

[Math recitation finsihes.]
Stone: OK, let's begin those reports.
          (Kids get out paper and split into small groups. Tom, Bob, Rick, Scott, and Paul all gather by Tom's desk. Talking.)
Stone: What are you doing?
Bob: We're trying to decide groups.
Stone: I thought you had it worked out yesterday. You told me Tom, Rick, and Bob were going to work together. And, Scott and Paul were going to.
Scott: Well, Paul wants to change. He likes their topic better.
Stone: Well?
Tom: I'm going to work with Scotty.
Stone: That's OK, just get some work done. I don't care what the groups are.
[Two days later, Tom moved his desk up by Scott and Paul moved back by Bob and Rick.]

Whereas peer groups in Hunt's and Field's room remained quite constant after the tenth week of school, friendship groups constantly changed in Stone's room: In eleven weeks, there were two changes in Hunt's, three in Field's, and nine in Stone's classroom.

Peer relations in Park's classroom also were fluid and independent of relative academic performance. No more than three friendship pairs (of seven or eight groupings) contained only academic equals. Because peer groupings constantly shifted in this classroom, nearly every pupil belonged to a friendship group with every other pupil of the same sex at least once during the year. The only exception was two girls who remained a cohesive pair throughout the year. Park's children seemed to change friendship groups as often as interests in projects or hobbies changed. During the period this class was observed, the children initiated nineteen seating changes due to shifts in friendship groupings, approximately one per week. The children in Stone's class initiated twelve shifts; there were seven such shifts in Field's class, and four in Hunt's class. Illustrative of the fluidity of peer associations in Park's class was the formation and subsequent dissolution of the Nancy Drew Mystery Book Club. Two seating shifts established the club among six girls, while one change reflected its demise into three separate pairs. Other shifts occurred when groups formed among several boys who played war games during free-time periods, among football fans during that season, and among children having common task interests. Because there were often many different tasks going on at the same time, Park's children could easily change groups when they became uninterested in a project.

[Multi-task]
Ellen: (going up to Park) Ms. Park, I really don't want to work on the mountain (project building a papier-mâché mountain).
Park: OK, Ellen. What do you want to do?
Ellen: I think I'd like to paint.
Park: OK, go over by Terry and Kathy and get started. They can help you.

The multi-task activities allowed a freedom of choice that did not exist in the recitation-dominated classrooms. The children themselves were responsible for selecting and organizing many of their tasks.

Multi-task activities do not allow for the observation and comparison of task performance among pupils, so that achievement rarely became a concern in peer relations. Few children completed the same task, and when they did, task performance never became a criterion for special privileges. There was no math honor guard or castle committee. It made little difference who had finished their work first or who was ahead in their language booklet. When the children did work together on common tasks, such as a math assignment or spelling, they did not form into performance-homogeneous groups. In fact, when Park often asked children to help each other on assignments, she did so with little regard for the pupil's academic performance levels.

[Conversation]
Park: My kids have to be able to work together. Things really don't go well otherwise. I can't police one group while I'm working with another. It's good that I have several helpers this year. Terry is so good. She doesn't boss the kids and can really help on some things. Though, it was funny the other day — you weren't here — to see Ted helping Charles with his math. Talk about the blind leading the blind.

Within this classroom there was very little competition. Occasionally, some comments were made about a pupil's achievements in math, spelling, and on the language booklets. However, this rarely seemed to affect other friendship choices. In all, these pupils were open about their acheivements and failures. For example, at the end of every spelling test Park would give two 'hard' words not on the regular spelling list. None of the children seemed afraid to share their performance on these 'hard' words with their classmates, even if they spelled both words wrong. This was different from the competition in the Hunt's and Field's classrooms.

[Spelling test]
Park: OK, now for the hard words. The first one is 'dictionary'. I

looked up the word in the 'dictionary'. The next one is 'establishment'. This is a good 'establishment'.
(Kids write down words.)
OK —

Ellen: Spell the hard words. (Several kids say how many they think they got right.)
Park: 'Dictionary' is d-i-c-t-i-o-n-a-r-y. 'Establishment' is e-s-t-a-b-l-i-s-h-m-e-n-t.
Ellen: Yeah, I got them both.
[Kids discuss how many they got right.]
Mike: Oh, I only got one.
Ted: Well, I tried anyway.

[Checking math homework — Hunt's class]
After every answer she gets correct, Laurie cheers and waves here hands over her head.

Laurie: (to George) How many are you getting right?
George: None of your business. (He covers his book.)
Laurie: Let me see. (She tries to uncover his hands over the book.)
George: You don't need to know.
Laurie: Well, I got every one right so far.

[Lunch — Field's class]
Fred wanders up to the SRA box and starts looking through, commenting on the progress of everyone else. He laughed at Mark's booklet because Mark is only on red [the first level].

Only one pupil in Park's classroom mentioned academic performance in selecting friends: He was a pupil in Hunt's class the year before. Because there was little competition, few children were categorized by their peers in terms of performance levels. Two exceptions were Terry and David. Terry's art skill was recognized by everyone in the class, and David was aptly called the 'math brain'. However, these distinctions were much more task specific than comments made by the children in Field's and Hunt's classrooms, where the children rated each other in very general performance categories, like 'top', 'average', and 'stupid'. Terry's and David's distinctions, moreover, did not hinder them from working with anyone else in the class. Most of the children agreed with the statement one boy made, that 'the kids in this class are mostly nice and friendly. I get along well with them, and have fun. You help each other when you can.'

Friendships Through Third and Fourth Grade

Interesting to note are the similarities and differences in patterns of peer associations exhibited among the thirty-five children who experienced similar or different classroom task structures over the two years of this study. In the third grade, these children all tended to follow the patterns described earlier. Pupils in Stone's room were willing to associate with most of their fellow classmates, and peer groupings changed frequently. Children in Hunt's room formed friendship groups that remained very stable and reflected the academic performance hierarchy within the class. Among those children who went from Stone's room to Park's or from Hunt's to Field's — classrooms having similar activity organizations — there was little change in the patterns of the peer associations. Stone's pupils continued to be involved in a variety of friendship and work groups without regard for academic performance, whereas Hunt's pupils still associated primarily with children of similar acheivement levels. However, children who were in a fourth-grade classroom with a different task structure exhibited considerable changes, In Park's room, Hunt's former pupils became less competitive and began associating freely among fellow pupils. Stone's former pupils, who had been very cooperative the previous year, became increasingly concerned with their academic performance in Field's room and began associating exclusively with children performing at their same level.

Conclusion: Tasks and Peer Relations

The consistency in forms of peer group structures, both between classrooms having similar instructional organizations and within the same classroom over the two-year study period, as well as the friendship shifts that occurred among students who changed classroom types, demonstrates the impact of the organizaton of instruction. The varying importance that academic performance played in the selection of friends and workmates cannot be attributed to differences among the children. These pupils adapted readily to the influence of task and reward structures and responded to the dominant organization present in their current classrooms.

The structure of recitation allows for individual comparisons and when accompanied by comparative assessments of performance, fosters the development of a competitive status system with the classroom. Status and interpersonal bonding depend on individual performance. This decreases overall group cohesion and reinforces social relationships that support both the pupil's productivity and chances for obtaining rewards. In recitation-organized classrooms, children separate into performance-homogeneous friendship groups, that remain exclusive and fairly stable throughout the year. By contrast, the structure of the multi-task organization does not involve comparative assessments of pupil performance. Status, based on academic achievements, and competitive peer interactions do not develop. Pupils are free to establish a variety of social relations without regard for their instrumental value in obtaining performance recognition. They choose friends and workmates often on the basis of task or hobby interests, changing groups as their interests shift.

One consequence of these different patterns of peer associations in the four classrooms was the extent of cooperative behavior among pupils. Most of the children in both Mr. Stone's and Ms. Park's classrooms were willing to work with each other in groups. In Ms. Hunt's and Ms. Field's classrooms, by contrast, the competitive attitude of the children, particularly the top achievers, resulted in segregated work groups according to performance level.

In summary, a classroom's task organization specifies who interacts with whom as well as the context in which the interaction occurs. Differences in work organization affect the patterns of teacher-pupil and peer interaction that arise within a given task activity and within classrooms utilizing distinctive activity structures.

Viewing classroom structure as an activity organization provides an important analytic tool for delineating the forces that shape social interaction within schools and for differentiating classroom patterns.

References

BOSSERT, S. (1979) *Tasks and Social Relationships in Classrooms*, Cambridge, Cambridge University Press.

JACKSON, P. (1968) *Life in Classrooms*, New York, Holt, Rinehart and Winston.

THIBAUT, J.W. and KELLY, H.H. (1959) *The Social Psychology of Groups*, New York, Wiley.

10 The Culture of the Primary School Playground

Andy Sluckin

The Lessons of Playtime

The lessons that children learn in the school playground are usually considered by them as far more important than those which take place in the classroom. And yet teachers rarely notice that their pupils social, emotional and often intellectual development is heavily influenced by this world of peer pressure. Indeed some of the most stubborn pupils in the classroom situation are highly motivated to succeed in the playground. Through their games and conflicts they learn all the skills that are necessary for adult life, but which their teacher and parents hardly dare admit to, let alone openly encourage.

In my book *Growing up in the Playground: The Social Development of Children* (1981), I showed how the traditional worlds of childhood, as described by folklorists Iona and Peter Opie, continue to thrive today, despite the impact of television and other aspects of modern culture. In their books *The Lore and Language of School Children* (1959) and *Children's Games in Street and Playground* (1969), the Opies describe the seasonal customs, initiation rites, superstitious practices and beliefs, rhymes and chants, catcalls and retorts, stock jokes, ruderies, riddles, slang epithets, nicknames and innumerable traditional games common in playgrounds throughout the British Isles. But although their findings have become widely known, the teachers and parents that I have met have been sceptical that this world extends into their own backyard. However, in the Oxford First and Middle School where I chose to observe, I can report that the playground world lives on.

During my three years as a playground sleuth, watching and wondering, observing and discussing, I came to three important conclusions. Firstly, I noticed that there is order amongst the apparent chaos of playground life. You do not have to look very closely to realize that children at playtime are not just like little savages (as some of their teachers describe them). But there is indeed a sense in which playground life can be said to be primitive. My second conclusion was that although the activities or content of the children's world usually differ from those of adults, the means or processes by which children and adults manage their worlds are remarkably similar. According to the Opies (1969), the day-to-day running of playground life involves affidavits, promissory notes, claims, deeds of coveyance, receipts and notices of resignation, all of which are verbal and all sealed by the utterance of ancient words which are recognized and considered binding by the whole community. My third conclusion was that experience in the playground provides an important preparation for adult social life.

In this chapter, I want to share some of the observations that led to my three conclusions. I also want to provide a model of psychological theory, research and intervention that will help teachers to better understand their pupils' development, rather than seem irrelevant to it.

Watching and Wondering: Naturalistic Observation

In an effort to make psychology a respected science of people, many researchers have tried to copy the patterns of investigation use by physicists and chemists. Having noted an interesting 'natural' phenomenon such as, for example, attachment behaviour, they have attempted to study it under carefully controlled laboratory conditions, so as to be able to separate out cause and effect. However, applying this approach to social and developmental psychology has led to 'elegantly designed experiments involving situations that are unfamiliar, artificial and short-lived that call for unusual behaviours that are difficult to generalise to other settings' (Bronfenbrenner, 1977). In other words, these laboratory-based studies have led to a psychology which is 'the science of the strange behaviour of children in strange situations with strange adults for the briefest possible periods of time' (*ibid*).

Although laboratory-based studies have dominated post-war psychology, there has always been an alternative tradition of studying 'life in the raw'. Zoologists, such as Konrad Lorenz and Niko Tinbergen, who stressed the need for 'watching and wondering' leading to careful and systematic observation in natural surroundings, called themselves ethologists. They tried to understand behaviour from a perspective not only of what triggered it off, but also considered the benefit that any behaviour might give to the individual and the species.

Some years ago, under the influence of the discipline of 'human ethology', I observed all the hostile interactions over a month in two pre-school playgroups. Interestingly, it proved possible to construct from this data a dominance hierarchy for the children. In other words, as with chickens, there was a strict pecking order in both groups. But children are not chickens and the fact of a pecking order tells us little about how exactly conflicts are resolved, nor how the children understand and adapt to their world. The discipline of anthropology led me later to wonder what are the rules, roles and rituals for conflict situations that children must learn in order to live together and when, how and from whom do they learn them. In my present work as a clinical psychologist and psychotherapist, I am continually investigating situations where these roles, rules and rituals have in some way broken down. Much of the time I am engaged in a process of discovery of how each member of a family or peer group understands and deals with conflicts. But before considering the implications of my study of the playground culture, let me outline how I investigated the skills that children show as they play games and relate to one another in a world where they are largely left to their own devices.

'Hey, Mister, Can I Be in Your Book?'

Children are inevitably interested in a strange man talking into a pocket dictaphone and walking round their playground, but they are not nearly so self-conscious as adults. Over a period of three years, I attended roughly six months of playtimes in a single Oxford first school and later followed up some of the children who went to a nearby middle school. At first I collected basic information such as who was doing what with whom. This led to a catalogue of activities. Later, I collected episodes of potential or actual conflicts, trying to note as far as possible exactly what the children did and said to each other. I followed up my observations by talking individually to every child about playtime. These chats took place during lesson time and the children soon learnt that I would not respond to them at playtime. Nevertheless, before they allowed me to melt into the furniture, they attempted first to provoke a reaction from me and later to explain away my presence.

'What do you use that radio for? Who are you speaking to with that sort of thing? Because it won't do you any good, unless you're operating for someone to smuggle us away.'

'Hey, you man, speak!'

'I'll make him wake up.'

'He doesn't speak, he's a bastard.'

'If you don't speak, I'll just have to smack you.'

'I won't leave you alone, till you tell me what that thing's for.'

'He's a nutter.'

'He's a deaf man.'

'He's a spy.'

When I went up into the middle school, the first school children that

I knew explained my harmless presence to the other children. For my part, I offered these older ones the explanation that 'I'm writing a book about playtime' and they too were content to let me get on with my business, though occasionally they asked, 'Hey mister, can I be in your book?'

'Eeny, Meeny, Macka, Racka' . . . A Catalogue of Activities

I went to a Chinese restaurant
to buy to loaf of bread.
They wrapped it up in a five-pound note
and this is what they said:
'My name is
eeny, meeny, macka, racka,
Ar, I, domma, Knacker,
Knicker, bocker, lolli, popper,
Om, pom, push.'

Many of the activities that I saw at playtime were not just made up on the spot but had been handed down from generation to generation. According to the Opies, children know the rhyme above as 'Chinese counting' and it is relatively modern, having come into play during the 1920s. Not only are these rhymes handed down from child to child, but also direct teaching by parents or even grandparents may also serve to secure their survival over the decades. Eight-year-old Clare told me she had learnt the following rhyme from her grandmother:

Ar, ar, chickerah,
roney, poney,
pom, pom, piney,
hari, gari, gasha,
Chinese sea.

This is obviously a continuation of a rhyme that even in the 1890s stretched from Scotland to the United States. The Opies record two versions:

Ra, ra, chuckeree, chuckeree,	Rye, chy, chookereye, chookereye,
ony, pony	Choo, choo, ronee, ponee
ningy, ningy, na,	icky, picky, nigh,
addy, caddy, westee	caddy, paddy, vester
anty poo,	canlee poo,
chutipan, chutipan,	itty pau, jutty pau,
China chu	Chinee Jew
(Fraserburgh, 1891)	(Pennsylvania, 1897)

My observations at playtime revealed a whole catalogue of traditional pastimes, essentially similar to those indulged in by the children's parents and no doubt by their grandparents, too. Fashions change but essentially the same rule-structure of games remain. For example, the 9 November 1956 edition of *The Goon Show* was the source of infection for the 'dreaded lurgi' which has maintained its place in chasing games. Similarly, in *White Horses* all but one of the older girl players lined up along a wall and each child took a name from a particular class of names i.e, TV programmes, pop stars etc. The one left out was 'it' and was told these names, but not which individuals held them. She called out a name at random and the person so selected had to race against her to the opposite wall and back, shouting 'White horses' on her return. The winner became the new 'it'.

And so the catalogue continues with new variations reflecting today's values. Girls who recount Susie's stages of life now add a verse for her as a teenager when 'she left her bra in her boyfriend's car and doesn't know where her knickers are'. Other 8-year-old girls sing 'Roll me over, lay me down and do it again', but we need not assume that they are recounting their own sexual adventures. And even 5-year-olds tell each other:

> Humpty Dumpty sat on a wall,
> ate a black banana.
> Where do you think he put this in?
> down a girl's pyjama.

In learning these rhymes and games or indeed in finding a way to take part in playground life at all, children are continuously faced with a stream of social problems for which they need to find solutions. It is these skills that I shall examine next.

'Bagsee No Bagsee' — The Power of Ritual Words

From a biological perspective, individuals strive in a group situation to get their own way without becoming so obnoxious as to be excluded from the group. From a humanistic perspective, the rewards of the group interaction lie in making satisfying contact with other individuals in such a way that the needs of both partners are met. Both these models of group behaviour have something to offer us. Rules, roles and rituals can at times help to structure our interactions so as to promote contact. At other times these very same rules, role and rituals limit our possibilities of mutual contact, whilst ensuring that one individual's wishes are met to the detriment of the other. In my study of conflict resolution, it is possible to see both sets of skills — those useful for cooperation as well as those needed for competition.

The single word 'bagsee' has tremendous power within the school playground. The Opies claim that 'bags' or 'bagsee' is in general use throughout Britain. 'Bagsee mine' gains possession, 'bagsee me first' claims precedence and 'bagsee me not it' avoids a role. The use of 'bagsee' enables a child to predict better what will happen next. For instance, an individual who makes a request but omits the word 'bagsee' cannot be sure what the reactions of others will be.

There are other ritual words in use in the playground. 'Crucems' is a local Oxford word which, together with the appropriately crossed first and forefinger on each hand, enables you to drop out of a game for a period.

'Taxi' and its associated sign also solves a problem. The thumb is first dabbed on the tongue, then placed on the forehead with the palm out-stretched and lastly the word 'taxi' is uttered. The child who says it is ritually denying that it was he or she who passed wind and the others in the group quickly follow suit. In the middle school the gesture is far simpler, for only the thumb and outstretched palm placed on the nose are retained. The meaning, however, is completely reversed for now it is the child who 'farts' that needs to say 'taxi'. Should he or she fail to utter this word, then any companions are liable to say 'sixes' and punch the offender six times.

'Bagsee', 'crucems' and 'taxi' represent the height of verbal achieve-ment in the first school playground and are used only by the 7 and 8-year-olds. The younger infants take two years to learn how and when to use these formulae, whereas the older middle school children become so adept at using them that the rituals lose their power. The children begin to turn the power of these words back on themselves.

Lynn (9):   Crucems
Dottie (9):   We're not having crucems
Lynn: Bagsee no crucems.

Playing With Words To Get What You Want

Ritual words have a well-established and clear meaning in the community. Other aspects of our actions, either what we do or say, may be more ambiguous. It is often the case that although we know what we intend, others interpret our actions differently. This can both be the cause of social problems as well as a way of solving them. Sometimes it is necessary to reassert the context within which an action is to be understood, whilst at other times it is this possibility of different interpretations that provides the solution. Although these various ways of playing with words are extremely subtle, they are not confined to adulthood. Children in the playground are equally adept in their use.

Since hitting and wrestling can occur in either a friendly or in a hostile context, it is important to know which situation prevails. Dinner ladies appear even less skilled than children in recognizing the context of these behaviours and many are not prepared to allow any pretend fighting at all out of fear that it could 'turn nasty'. And it is, of course, precisely this ambiguity in meaning that children exploit in order to control one another. For instance, if you are approached by a 9-year-old who threatens to 'smash your face in', it may pay off to smile back and graciously 'let him off this time'. If Graeme had not turned this presumably real aggression into a joke, then he would have had to either fight or run away. But the most striking example of this strategy involved a group of 7 and 8-year-olds who relentlessly attempted to redefine a fight between two brothers, first as a game and then as a wrestling match. They were acting to allow the older brother who did not want to fight, a way out of the conflict without losing face and being seen as scared.

Whereas redfining the situation places an action in a different light, another strategy is to redefine the person responsible for the action and in this way to discount what he or she does. I once saw a 6-year-old girl who was breaking the rules of hopscotch tell her 8-year-old companion, 'It doesn't matter, we're only little'. Likewise, in games children are continually denying agency with 'It wasn't me'. Indeed, nothing can infuriate an adult more than a child who insists 'it wasn't me', despite the inescapable evidence of our own eyes.

If 'I didn't do it' is often difficult to believe, then 'it didn't happen at all' must be even harder to accept. Yet children are remarkably successful in this ability to deny all sorts of occurrences, particularly being caught in a chasing game. Another less drastic way of redefining what has happened is to give the actions a new label and so place them in either a better or worse light. Aggression can be relabelled as merely 'self-defence' and scoring a goal is relegated to 'showing off'.

The impression that comes over again and again from examining episodes of playground conflicts is just how powerful words alone can be. A skilled mouth is an important asset and it makes playtime predictable, for by and large children's expectations are fulfilled. In these situations words enable a child to get what he or she wants, often at the expense of the other's wishes. In my book I examine how these strategies help to resolve all sorts of everyday social problems, such a joining in a game, excluding others, avoiding a role, starting and stopping fights, insulting, threatening, bribing, gaining a reputation and the public and private management of friendships with the opposite sex.

Neill — The Boss of the Playground

Using the perspective that I have outlined above, I studied one child in greater depth. All Neill's peers in the first school called him 'the boss of the playground' and I was lucky to have collected a good deal of information about his style of conflict management, since he figured highly in my sample of conflict episodes.

In the first school Neill got away with cheating, joined games without the owners permission, ignored the power of bagsee and was extraordinarily successful in making his opinions stick. He was a boy who was obsessed with winning races. He would redefine himself as 'ill' if he lost or, in a timed race, lasooed a leading competitor with a rope and preferred to be called a cheat than to concede defeat. Neill was intolerant of any opposition to which he occasionally reacted with physical violence or more often with the threat of exclusion. But, by and large, Neill's most successful skill was to avoid fights, whilst maintaining his tough image.

His dedication not to be seen to give in during verbal battles, while at the same time avoiding fighting, can be seen in the following long episode, which was collected over a twenty minute period during a midday playtime. First, a synopsis of the plot.

Neill and a few other boys have been disrupting the girls' game of 'roll over'. Neill's insistence on joining in as captain was the last straw. The girls throw verbal abuse at the boys, which they faithfully return. The sexes call each other names, glare and claim that they could easily inflict some terrible harm, such as the breaking of fingers or the smashing of skulls. Two rather conflicting accusations are flung between children. 'I'm not scared of you' reveals the value attached to a lack of fear, while 'He wants a fight' shows that the actual initiation of violence is frowned upon. Nobody, it seems, wants an all-out fight, but equally nobody wants to be seen to give in. This leads to a stalemate from which there seems no way out of the accusation/counter-accusation routine.

At this point Neill produces a most striking solution. He pretends to go to sleep, and as the girls around continue to taunt him, his definition catches on with the other boys. In this way the problem is solved. An all-out fight is avoided, and the boys are not seen to be giving in, for 'sleeping dogs do not have to answer to bitches' taunts'. But as we shall see, the girls do not give up that easily. Eventually an end to playtime terminates the espisode; the adult world has intervened. Surprising though it may seem, the social upheaval caused by this battle was quickly glossed over and the following lunchtime I only heard brief references to the 'events' of the previous day.

Pete (9.4) (accidentally) knocks over Jane (8.10). Jane gets really angry, and glares at him, hits him, and now chases after Neill.

Jane: Neill is a baby, Neill is a baby.

[Neill, Pete and some other boys are trying to disrupt the girls' game of 'roll over'].

Jane: Just because he can't be captain (about Neill).

157

[Now the girls all start chasing the boys. Graeme (9.3) rushes up to Ginny (9) and gets down on his knees.

> Graeme: Spare me, spare my life! (redefine the situation — real to pretend).
> Ginny: Not sure that I will.
> Ginny to Neill: Big Ears, spoilsport, he wants a fight.

[John has been knocked over in a scuffle and on regaining his feet goes after Ginny.]

> John: I'll get you.

[John 'paces' Ginny round the playground; as he walks he glares and Ginny recedes backwards.]

> John: I'm not scared of you.
> Ginny: I'm not scared of anybody.
> John: Flubbadubba [and a smile appears on his face (redefine the situation — real to pretend)].
> Ginny: Look, he soon changes his tune (thwarts attempt to change definition of situation).

[John regains his glare and goes off (he can either fight or withdraw).]

> Boys: What are little girls made of?
> Girls: What are little boys made of?

[After a moment]

> Neill (to Ginny): Who's scared of you now?
> Ginny: Neill's got a little dust on him.
> Jane: One of the loonies has escaped.

[Jane and Pete tussle.]

> Pete: I could have broken your fingers.
> Jane: I could have broken yours as well.

[Now Pete tussles with Ginny]

> Ginny: He's scared of me anyday. (To the other girls) They're scared of my little hands.
> Ginny to Clare (9.2): I want to do like that.

[She slaps her hand down in the air.]

> Ginny to Pete: He's scared of me, he's scared of me, he's a baby.
> Pete: Who's scared?

[Ginny gently punches him on the cheek.]

> Pete: I'm not scared.

[Meanwhile, in the background a number of boys and girls are announcing their impressions (ie. play acting) of certain members of the opposite sex.]

John to Pete:	Here's an impression of Pete Bond.
Pete:	Look, you're on my side, you dummy.
Neill tells Ginny:	I'm not ticklish.
Ginny:	Oh no, put your arm up, itchy bum.
Pete:	Get down there, sit down there.

[He pushes Carole (7.8) to the ground.]

Jane:	You could have broken her skull doing that.
Pete:	Yeah?

[The two glare at each other. Pete lets his coat drop from around his shoulders (it looks like in preparation for action)]

Ginny smiles and says: Batman, Batman.

[Pete and Jane smile at each other, (redefine situation). Neill now lies down on the ground]

Ginny, Carol and Sara: He likes this, he likes this.

[They place their feet on his prostrate body.]

Jane: He don't like this.

[She puts her feet over his groin and Sara does the same.]

Ginny: Ah, Garratt's (Neill) surrendered at last, he's ticklish.

[Pete gets down on the ground to join Neill.]

Clare:	Overgrown baby.
Dinner-lady:	[Comes over to Neill and Pete.] Get up.
Ginny:	It started just because he couldn't be the captain of 'roll over', he starts making war, he starts bashing us in.
Dinner-lady:	Go on, get up, you silly boys.
Neill:	Miss, I want to sleep.
Dinner-lady:	Come on, children want to run round, they'll fall over you.

[Neill goes over to the corner of the playground and lies down. The girls follow him over.]

Carol:	When he sits down, he's got a split in his bum like this.
Ginny:	Oh, we want to see his face.

[Neill has covered his face with a coat.]

Carol: Oh, what a silly face.

[Neill, Pete and Graeme all pretend it is bedtime and pay no attention to the girls. (They say 'Goodnight' to each other.) Carol sticks her foot on Neill's head and then his tummy. Joy and Sara kick Neill on the side.]

Ginny: Look what you lot have done.
Neill: I never.
Ginny: Touch me, so I hope to die, that shows you ain't going to touch them any more.

[Sare (8.3) puts her foot out.]

Neil grabs Carol: Now I've got you, you bastard, you just shut up bothering us.
Carol: I'm telling Miss.
Ginny: No, I ain't going to leave you alone, not now. I'm going to annoy him all the time; I will, don't worry.

[Carol slams her foot down on Neill.]

Four girls sing: Baby, baby on the treetop, when the bough breaks the baby will fall, etc.

[Neill still pretends to be asleep.]

Ginny: My talons would scratch you to pieces.

[Jane tries to touch his groin. Clare hits Neill all over with a wooden spoon and he lies doggo. Graeme attacks Clare and wrestles the spoon off her and hits her with it. He misses Clare and hits Sara.]

Beckie: Give that to me, it's not yours, it's mine.

[Jane wrenches the spoon off Graeme and gives it to Beckie.]

Clare: It's probably got poison on it.
Ginny: He opened his eyes (Neill), he ain't dead, what a shame.
Neill: I'll tell you where you can't disturb us, (to boys) come on, you lot, let's get off.

[Pete, Neill, Graeme and John all go to the boys' toilets.]

Clare: I tell you what, I tell you what, upstairs you can see the boys in the boys' toilets.
Another girl: We're not allowed upstairs.
Clare: I know, I know.

[Carol forays into the boys' toilets (or at least the area of them)]

Carol: Eeeh, Neill Garratt's doing a piss-piss, his piss-piss is green.

[The boys emerge from the toilets]

Graeme says to Helen:	Let's have a staring match, see who can outstare each other'.
Neill complains to the Dinner-lady:	Carol keeps on coming into the boys' toilets.
Dinner-lady tells Carol:	Don't go there.
Neill:	See, see, don't tell fibs.

[Graeme 'paces' Carol around the playground and they glare at each other. Carol backs away. She runs to the other side of the playground]

Carol shouts: Scaredy boots, Welly boots.

[Neill goes back to 'sleep' with Pete.]

Mary (8.9):	Playing Mummies and Daddies, are you?
John:	Look what I've got, look what I've got.

[John has captured Carol]

Carol: I'm telling Miss.

[John punches Carol and lets her go.]

Neill:	Let her go. I'm going to sleep.
Carol:	Don't touch us again, Welly boots.
Clare:	Look at his fat bum.
Beckie:	Oy, Ginny, they're all snug and warm.

[Jane, Ginny, Carol, Helen, Beckie and Sara are the girls now involved.]

Ginny:	Look at the little babies asleep. Do you want your bottles?
Mary:	Bond, Bond, Miss wants you.

[Pete takes no notice]

Neill:	Why don't you go away?
Ginny:	No, you started annoying us, now we're going to annoy you.
Neill:	Miss, we can't get any peace.
Ginny:	You shouldn't have annoyed us in the first place.

[The boys smell a pungent odour.]

Neill: Who's done it?

In turn the boys go 'Taxi, taxi, taxi', which with the appropriate sign of thumb on tongue, and then dabbed on forehead with the palm outstretched, is the ritual means to deny responsibility for the smell. Graeme touches a dead frog that he sees and, as all the other boys shout 'Welland's got the lurgi', the whistle calls an end to playtime.

Along with ten of his peers, 9-year-old Neill progressed from first to middle school and I observed him in this new environment to see how his reputation as 'boss' would fare. Alas, for him, he was no longer called the 'boss', had started to ask for permission to join in, was at times excluded from games and what was worse, his bribes of sweeties were no longer successful. However, as before, he was dedicated to winning races, intolerant of opposition and studiously avoided fights, even when the perpetrator of a crime was dragged to him for punishment.

What does it take to become 'boss of the playground'? First and foremost, Neill had great dedication to rise up the pecking order. In order to get there, he developed the necessary aggression to secure roles and knew how to impose his wishes without the group breaking up. His skill was to balance his determination to control and his intolerance of opposition with the attractiveness that he offered of original solutions and exciting ideas. But his desperate need for control limited his possibilities of long-term satisfaction in relationships and hence his long-term success in the playground.[1]

What Do Children Learn in the Playground?

My observations clearly demonstrate the order that exists amongst the apparent chaos of playtime. We have seen also that the processes by which relationships are maintained are essentially the same as those used by adults. For example 'bagsee', 'crucems' and 'taxi' prepare children to use the formulae of adult social life such as the marriage ceremony or the State Opening of Parliament. What all these rituals have in common is that they are systems of signs which convey other than overt-messages. Only members of the particular community in question fully understand their significance and part of this significance is the strong feeling of obligation to follow the ritual that all individuals within the community feel.

Another example of parallels between the methods of playground management and adult social life are the ways in which children define and redefine their own and other's actions. This skill can already be seen much earlier in the nursery school. Name-calling also pervades all ages. Contrary to parents' wishes, children do not grow out of it, they merely become more expert in its use as they grow up. The same is true of the way adults threaten and bribe each other. They no longer offer sweets in order to be allowed in the game, but develop sophisticated ways of making 'an offer that you can't refuse'.

How important is experience in the playground for social development? My observations lead me to conclude that games serve as an introduction to culturally specific attitudes, values and sex-roles. Brian Sutton-Smith (1973) has spent over a quarter of a century researching into games and he summarizes his findings as follows:

In the child's game we find a distillation of human relationships, particularly those having to do with power. As models of power, games serve to prepare children for expected life experiences. They are models of ways of succeeding over others, by magical power (as in games of chance), by force (as in physical skill games), or by cleverness (as in games of strategy). We have speculated that in games children learn all those necessary arts of trickery, deception, harassment, divination and foul play that their teachers won't teach them but are most important in successful human relationships in marriage, business and war.

The games that I saw in the Oxford playgrounds prepared the children for life in a world involving voluntary cooperation, regulated competition, contracts, and a judicial system that is meant to protect the rights of weak and powerful alike. It is precisely these values that are enshrined in the rule systems of the playground games. And in each culture where games have been studied, similar parallels are evident.

Most important of all is that growing up in the playground offers a setting where children have a high motivation to learn how to get on with their peers. During games they are able to initiate, discuss, influence and change rules in a way that just could not happen between child and adult. Indeed, when teachers supervise play, it is all too often precisely these types of opportunities that are missing. It is simply not the case, as one headteacher claimed, that anything a child learns in the playground could equally well be learnt in the classroom. As adults we need to have respect for the self-motivated learning that takes place away from the direct influence of adults and yet provides just those experiences that help prepare for adulthood. As one 5-year-old told me, 'playtime makes me grow up extremely slowly'.

Note

1   I do not know how Neill stands now ten years on in relation to his peer group, but I doubt whether he has lost his motivation to be a leader. His strategies may have changed in response to his new environments, but he is unlikely to have had the opportunity for the sorts of experiences that could release the emotions which underlie his need to control others. This sort of change usually happens within psychotherapeutic relationships, in which an individual at first tests out the safety of experiencing his anxiety in relationships and then later reveals to himself and the therapist and/or to the therapeutic group, those feelings that he or she has been trying so hard to conceal. This sort of experience brings about changes in behaviour, since the individual's real needs have at last been recognised, even if they cannot be met. For a further discussion of the process of therapy in children, see my articles on 'Children's dreams and nightmares' (1985) and 'Gestalt therapy and renal failure' (1986) or Violet Oaklander's excellent source book *Windows to Our Children*.

References

BRONFENBRENNER, U. (1977) 'Towards an experimental ecology of human development', *American Psychologist*, 32, 7, pp. 513–31.

OAKLANDER, V. (1975) *Windows to our Children: A Gestalt Therapy Approach to Children and Adolescents*, Moab, Utah, Real People Press.

OPIE, I. and OPIE, P. (1959) *The Lore and Language of Schoolchildren*, London and New York, Oxford University Press.

OPIE, I. and OPIE, P. (1969) *Children's Games in Street and Playground*, London and New York, Oxford University Press.

SLUCKIN, A. (1981) *Growing up in the Playground: The Social Development of Children*, London, Routledge and Kegan Paul.

SLUCKIN, A. (1985) 'Dreams and nightmares,' *Changes*, 3, pp. 123–5.

SLUCKIN, A. (1986) 'Gestalt therapy and renal failure,' *Changes*, 4, pp. 232–5.

SUTTON-SMITH, B. (1973) *Children Psychology*, New York, Appleton-Century-Crofts, pp. 356–7.

SUTTON-SMITH, B. (Ed.) (1973) *Readings in Child Psychology*, New York, Appleton-Century-Crofts.

11   Goodies, Jokers and Gangs

Andrew Pollard

Introduction

This chapter is concerned with the perspectives of children in their final
year at an 8–12 middle school.[1] The school was situated in a predominantly working-class area on the perimeter of a Northern textile town. Data
was collected at 'Moorside Middle School' over a period of two years using
ethnographic methods. With regard to the children this included observation, a sociometric analysis and extensive use of interviews which were
carried out with the partial assistance of a child interviewing team.[2]

The present chapter is particularly focussed on children's attempts to
'cope' with school life and on their immediate interests in the classroom.
Of course, the greatest potential threat to children's coping in school is
associated with the power of the teacher, and it has been argued (Pollard,
1979) that they orient their actions with particular regard to this power.
However, it is necessary to break down the assumption of homogeneity
which the unproblematic use of the category 'children' implies. This is
attempted in the present chapter which reports on the tendencies and
parameters of children's perspectives through the identification of three
analytical 'types' of friendship group. These range from those children who
were 'good' and normally conformed to teachers' wishes, through 'jokers'
who would 'have a laugh' with teachers and commit acts of 'routine
deviance', to those 'gang' members who acted more with regard to peer-
group expectations than to those of the teacher.

Goodies, Jokers and Gangs

We can begin the analysis by considering the three types of child group
which were identified. The sociometric analysis yielded twelve friendship
groups and distinctions between good groups, joker groups and gang groups
were derived from comparison of the perspectives of children in these

groups, particularly regarding their attitudes to themselves, to other children and towards teachers and school. There were clear differences between the children in such groups. Children in groups that other children termed 'good groups' regarded groups which they called 'gangs' very negatively for their 'roughness' and 'destroying' behaviour. Groups which I termed 'joker groups' puzzled at the quietness of Good groups, regarded each other as 'good fun' and 'sensible' but were also clear about the 'bigheaded', 'thick' 'roughness' of gangs. Gang groups condemned Good groups as 'soft' and 'goodie-goodies' and Joker groups as 'show-offs' and 'big heads'. Whilst their own gang was regarded as 'great' other gangs were usually labelled as 'soft', 'rubbish' or 'cocky', thus reflecting the extent of intergang rivalry.

Using such data it was possible to construct an inter-group sociogram to represent the children's social structure. In figure 1 the sizes of each group are represented by the area of the group's symbol. This shows the nine children in Good groups, thirty-eight in Joker groups and twenty-eight in Gangs.

The ethnographic data which documents the perspectives of each of the twelve groups is too extensive to be included in full in this chapter but an illustration of the perspectives of a group of each postulated type is essential. For this purpose I offer data from three friendship groups of girls — a choice made not because of any particular significance of the girls' perspectives to my argument but simply because girl's perspectives have tended to be under-represented in the literature in the past. So here we have three groups — the 'Good Girls', the 'Netball Group' of 'jokers' and 'Samantha's Gang'.

The 'Good Girls' (Group 5)

The four girls in this group were considered by teachers to be of 'moderate ability'. None of the girls felt themselves to be good at sport and indeed none of them had ever been selected for the netball team. Thus in two important respects they were distinguishable from the academic and sporting netballing girls which tended to be the dominant girls group. In fact their attitude to that group was a mixture of admiration and disdain:

> *Linda:* Some people that we don't like are Paula and Julie — they talk too much and are show-offs. Some of that lot dress too old for their age but they are all in the top sets for everything. I am trying to do my best to get up to the A set for English but I haven't yet. I am in the next to top group now.
>
> *Kisty:* Tessa, Heather and Donna — I think they are nice but they

Figure 1: An intergroup sociogram

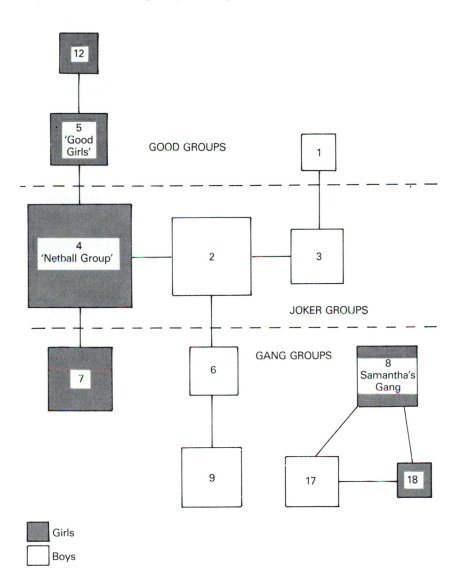

don't like the things we like to play at, they play with boys too much.

The good girls generally preferred quieter activities.

> *Kirsty*: We like to sit in the classroom and talk. We talk about fashion and animals or what we have been doing in lesson times. In the playground we play Letter Tig. We like to do ballroom dancing together.
>
> *Linda*: We like to sit around and talk to each other. We sometimes all play games in the middle playground.

The girls had constituted themselves into a 'Club':

> *Linda*: We call our club the Lion Club and it is very successful. We are all friends in it. We are honest and fair. We all have nicknames for being in the club, mine is 'Rory', Caroline's is 'Little Boots', Mandy's is 'Shelly' and Kirsty's is 'Thackey'. Ours is a friendly group, we never fall out, or if we do it's only because of silly things.

Such a 'small, friendly group' was distinguished from a 'gang':

> *Caroline*: In school there are many gangs. I think it's terrible being in a gang because when we grow up we would be involved in some kind of trouble with the police.
>
> *Kirsty*: I think gangs are not at all nice because they are rough and I am nearly always getting bashed in so I have to stay clear of them. I do not think it is fun at all. I hope there is not going to be any more gangs made.

The attitudes of the girls to school and to the teachers was generally favourable and deferential:

> *Kirsty*: School tries to help us a lot and you feel very good when they encourage you to do things. They try to help you with your work for instance when I was in the first year I could only write a few sentences in real writing but look at me now.
>
> *Linda*: School rules are fair because they are good for us or for our own safety so they are fair really. I think children should be good in school because it helps everyone so that the teachers don't get in a bad mood.
>
> *Caroline*: I think school helps us a lot because if there was no teachers we would never learn anything and when we were up to the age of getting a job we would not know a thing about it or what to do, or if you worked in a shop you would not be any better off because you would get shown up.

However, the girls were not at ease with teachers, as Kirsty commented:

Kirsty: Talking to a teacher is very hard. If you know what to say before you still get so nervous that you just mumble something out and hope for the best and to get it over and done with. At home it is more relaxed but at school it's easy to get the words all jumbled up which is very embarrassing and it's very hard to show that you are not that way really. It's horrible, and you feel as though you are going to cry about it anytime, but you can't.

As with the boys of Group 1, another 'good' group, these girls were hesitant about having a laugh and wished to avoid getting into trouble.

Kirsty: You should only laugh really when the teacher is laughing, then it's alright, but in some of the lessons we get people messing about all the time. Having a laugh is a good thing sometimes 'cos it brings out the happy side of you and makes you cheery and bright, but we shouldn't do it too much at school or we'll never get any work done.

Mandy: We don't like getting into trouble because when we get told off we get upset. It's not very nice 'cos you don't know what to do. Usually we try and keep out of trouble then it's OK.

It was this reluctance to get involved with any form of deviance which had led to the group being termed as 'goodie-goodies' by many of the other children. The girls appeared to have countered this position as a minority and 'out' group *vis-à-vis* the majority of children, and also their only moderate academic success, through the closeness of their friendship, the protection of their 'Club' and by their determination to avoid trouble either with 'rough gangs' or teachers.

The Netball Group of 'Jokers' (Group 4)

This was a large group of twenty girls and the sociomatrix showed that it was made up of numerous interlocking and chaining trios and pairs. Ten of the girls were in the school netball team and practised regularly at dinner-time. Eleven of the group were in the choir and all four girls House Captains were members of the group. They were almost all regarded as being 'bright' academically.

The Netball Group of girls was very comparable to the other main 'joker' group, the Football Group of boys (Group 2). They were similarly successful both at sport and academically, and their perspectives on many issues were very close. For instance, they both regarded themselves as 'sensible' and showed disdain for some other groups. Here are some comments from the girls:

Jo: There's us lot, er ..., you could call it the netball team and their friends, and then there's the other lot which is Samantha's [Group 8], Janine's [Group 7], people like that. It's two different bands, and really we're always against one another — there's a difference.

Donna: People in the first band, they seem to be sensible, they do work, they like the teachers and everything, but the others ... they cause trouble — I don't know, you can't really understand it, but they don't seem to like the teachers. They act about and they're always getting into trouble.

Becky: We like to be able to be doing activities such as netball, choir, Gym Club, and helping teachers. We think we are too old to play games as it seems to be silly to us. There are also groups of people that go round together like Jenny's and Janine's [Group 7]. These girls are very silly and play silly games. Sometimes they get very bossy and begin to boss people around. I don't like gangs because they're always bother causers.

In the playground Netball Group members almost always played netball when a court was available. A few of the girls would also usually be involved doing telephone duty, 'helping teachers' or 'doing a job'. Others 'just walked around':

Jo: The thing that we like doing is just walking around about the school — touring round, talking and watching everything.

Louise: We don't exactly do anything much, we like to go around together and see what's going on, and we talk a lot about school and what we'll do when we get home and things like that.

Sometimes games were more active:

Gill: We like playing with a ball and skipping and playing out in the playground. We like to talk and have a good laugh. Sometimes we play chasing with the boys or watching them playing football.

The 'boys' referred to by Gill above were, of course, members of the Football Group. However, the girls had clear conceptions of the parameters of 'respectable' behaviour with boys. For instance Becky commented on the activities of two 'gang' members:

> *Becky*: Last night I saw 'em necking in the corner. It's getting out of hand. It's disgraceful.

In lesson times the girls generally wanted to do their work, learn and 'get a good education'. However, as with the Football Group they enjoyed a fairly close rapport with many teachers which was one of the main distinguishing features of the 'joker' group.

Jayne:	See, I've found out with Mr. Matthews and all the others that are friendly, you get on well with them and get on with your work . . . and Mr. Jackson, when we didn't do our work and we hadn't got time, he didn't play heck with us as Mr. Smith would have done.
Tessa [interviewing]:	Do you think all teachers should be like that?
Jayne:	Yes, but you've got to get it done, you haven't just to leave it.
Julie:	You haven't to joke about as much as Mr. Matthews does sometimes tho', he doesn't let you get on with your work sometimes.

Julie's comment above shows the girls' concern to be 'sensible' and not prejudice their learning, but at the same time they were very keen on having a laugh to overcome boredom:

> *Becky*: It's boring being in general studies, when we have to stop and think, you're looking around the room you've nothing to do, thinking, wondering what to do, run out of ideas, looking at the paper, sighing and can't think properly, thinking of something else and can't concentrate on what you're doing — you need a laugh.
>
> *Jayne*: We can have fun with most of the teachers. Like in maths we have fun and if the teachers were strict the lessons would get boring, everybody would start fidgeting and they would not listen. If we have a laugh at school we can, sort of, be normal, and it's more relaxing instead of having to be a little Miss Innocent.

There was also a good deal of talking in lessons and note writing about school work and other interests.

> *Carol*: In lessons we usually talk to each other or me and Julie sit next to each other so we talk, and Donna sits near so we sneak across and talk. In sewing Julie is with Louise so I get with Donna and Hazel so we can talk.

Thus the netball girls took the overall view that:

> *Donna*: Children should be good in school, but not good all the time because we can't all be goodie-goodies.

In most cases their rapport with teachers led them to like them and respect their authority:

> *Jo*: Teachers can joke with us and it's good fun. The school rules are for our own good and they're usually fair. In these ways school helps you and learns you all it can so that you grow up well educated. To help teachers learn you you should be good and help the teachers by being quiet and obedient.
>
> *Tessa*: Like Mrs. Graves, if you've been really naughty she'll give you the slipper but otherwise she'll just shout at you — or sometimes she'll just leave you but if you carry on after a period she'll give you a smack or whatever. I think that's right. Teachers can't be patient all the time, they have to teach us.

However, this respect did not prevent them condemning teachers who exceeded their perceived authority, particularly by 'picking on people' or 'going mad':

> *Jayne*: I don't know, I think when teachers pick on people and go mad it's probably because they've been arguing with their husband or wife at home, or there's been summat happening at home and they take it out on the children, they come to school because it's the law. It's not fair that some kids get upset by teachers when they're just in a bad mood.

In circumstances of being told off the friendship group was important both as audience and support, with the event being retrospectively taken to build solidarity.

> *AP*: Well how do you feel about a telling off? Does it matter?
>
> *Tessa*: It matters alright 'cos you know you've got into trouble — you go bright red and when you go back sitting with your class you try to talk, to be cheerful with your friends, but they know that you've got into trouble and you're blushing an' that. You try to laugh about it and everybody's looking. Some folks say ... 'I'm not bothered' ... and they get on with their work, and eventually they get right happy and laugh about it when the teacher's not there and in the playground.

The girls tended to have fairly traditional attitudes regarding gender. For instance they allowed the initiative for most classroom laughs to come from the boys and the desire to be seen to be 'sensible' often took the form of 'clearing up' for teacher, thus mirroring dominant domestic expectations. A New Year's resolution from a jotter read:

> *Dawn:* My New Year's resolution is to help my mum by keeping my bedroom tidy and as well to help Mum to do the shopping and to help her to do the washing because I like washing.

However some were conscious of iniquities in the roles which they were allocated:

> *Jayne:* My Dad, he says ... 'Look you'll get a chance for choice when you grow up, so you'll get the chance not to wash up when you grow up but you've got to do it now' — and my brother, he always get out of stuff like that, all he has to do is fill the coal hod and then he can go out and play as long as he wants, and he could do that when he was our age and that's all he had to do. Now we're our age we have to clean up, wash up and all sorts.
>
> *AP:* And why do you think that is?
>
> *Jayne:* It's 'cos he's lazy.
>
> *Tessa:* It's 'cos we're girls.

Thus in summary, this large group of girls were intelligent, were successful at work and got on well with teachers. They enjoyed a laugh but considered themselves to be 'sensible' in terms of doing their work, playing nicely, being 'kind', dressing appropriately, helping teachers and not 'going too far' with boys. They were popular with most of the other groups and with the teachers. They participated in a large number of school activities and clubs, and were particularly good at sports.

Samantha's Gang (Group 8)

The members of this group of seven girls were the least successful academically of the girls. However, the most distinctive features of the group were their relatively greater 'roughness' and their very uneasy degree of cohesion. One of their perennial activities was that of falling in and out of friendships with each other:

> *Tina:* I have a good group of friends when I don't fall out with them. Katherine is always falling out with me and going off with Carly. If that happens, like, she has pinched my friend, then Carly is a fat cow. When I am friends with Susan, just because I am small for her age, she always pushes me around and blames me for things, but Lucy, if we are friends and we play hitting one another it's good fun. But if I hit her too hard she will not play at all. She can be a baby sometimes.

Some more quotations will give the flavour of other activities.

> *Samantha:* Carly is good fun. Every time we go in for dinner she always puts her foot in the mud and kicks it in our hair and sometimes on our clothes. One day Louise got it right up her skirt and all on her face. Then we try to do it back to her but it's hard to get her.
>
> *Lucy:* Our gang is very exciting. It's an exploring group. We like going to Mecca Ice Skating. We have a marvellous time falling and bumping into one another.
>
> *Katherine:* In the classroom we like to chase each other. We run through Mr. Taylor's room and hide in Mrs. Clark's. Sometimes we run round Mr. Matthews' and through the kitchen. When we catch whoever is running we pretend to put them in our powers and then they must count to 20 and come after us.
>
> *Carly:* Our group always likes to have fun, like we play off-ground-tig or chasing or teasing someone. We like running down the banking or over the grass near the staff-room.

One of the most significant activities was that of 'braying' or 'gobbing' members of other gangs, and being 'got back'. Most of this fighting was with the girls of Group 18, Sarah and Diana, or the boys of Group 17, Malcolm, Robert, Nigel and Andrew. Sometimes the fighting would involve alliances between, or with members of, these groups with consequent variations in attitudes to them:

> *AP:* What about Nigel and Robert ... that lot? [Group 17]
>
> *Samantha:* They're awful.
>
> *Lucy:* They can be rough and nasty.
>
> *Tina:* Like when I was friends with Sarah and we was going home and Malcolm brayed me, just for no reason at all.
>
> *Samantha:* He said it was because she'd told Robert to gob him.
>
> *AP:* Do you like playing with these boys?
>
> *Carly:* Yea, especially when I'm not friends with these [referring to Tina, Lucy and Samantha].
>
> *Tina:* But he, Nigel, he comes over to our table and starts teasing us ...
>
> *Samantha:* ... and being rude.
>
> *AP:* What does he say?
>
> *Samantha:* He calls me awful names, I'm not saying them.
>
> *Carly:* Sometimes they call her 'Sticklesons'.
>
> *Samantha:* Oh that's nothing, it's rude what they call me, four-lettered ones.

AP:	Does it get you upset?
Samantha:	Yea, but we get our own back later.

With regard to the boys there was some excitement, concern and teasing at their intentions.

Samantha:	Well y'know what they want don't you? Like when Malcolm and Tina went in the woods, and Nigel, well he went chasing after Carly and touching her up, you know.

Such activities generated much teasing and thus more 'gobbing' and 'braying' to 'get back at' the teaser. 'Sexy' jokes and rhymes were also a source of amusement. For instance, a rhyme from Katherine's jotter:

> Eh by gum,
> Can your belly touch your bum,
> Can your tits hang low,
> Can you tie 'em in a bow,
> Can your balls go red,
> When you rub 'em on your bed,
> Eh by gum,
> That's it!

Samantha's gang were often involved with other groups, apart from those mentioned, except for occasional insult-exchanges with Janine's Terrors (Group 7). Groups like the Netball girls were regarded as a 'rubbish group' and 'big heads' but Samantha's gang were not completely immune to other opinions and did feel it necessary to neutralize their own relative lack of school achievement.

AP:	What about Tessa's group? [Group 4, Jokers].
Samantha:	Well, they're swell heads, just because they're in the top groups 'n that, but ...
Katherine:	... yea, they think they're 'brains' just because they've got more brains than other folk.
AP:	Do you think that's true?
Samantha:	No, no.
Tina:	Like Liz, she's a good worker.
Liz:	I'm not, I'm not.
AP:	What do you mean?
Liz:	I try but I never get anywhere.
AP:	Why do you think that is?
Samantha:	Well like, they get help, like Carol, her Mum's a teacher so she's got a better chance than us lot.
Liz:	It might run in their family to have brains.
AP:	Do you think it's right that they should be in the top groups?
Samantha:	No, but we've not bothered.

Many of the other children were also regarded as being privileged and 'posh' in their home backgrounds.

> *Carly*: Lots of people act as if they are posh, just because they go on holidays each year and buy expensive things for their homes and make their kids look nice and take them to school in the car thinking one of the teachers should see her, and try to see how her child is getting on at school. Most people act as if they were posh but put it on an' show off about something new. They ask their Mums if they can have this, that and the other. They try to get the nicest present for a party. But them who are not that well off, they act normally. They admit that they do not get very much but they are still thankful for what they have got. If you have a lot you can't have very much more so I don't care really.

This disdain for many of the children at school meant that Samantha's gang were prepared at times to upset them as well as teachers.

> *Tina*: One good laugh we had was in games with Samantha because we kept slowing our team down and when it came to skipping together we kept falling over and having a right laugh and everybody was looking at just us and getting narky but we had a great laugh.

As with other groups the girls would have a laugh in lessons when they got bored or 'couldn't be bothered to do any work' but they were more prepared than many groups to laugh *at* a teacher or despite a teacher:

> *Anna*: If we have a laugh and the teacher's in a bad mood well that's hard lines, we don't care.
>
> *Lucy*: You can have a laugh about something and then if someone gets told off you can have a laugh about that 'cos it's only a warning. That gives you a laugh too when you get into the playground.
>
> *Carly*: When Mrs. Jones caught us fooling about and my boot wouldn't come off, she said 'you two are making fools of yourselves' and I was laughing all the time when I bent down to put my boot on. Then she said — 'Let's hope you come in a better frame of mind tomorrow', and we was laughing all the way home.

Attitudes to teacher authority and school rules acknowledged a degree of well-meaning intent but were clearly unfavourable in many other ways:

> *Anna*: I think some teachers try to be fair and some are stinking ratbags and are always on to you. The school rules are not fair because if someone starts trouble and you bash them up then

> teachers interfere and you get into big, big trouble. The school tries to help you sometimes but they treat us like dirt so at other times they don't try to help us one little bit. If we were good in school there would be no fun at all.

> *Tina:* If you can't spell they learn you how and if you can't write properly they will learn you how to do but when we get done and they shout at us, it's not fair.

The girls were particularly incensed if they felt they were being 'picked on'.

> *Katherine:* Teachers are too bossy. They always stop me and Lucy sitting next to each other in lessons or they might keep us in.

> *Samantha:* Sometimes they tell us off for nothing, so then we should not be good, we should get our own back on them, not let them get us into trouble for nothing.

> *Liz:* I hate Mr. Smith, he shows off too much and he shouts too much and he's always picking on us.

In summary, Samantha's gang could be regarded as having anti-school values in many ways. Compared with the other groups of girls they were relatively unsuccessful both academically and at sport. They were less popular. They caused more 'bother' in school and 'got done' more often. They had less respect for teachers and they looked forward to leaving school to get a job.

Parameters of Classroom Action

Clearly the children in 'good', 'joker' and 'gang' groups have very different perspectives on many aspects of their school life. However, I want now to focus more specifically on the ways in which they seek to cope in the classroom. In order to do this I will draw on a symbolic-interactionist view of the negotiating processes which take place between children and teachers in classrooms. In this perspective it is argued that negotiation leads to the establishment of particular definitions of the classroom situation (Stebbins, 1981; Ball, 1980) and that these provide guides for the action of the participants. Further, because of both the teachers' and the children's perceived necessity of 'coping' with daily life in classrooms, it is suggested that they routinely accommodate their definitions of the situation into a 'working consensus'. This represents a set of shared social understandings which structure and frame the classroom context in terms of routines, conventions and expectations and it takes its dynamic from the power of the children to threaten the teacher because of their numbers and from the power of the teacher to threaten the children because of their role and authority. In that each can pose a threat for the other the working consensus should be seen as a mutual accommodation and, in this sense, it represents a 'truce' rather than a consensus — an acceptance by both parties that the other has the power or resource to threaten their own ability to 'cope' and 'survive' (Woods, 1977) in the classroom situation. Of course, we then have to reject that implied assumption of child homogeneity and to analyse the parameters of the action decisions of particular children. If this is done, using the analysis of types of group which has been presented, it yields figure 2 below.

Figure 2   Parameters of action decision

	Actions derived from the working cosensus		Actions derived from peer culture
Child position in social structure	Conformity	Routine deviance	Rule framed disorder
'Good' groups 'Joker' groups 'Gangs'	⟶	⟶	⟶

Both the good group members and the joker group members are indicated here as acting within the bounds of the working consensus. However, the gang group members are shown as being prepared — in some situations — to act outside those understandings. What we have here then are three characteristic or 'ideal types' of child coping strategy, an important and formative component of which stems from the quality and nature of the child's interaction with the teacher. The parameters of children's actions are thus determined to a significant extent by the actions of their teacher.[3]

Children's Interests-at-hand

Up to this point in the chapter I have used the term 'coping' without much clarification. Yet it is a crucial concept for it provides a link between the discussion of the parameters of children's action and the analysis of children's interests in the immediacy of the classroom which forms the second half of the chapter. In my use of the term 'coping' I have again drawn on symbolic interactionism and in particular on Mead's (1934) conception of 'self' with its social and biographical origins. Following symbolic interactionist analysis 'self' should be seen as a core concern for any actor. Thus in the classroom context 'coping' can be defined by how closely each participant can satisfy this concern — both from the presentational point of view, which is associated with the actors' role, and from the more personal point of view which is associated directly with their biography. This attempt to satisfy the concern for self in the immediacy of classroom events can then be analysed in more detail using the concept of 'interests-at-hand' for it can be argued that interests-at-hand represent various facets of self which are juggled in the ebb and flow of classroom processes to produce an overall level of satisfaction for self — and hence of 'coping'. The remainder of the chapter thus seeks to identify the major interests-at-hand of the children at Moorside and, in doing so, to distinguish between the priorities of goodies, jokers and gangs.

In beginning this task we must remember a crucial fact of the social situation within a classroom which is that two relatively distinct social systems exist beside each other. The official system of the school with its hierarchy, rules and particular criteria of evaluation exists alongside the children's own social system which may appear to be less formal but also has its own hierarchy, rules and criteria of judgment. In lessons the official school system is represented by the teacher whilst the children's own social system is represented by each child's peers. To which party and to which social system should each child refer his or her actions, and with what consequences?

I would suggest that the most important factor in each child's solution to this dilemma is their structural position within the school and class and therefore that their solutions can be seen as being patterned around the Good, Joker, Gang distinctions. It seems to be the case that Goodies conform to teachers and the offical school system during lessons, whilst Gangs tend to reference their actions more to their group of peers. The success of Jokers lies in their skill and flexibility in bridging both types of social system. I am thus arguing that Jokers are able to square their reference groups in both systems in ways which Goodies do not attempt and which Gangs would not attempt.

From the analysis of the Moorside data it was possible to identify particular issues which were salient to the children. These appeared to be bound to their instrumental concern with prediction and control in their classroom and could thus be grouped by purpose, which made it possible to infer interests. This procedure yielded six groupings and it seemed analytically useful to draw a distinction between the primary interest of 'self', which has several facets, and more secondary interests, which are enabling interests' in an essentially means-end relationships. These interests are shown in table 1 over page.

Of course, it is possible to argue that most children in primary schools share these interests-at-hand in classroom contexts and indeed I would want to do so drawing on a number of other studies. However, for reasons of space I have continued here on the Moorside children.[4]

Table 1. The interests-at-hand of children in classrooms

Primary interests-at hand	Enabling interests-at-hand
Self • Maintenance of self image	Peer group membership
• Enjoyment	Learning
• Control of stress	
• Retention of dignity	

'Self-image': A Facet of the Primary Interest of 'Self'

As we have seen the children at Moorside had clear images of their own identities. These were related in many ways to their friendship groups. The Good groups thought of themselves as 'kind', 'quiet', and 'friendly', the Joker groups believed themselves to be 'clever' and 'good fun' but 'sensible', whilst the Gangs regarded themselves as 'tough' and 'rough'. These identities were further highlighted by denigrating concepts such as reference by Joker groups to Gangs as 'thick, silly yobs' or by Gangs to Joker groups as 'snobbish, creeping, pansies'.

It was clear that when interacting in their classrooms the children would act to maintain their self-image *vis-à-vis* their peers, often even when other interests were threatened. Perhaps the most regular and obvious instance of this was the number of Gang members who would assert their toughness by defying teachers and 'taking' the punishments and sanctions which followed. Clearly children have to manage their self-image in ways which are advantageous to them and this presentational problem can be acute in the classroom when the expectations of peers and the teacher or parent may clash. Maintaining their self-image and sense of identity in this context is an ever present concern.

'Enjoyment': A Facet of the Primary Interest of 'Self'

Enjoyment here refers to the degree of intrinsic self-fulfilment to be obtained from interaction with other people. Children will hope to experience a sense of positive reward from interactions so that they are supportive of self.

Of course there are many forms which such enjoyment can take but one which stands out in the literature, as at Moorside, is that of 'having a laugh'. As Woods (1976) has put it:

> ... pupils have their own norms, rules and values and ...
> their school lives are well structured by them.... In their lives,
> laughter has a central place whether as a natural product or as a

life-saving response to the exigencies of the institution — boredom, ritual, routine, regulations, oppressive authority. (p. 185)

However, not all 'laughs' are oppositional. Humour in the classroom also
often enables teachers and pupils to step out of their role and to express
themselves and to communicate in less guarded ways than they might
usually adopt. As such, humour can also be seen as a source of reinforcement and development of teacher-pupil relationships, in that to share and
'get the joke' reasserts and constructs the 'culture of the classroom'
(Walker and Adelman, 1976) and thus gives security to all 'members; within
that setting.

Stebbings (1980) has noted that for teachers humour is both a strategy
used for control and as a form of self-expression. 'Having a laugh' can be seen
for children in similar terms. It can be a strategy of opposition which
challenges teacher control or it can be enjoyable as a form of collective
relaxation. At Moorside the different types of friendship groups had characteristically patterned aspirations. In the case of Gangs, their greatest
enjoyment appeared to come from forms of action which were essentially
oppositional to teachers. Thus, they emphasized incidents of 'causing
bother' and 'mucking about' as highlights of their experiences and they
liked the excitement from such activities as 'cheeking off' teachers or
playing at 'dares' in lessons. Joker groups also enjoyed excitement but
appeared to derive it in lessons from less disruptive actions such as
sending notes or drawing in jotters. Rather than 'act daft' and 'cause
bother' they would derive their greatest enjoyment from 'having a laugh'
with teacher participation and they also reported enjoying lessons which
were particularly 'interesting'. Good groups also emphasized enjoying
'interesting' lessons and mentioned enjoying lessons sometimes when
teachers 'told jokes'. In most instances, however, their great desire to
avoid stress meant that they felt most relaxed in ordered, routine and
predictable lessons.

The references to enjoyment from 'interesting lessons' of course
relates to the other main source of positive reward for children — the
sense of self-fulfilment produced by success and achievement in learning.
At Moorside many children, particularly in Joker and Good groups,
wanted to succeed in academic terms — after all these were the official,
adult criteria by which they would be evaluated and by which to some
extent they evaluated themselves. The key to this though was balance.
Children wanted teachers who would 'have a laugh' *and* 'teach things'.

'Control of Stress': A Facet of the Primary Interest of 'Self'

The main source of stress for children in classrooms derives from teacher
power and the evaluative context of schooling. For 'good' groups at Moor-

side stress avoidance seemed to be a particularly prominent interest-at-hand, largely, I would argue, because their self-image as quiet, studious, and conformist was undercut with few defences if rejected by a teacher 'getting mad' with them. They were also vulnerable and relatively defenceless if in conflict with other groups of children. They thus tended to be wary and to concentrate on 'avoiding trouble'. In contrast Gangs almost needed stress by which to assert their 'toughness'. At the same time though, few children actually sought out, say, a severe telling-off from a teacher, If such a thing occurred, then it was used to build a tough identity but it was not enjoyed in itself. Joker groups were also concerned to avoid stress, be it from academic failure or acts of deviance. They very much disliked being told off because it negated the type of relationship which they tried to establish with teachers. At the same time, though, it is clear that a lot of their 'good fun' and 'enjoyment' was derived from juggling with the risks of 'getting done' by teachers. If their judgements were correct then routine teacher reactions would not result in much stress. Indeed, spice and zest would be added to classroom experiences from such 'exploration of the limits' without serious sanctions resulting.

Stress is thus a double-edged interest-at-hand. Usually children seek to avoid the potential stress to which they are permanently subject because of teacher power and because of the constant evaluation of their learning. However, there is no doubt that other sorts of stress are wilfully introduced by children from time to time as a source of enjoyment and as an antidote to routine or boredom.

'Retaining Dignity': A Facet of the Primary Interest of 'Self'

This was one of the important interests-at-hand for all the groups of children, being crucial for the preservation of self and peer-group esteem. Of course there is a close relationship between dignity and perceived 'fairness' and this was particularly clear at Moorside. Thus teacher actions and censures would be constantly assessed by the children for legitimacy. 'Getting done' could therefore be accepted without loss of dignity if it was 'fair', but if the teacher went 'mad' and particularly if they started shouting and denigrating a child, then this would be regarded as a most 'unfair' assault by all the children. Other, more specific, threats to dignity came from being 'picked on', or teased by teachers as well as by having one's name forgotten. Being picked on was felt particularly deeply as a personal attack by the Gang groups. It was regarded as unfair because it was seen to arise from unusual levels of teacher surveillance and from particular attention being directed towards them. Similarly, being 'shown up' was recognized as a specific act of depersonalization intended to set an example. For instance,

Malcolm: He only showed me up like that in front of everyone just to make me look stupid ... and just to try to make us all learn the notes better. He's always getting on at us for it and just 'cos I couldn't answer his questions he picked on me.

On the other hand, being teased was something which the Joker groups seemed particularly conscious of. The girls related that one teacher often teased them about boyfriends which in some cases upset them because it made them 'go all red and look silly'. The relatively quiet members of Good groups were the main group of children who reported having their names forgotten. They clearly regarded this as insulting and resented it.

With regard to retaining dignity *vis-à-vis* the other children similar issues seemed important. The inter-group rivalry at Moorside was reflected in mild forms of teasing and in more serious episodes of name calling or fighting similar to that recorded by Sluckin (1981) in Oxfordshire primary schools. In all cases though the children's comments on such incidents revealed both defensive and aggressive actions to be forms of assertion of particular self-identities with particular group associations. The defence of personal dignity thus seems to be a very prominent interest-at-hand for children in all school contexts.

'Peer Group Membership' and 'Learning': Two Enabling Interests

It was suggested earlier that peer group loyalty and learning should be seen as enabling interests rather than as facets of the primary self-interest. They thus take on the same role for children as order and instruction do for teachers (Pollard, 1980), in that they articulate between the social ascriptions of respective reference groups and facets of the primary interest-at-hand of the participants. In the case of teachers, order and instruction can be seen as the two main aspects of their role expectation, which they have to come to terms with if they are to avoid external pressure. However, order and instruction are also the means of achieving a satisfactory level of satisfaction of more personal interests. In the case of the children, peer group membership and learning seem to relate to the social ascriptions of the child culture and social system and of the adult educational culture and wider society respectively. As such they reflect the ambiguity of each child's structural position and of course to some extent they offer alternative ways of enabling the primary interest-at-hand to be satisfied. They also pose severe dilemmas for the children when they come to make strategic decisions concerning action and to juggle with their interests in the dynamic flow of classroom processes.

Peer Group Membership

At Moorside peer group membership was linked to both the assertion and defence of self. Enjoyment, laughs and 'great times' almost exclusively derived from interaction between the children and their 'mates' or 'friends' with or without the positive participation of the teacher. A supportive audience was thus crucial and could only be guaranteed by the secure membership and solidarity of a peer group. Peer group 'competence' sometimes had to be proven if a child was to avoid being rejected as 'wet' or 'stupid' but would of course vary in its nature depending on the type of group. Group membership was also of defensive value both against the threat from teachers and from other children. The solidarity which existed within groups provided a powerful resource for individuals in exposed situations both in the classroom or playground. Group members were expected to 'stick up' for each other and certainly one of the worse actions imaginable was to 'snitch' or 'tell tales' on a friend. Peer group solidarity was a particularly important interest for gang groups because of the consequences of their frequent rejection of teacher authority. Children's concern to be seen as a full and competent member of their peer group can thus be seen as an enabling interest in the context of their primary concern to protect their self and 'survive' the variety of situations at school which they encounter.

Learning

Whilst the enabling interest of peer group membership responds to the children's social system, the interest of 'learning' is a primary means of coping in the adult evaluation systems of teachers and parents. Teachers and parents expect children to 'learn'. Thus one way of satisfying them and of negotiating their power and influence is simply to do just that. However, within children's social structures there will be considerable variation in the degree of commitment to this strategy. For instance, at Moorside the children would constantly assess the 'cost' of trying to learn by evaluating how 'interesting' or 'boring' the lessons were. Of course there were variations not only in those judgements but also in the responses then made. Good groups might consider a lesson as 'boring' but put up with it anyway, accepting it as 'good for them' and not wishing to compromise their identities with their teachers. Joker group members would be more inclined to attempt to direct the lesson into more 'fertile' activities whilst Gang members would be likely to attempt to subvert the lesson directly. Good and Joker group members reported far more intrinsic satisfaction from lessons than Gang members. The latter were far more likely to see lessons as a 'waste of time' or time spent on 'doing nothing' unless a direct link with future work possibilities was drawn. They thus generally had a more exclusively instrumental approach than the other, more academically successful, types of group. Obviously their perceived academic 'failure' meant that learning did not seem to provide anything more than a very limited means of enabling them to cope with their situation. On the other hand, for Joker group members their success at learning earned them the credit with teachers and parents with which they were able to relax and cultivate laughs. For the Good group members the studious sincerity of their attempts to learn enabled them to accomplish lessons without incident.

Of course academic achievement feeds back directly to the development of each child's identity and self-concept so that to learn in lessons is not an interest-at-hand simply by virtue of the need to accomplish the particular situation. It is linked to the maintenance and development of self-image, to enjoyment, to stress-avoidance and to dignity — facets of self which, though experienced with immediacy, accumulate over time into more established identities. Thus not only teachers but each child himself comes to 'know' who is 'thick' and who is 'bright', and of course so do other children. This last point is of considerable significance for it influences children's friendships groups and the nature of interaction within them considerably. Learning is thus an important interest in terms of developing a particular identity for children within their peer group though its main significance as an enabling interest clearly stems from its articulation with teacher concerns and with the official curriculum and purposes of school.

Conclusion

We can finally consider how these child interests-at-hand — maintaining self-image, enjoyment, control of stress, retaining dignity, peer-group membership and learning — might be used in the immediacy of classroom situations to produce forms of action. As a consequence of the understandings negotiated between the teacher and children and which form the 'working consensus', it is possible to see classrooms as being 'rule-framed' (Pollard, 1980). The nature of the rules 'in play' at any point will vary depending on the particular configuration of time, space, purpose and personnel and it is evident that contrasts in particular types of rule-frame situations will not affect all child interests in the same ways. The levels of satisfaction of different interests are unlikely, therefore, to vary together, and various degrees of imbalance in interest satisfaction will result. For instance, for a 'Joker' a low frame humorous interlude in a lesson may well be extremely enjoyable and offer many opportunities for establishing a strong identity as a peer group member, but it may also result in very little learning and a great deal of stress if called to account finally by the teacher. The point which I want to argue, therefore, is that the three major child interests of self, peer group membership and learning, whatever their relative prominence or nature for each type of group. are mutually interrelated in the way in which they affect coping. For each individual coping in the long run depends on evolving viable strategies by which to accomplish their structural position and hence must derive from some form of accommodation with it, in which an acceptable *balance* of self, peer group membership and learning is necessary.

I would suggest that the types of group which have been identified represent different types of solution to the problems posed by school life. The situation is difficult for children. Some will seek to cope with it by conforming and seeking to 'please the teacher' as much as possible; some will reject the whole experience, treat it as an attack on their self-esteem and resist it; some may try to negotiate their way through the situation by balancing their concerns with those of the teacher. Thus we have the strategies of the 'good' groups, the 'gang' groups and the 'joker' groups. One important consequence is the possibility that the adoption of particular strategies by children may result in further reinforcement and elaboration of the associated identity from interaction with teachers and from organizational amplification. Child adaptations and perspectives of the sort which I have been considering could therefore lead into an analysis of typing and 'career' and hence become directly related to the major sociological issue of the role of schooling in social reproduction.

Notes

1 The chapter forms part of a broadly-based interactionist analysis which is reported elsewhere (Pollard, 1981 and 1985). It directly parallels an account of teacher interests-at-hand (Pollard, 1980)
2 For methodological accounts see Pollard (1984 and 1987).
3 For a fuller discussion of the implications of this model see Pollard (1979).
4 See Pollard (1985) for a fuller account which incorporates other research on primary school pupils.

References

BALL, S. (1980) 'Initial encounters in the classroom and the process of establishment' in WOODS, P. (Ed.) *Pupil Strategies*, London, Croom Helm.
MEAO, G.H. (1934) *Mind, Self and Society*, Chicago, University of Chicago Press.
POLLARD, A. (1979) 'Negotiating deviance and "getting done" in primary school classrooms' in BARTON, L. and MEIGHAN, R. (Eds) *Schools, Pupils and Deviance*, Driffield, Nafferton.
POLLARD, A. (1980) 'Teacher interests and changing situations of survival threat in primary school classrooms' in WOODS, P. (Ed.) *Teacher Strategies*, London, Croom Helm.
POLLARD, A. (1981) 'Coping with deviance: School processes and their implications for social reproduction', unpublished PhD thesis, University of Sheffield.
POLLARD, A. (1984) 'Opportunities and difficulties of a teacher-ethnographer: A per-

sonal account' in BURGESS, R.G. (Ed.) *Field Methods in the Study of Education: Issues and Problems*, Lewes, Falmer Press.

POLLARD, A. (1985) *The Social World of the Primary School*, London, Holt, Rinehart and Winston.

POLLARD, A. (1987) 'Studying children's perspectives — A collaborative approach' in WALFORD, G. (Ed.) *Doing Sociology of Education*, Lewes, Falmer Press.

SLUCKIN, A. (1981) *Growing Up in the Playground*, London, Routledge and Kegan Paul.

STEBBINS, R.A. (1980) 'The role of humour in teaching: strategy and self expression' in WOODS, P. (Ed.) *Teacher Strategies*, London, Croom Helm.

STEBBINS, R.A. (1981) 'Classroom ethnography and the definition of the situation' in BARTON, L. and WALKER, S. (Eds) *Schools, Teachers and Teaching*, Lewes, Falmer Press.

WALKER, R. and ADELMAN, C. (1976) 'Strawberries' in STUBBS, M. and DELAMONT, S. (Eds) *Explorations in Classroom Observation*, London, Wiley.

WOODS, P. (1976) 'Having a laugh, an antidote to schooling' in HAMMERSLEY, M. and WOODS, P. (Eds) *The Process of Schooling*, London, Routledge and Kegan Paul.

WOODS, P. (1977) 'Teaching for survival' in WOODS, P. and HAMMERSLEY, M. (Eds) *School Experience*, London, Croom Helm.

12 Child Culture at School A Clash Between Gendered Worlds?

Katherine Clarricoates

Introduction

Gender differentiation is a pervasive influence in all schools and affects many dimensions of school life.[1] Gender differences are inter-woven with class differences.[2] At times they reinforce each other. Yet whilst the school and the educational system may determine the formal structure in classrooms[3], this does not preclude the pupils themselves influencing what takes place.

In this chapter I shall explore the ways in which girls and boys behave toward each other in primary schools. The empirical data reported here has been collected from four schools and their catchment areas, in and around a Northern dockland city predominantly composed of white people:

Dock Side: A traditional urban school within an inner city working class district

Applegate: A rural/suburban school in a predominantly middle class village

Long Meadow: A relatively modern school in the middle of a corporation housing estate

Lintonbray: A small school in a rural and predominantly working class village

As well as using participant-observation data from *all* the classes (reception, infants and juniors) in each school, tape-recorded conversations and semi-structured interviews were conducted with all-female, with all-male and mixed gender groups between the age of 9 and 11 years. The specific aim was to clarify the nature of social relations *between* girls and boys in primary schools.[4]

The first section of the chapter examines the nature of status amongst girls and boys and the 'qualities' that provided status within each institution. The next section concentrates on the spatial and verbal struggle for dominance between the two sexes. I shall also examine intra-group rivalry and the ways in which individuals competed against each other.

Status and Gender-appropriate Behaviour

By examining those pupils at the extremes, viz. those with high and low status within the peer group, one should be able to specify the behaviour and attitudes which influence the behaviour of others. However, before doing this, it is necessary to convey something of the overall attitude of the children to academic work.

Previous research has revealed how girls were vulnerable to the 'male definitions of achievement' (Rich, 1979) and were estranged from and even denied 'academic competence' or 'creativity' (Clarricoates, 1978 and 1981; Evans, 1979; Deem, 1980). Such definitions are even now evident in that Smith (1984) states that girls prefer 'familiar, straightforward, repetitive work requiring care and accuracy to new challenging concepts and problems' (p. 77). What researchers must do is to take into account 'the intuitive grasp' that children have of the social processes 'which mould their lives' (Holly, 1985), and that theorizing in 'terms of achievement or underachievement' is neither useful nor accurate (Mahoney, 1985). However, it is important to look at 'academic norms' amongst the pupils to ascertain what they mean to them and how they are used.

Academic norms were not high in Dock side, Long Meadow and Lintonbray, but this broad statement conceals the complexity of the stituation. The girls sought some scholastic achievement for a number of reasons. Many accorded peer group status to academic achievement although some do not work hard nor seek such achievements for the sake of status alone. For example, Wendy — a top junior pupil at Dock Side — enjoyed certain subjects for their own sake, being neither competitive nor boastful of her supposedly high scholastic position in class. However, it is interesting to note that the girls call forth Wendy's name whenever their status as a group was brought into question by the boys.

Another major reason why girls aim to do well came from their aspirations for their future despite their 'socio-economic class'[5] and regional high unemployment. Some of the girls in Lintonbray expressed a wish to do well and even acquire further education:

My mum wants me to do well and get a good job ... 'cos there's nowt in our village ...
I'm gonna be a nurse and my mum wants me to go away for the training ...

I was able to ascertain the opinions of various groups towards academic achievement and towards those pupils who deviated from the forms of behaviour which were considered 'appropriate' or who ranked highly within the peer group:

Dock Side Girls: Boys always make a noise and try to stop you working ...

I got three stars today ... Miss Simmons says I'm improving all the time.

They (boys) don't do their writing properly like we do

See that girl over there, Wendy Hagan ... she's the best in the class.

Dock Side Boys: Girls always try to answer the questions first.

Yeah, they think they're a bunch of clever clogs.

We don't have to do anything 'cos the girls will always answer questions first ...

These quotations illustrate the distinctive attitudes towards academic endeavour and peer group status which are held by the girls and boys. They also indicate the mutual scorn that they express for each other. A finding noted by other researchers (Stanworth, 1983; Mahoney, 1985).

In order to highlight further features of the differences in perspective we can now go on to focus on children who held views or occupied positions at the extremes. Research has shown that teachers encourage competitiveness between girls and boys (Clarricoates, 1980; Spender and Sarah, 1980). In the top junior class of Dock Side, the boys saw themselves fortunate in having Ian Johnson (the 'bright boy') on their side as they invariably won the general knowledge quizzes. It was interesting to see how the boys accepted one of their kind with high 'academic achievement' when it was of particular use to them. For the most part Ian did not conform to the dominant values of the boys in this type of school, in that he liked his lessons, did not fight and, though adequate if called upon to play football, he was by no means gifted at the sport.[6] He transcended his *peer group deviation* by helping them beat the girls, which appeared to be the boys' major occupation in their prize for dominance as the 'superior' gender. Danny, however, was a shy boy, afraid of anyone who approached him aggressively, and possessed none of the status-conferring attributes of both pupils *and* teachers (being considered poor in his school work). As a result, he was put down by teachers and open to abuse from pupils — girls as well as boys. He therefore can be categorized as an *outcast* whereas Ian, by helping the boys 'beat the girls' escaped abuse — and thus the status of outcast — becoming a *loner*.

It was also noted amongst the boys in Long Meadow that academic success and articulacy was fairly irrelevant. 'Sissy' behaviour — primarily fear of aggressive encounters and low football ability — ensured low prestige:

> Michael's like a great fairy . . . he goes around with the girls.

> He can't fight . . . he's always goin' on about how he makes buns and things . . . instead of playing football.

> When Miss Mackeson asked him what he wanted to be when he grew up he said he wanted to a be a butterfly. He's just a great sissy.

To all intents and purposes Michael was neither popular within his peer group nor applauded for his scholastic achievement by his teachers, though they admitted he was 'bright' his 'general behaviour' seemed to be of much more concern to them. The teachers in fact attributed his 'behaviour' as partly due to the fact of coming from a one-parent family (absentee father). Michael's overt 'lack of masculine qualities' makes him an *outcast*, despite his high academic achievement.

In the village school of Lintonbray the most unpopular person in the top junior class was Simon; a large awkward boy who possessed none of the skills of football and was presumed slow at his work. The girls voiced their dislike of him:

> Simon's lousy at maths, he can't count you know.

> He's too fat . . . he can't run fast enough in football.

> Sir's always telling him off. He makes him stay behind when the team's on 'away' matches and we have to put up with him.

Although Simon may at first appear to be an outcast he was, however, disruptive and aggressive, traits seen as 'boyish' and hence 'masculine' behaviour. His status was commuted to *outsider*. The examples of Simon and Michael also illustrate that these two boys were encroaching upon the girls' games and space which may have increased their dislike of them.

Over the last decade, research has indicated that teachers have rated girls more highly for good, 'conformist' behaviour (Ingleby and Cooper, 1974; Belotti, 1975; Byrne, 1978; Spender and Sarah, 1980). However, more recent studies have revealed the situation to be more complex (Davies, 1979; Griffin, 1985; Pollard, 1985). It is important to point out, also, that apart from Pollard's work such studies have concentrated on secondary schools. So, what of those girls who do not conform but in fact are seen to deviate from their gender-appropriate behaviour with regard to teachers' expectations?

How peer group status and academic performance can diverge amongst the girls is clearly illustrated by Kerry, a 9-year-old girl in Dock Side who was not scholastically bright and was also seen as disruptive by her teachers. She did however, manage to attain a reasonable status from most of the other pupils in her class both female and male. Kerry resolutely entered the 'male space' — played football and chose the 'best' dinner-table for her and her friends — and parried successfully any threat of challenge from the dominant group of boys. Being a muscular child for her age and very confident, she was not afraid of aggressive encounters with either males or females. For this reason she was able to make in-roads for other girls into those areas and activities which the boys usually dominated, and into which they normally would not have gained a foothold if it had not been for her leadership. Consequently Kerry was well rewarded with sweets, licks of lollies, the first bite of an apple and the odd packed lunch (that the owner did not want). Her status was assured during the games lesson when she was always one of the first to be picked by either the female or *male teams* for the various mixed game efforts. She thus had fairly high status among all the pupils and was a noted *leader* in her class.

Physical aggression appeared to be a respected quality within the peer group and the teaching staff accorded it a fair degree of tolerance:

Well, what can you expect in an area like this.

There was already apparent among the boys the hard core of the 'anti-school elite' who had high status in the eyes of the other boys and had considerable power to define proceedings both within the classroom and the playground. The girls, in general, did not go along with the boys' definition of situations and appropriate behaviour, of which gender specificity was a crucial component. Male-appropriate behaviour can already be seen at this stage of their schooling, whilst female-appropriate behaviour was much more complex simply because the majority of the girls (perhaps due to their age) did not seek status via their relationships with boys: they did not wear make-up nor seek to make themselves attractive to boys. What is more, in many cases the girls were inclined to interpret the boys' behaviour as evidence of their inability to be competent either scholastically or in their behaviour. However, certain qualities and forms of behaviour which are seen as 'appropriate' to the girls did become manifested, eg: their capacity to be more attentive in class, the fact that they formed the majority of the 'academic elite' and their tendency to stay together merely to avoid the aggressive overtures of some of the boys.

Disruption was invariably initiated by the boys, this disruption for a time halts further work advancement and the girls reacted by expressing resentment against the boys. They regarded the boys as 'silly', 'lazy' and 'thick'. One way of controlling the boys who were disrupting their chances of getting on with their work was to call upon the teacher to disapprove of the offending boys. Perhaps the teacher did not intercede but it had the required effect of curtailing the boys' action. The girls, in fact, reported that the boys seemed to want to 'get into trouble'.

So far, the picture that is drawn seems to be that of girls as archetypal 'good pupils'. However the 'conformist' interpretation of this behaviour has to be reanalyzed in the light of the young girls' needs for recognized competence and self-esteem, not merely as 'wishing to please the teachers'. The girls indulged in *non-conformist* behaviour far more than teachers realized i.e. they ate and shared sweets 'undercover' of their desk lids and secretly passed verbal and written messages to each other. They considered themselves 'clever' in not being found out. This sort of behaviour was neither meek and passive nor aggressive but in certain instances — when a teacher felt that some of the girls were subverting her/his authority — this did cause tension. However, because there is no behavioural typescript for deviant behaviour for girls (Davies, 1979) they were categorized as 'silly' by teachers who found their behaviour puzzling. The girls seemed to be less influenced by each other (which some sociologists may regard as proof of a lack of solidarity) than the boys, who tended to prove to each other that they were part of the 'in-group'. The girls did not automatically define female teachers as adversaries, and had many common understandings with them which may have been assisted by the sex of the teachers. Certainly, it is too easy to assume that academic striving and achieving are synonymous with 'conformity'.

As a comparison with these three schools, I would like to discuss the middle-class rural-suburban school of Applegate. The values of the high status members of this suburban school were in marked contrast to those of Dock Side, Long Meadow or Lintonbray — especially for the boys. Academic aspiratons were part and parcel of the value structure of both school and home. That was the central concern. Most of the children were highly attuned to these values and duly placed considerable efforts into achieving them. Whereas most of the Dock Side pupils would seek to end their schooling as soon as they reached the statutory age, most of these children would aim (as their teachers and parents hoped) to remain at school so as to further their education.

Most of the children revealed considerable diligence in their written work through all the age levels of the school. This was particularly obvious in top junior classes. Again in conversations with the girls, with the boys and with the mixed groups this was ascertained from them:

Girls: I really like writing compositions ... I'd like to do well ... even go to university.

'Sir' says this is the best school in the area ... and he wants us to do well when we go on to senior school.

Sometimes Peter Jenkinson's top of the class and sometimes Carol Thornham is ... aren't you Carol?

Yes. I'm better at maths though ... he's good at poetry and writing.

Boys: I'd like to get on in school and get some qualfications. My dad says it's important to do well at school.

The girls usually win in the general knowledge quizzes but we're not far behind.

193

> We have tests every week ... spelling, maths ... and it's
> always Peter Jenkinson or Carol Thornham who win them.

Both girls and boys regarded scholastic ability as an indicator of high status
in contrast to Dock side where scholastic ability conferred status among
the boys only when it was used to their collective advantage to score one
against the girls. At Applegate, the boys each sought academic achievement for the sake of their own individual status.

Disruptive behaviour, fighting and swearing was looked down upon
by the peer group even among the boys. One of the boys in the top junior
class, Robert, affords us with a picture of the situation regarding status.
He was loud, aggressive and prone to consistent swearing (if out of earshot
of the teachers). There was little love lost between him, his peer group
and the school authorities — his school work was defined as poor and he
appeared rough both in his manner and attire. He appeared to be failing
and discredited on almost every dimension that seemed important to both
pupils and staff. However Robert's own interpretation of the situation was
quite the reverse. He appeared confident despite the constant disapproval
and managed to have as his constant companions a small group of boys
who admired him for his 'couldn't-care-less' attitude. The attitudes of the
other pupils however, confirmed his status:

> Robert Smith is always fighting. He's a proper bully and you
> should hear him swear.
>
> If 'Sir' catches him, he's for it!
>
> He's really rough and he never does his work in class.
>
> He's absolutely stupid ... he's always in trouble ...

Robert was obviously considered a problem by the school; a 'trouble-
maker' who came from what teachers classed as a 'difficult' working-class
home background. Being working class was not necessarily against him
but intra-class differences were also crucial referents within both village
and school, and Robert and his family were seen as 'rough' and 'inadequate' in relation to the norms of working class respectability.[7] His parents
did not support the school's attempts to contain him, so within the
classroom Robert had considerable power to define proceedings. As such,
he was a threat to the rest of the girls and boys in the challenge he
represented to their widely and firmly held norms about class location and
educational performance. Plus he expressed his 'machoism' by not being
adverse to hitting girls, something very strongly disapproved of in Applegate.

For girls in Applegate exemplary behaviour was demanded and expected of them by the staff and each other. In certain respects a more
rigid regime of 'femininity' appeared to be in existence than in the other
three schools. Sarah, for instance, was another classic example of a 'deviant' female pupil despite the fact that she came from a middle-class

home. Her parents were both 'professionals' and owned their large rambling house on the fringes of the village. The teachers defined her 'deviancy' as something to do with her 'home background' (like Robert):

Her parents let her run wild!

They allow her to get up to all sorts of mischief.

Isolated both at school and outside it, unlike Robert who reigned supreme
within a group of admiring 'side-kicks', Sarah was regarded as a threat,
particularly by the boys. They complained bitterly about the way she
attempted to join in their games and challenge them when they tried to
coerce her from doing so:

She yells at you.

... and she slapped Sean Allison across the face the other day
and that's not on.

Unfortunately, even the girls found her difficult and at times withdrawn
apart from her erratic outbursts of 'unfeminine' behaviour:

She's not like us ...

Well ... she shouts at the lads ...

That's not all, she even fights with them ...

Sir's always on at her.

Overall, Sarah represented an unenviable picture, which reminded the
other pupils, especially the girls, what constitutes 'feminine' behaviour
irrespective of social class or scholastic ability — as Sarah was regarded as
'quite bright'.

Unlike Kerry in Dock Side, Sarah was unable to forge any allies
amongst the girls and we can compare her situation to that of the four
reigning 'Boadiceas': Elizabeth, Sally, Joanne and Dawn in the same
school. These four girls came from varying backgrounds i.e. two came
from relatively comfortable middle-class homes whilst the other two came
from working-class (albeit 'respectable') homes. Their educational performance also differed, though not greatly but they were inseparable from
each other. They exasperated the staff in that they neither courted a good
reputation among teachers nor seemed to want to be seen as serious by
the staff or other pupils. They were a source of amusement and diversion
to the other girls who admired them for daring to challenge the boys on
'their own territory' by insisting on a share of the space the boys dominated. Despite the fact that many attempts were made to separate them
these were never successful. To a certain extent the four were a rallying
point for the other girls, especially in the playground where boys tended
to secure for themselves the vantage of the play apparatus and the space.

Their behaviour brought them into serious conflict with the *boys*
rather than being a direct challenge to the *teachers'* authority. However,

because the boys were more threatened, it was they who indulged in grossly disruptive behaviour which forced the teachers into the position of admonishing the girls.

It was apparent in most of the classes that there was a fair degree of impermanence in the composition of groups; however relations between and within the peer groups were stable enough to demarcate areas of privilege and status. Such areas of privilege and status are, to a large extend based on gender criteria. It is also important to point out the variations among those pupils who had considerable power to define proceeding and those who appeared more vulnerable than others. Whilst Danny (from Dock Side) and Michael (from Long Meadow) were both outcasts from the peer group by virtue of their gender deviant behaviour, Simon (from Lintonbray) was an outsider because he deviated from school appropriate behaviour in a way that was disruptive to both his teachers and his peer-group which suggests that at certain times and in particular situations gender-appropriate and school-appropriate behaviour overlap. This can be seen in the particular case of Ian, a loner, though scholastically bright was not necessarily high on gender-based criteria but assisted the other boys in their assumed 'prize' as the superior gender. Robert (from Applegate) deviated from school-appropriate behaviour and gender-based criteria on the basis of the social class of the school he attended which also suggests that gender and class values overlap. His popularity may in part be due to the fact that Applegate was not entirely populated by an indigenous middle-class but still retained a minority of working-class residents.

A similar complex picture emerges when discussing deviancy and status amongst girls. Kerry (from Dock Side) and Elizabeth, Sally, Joanne and Dawn (from Applegate) deviate from school appropriate behaviour in varying degrees and yet have the support and status cf their peer group which suggests that girls were not wholeheartedly compliant with school-based values at primary school age and may be forming peer-group values of their own, distinct and apart from their school and its environs. Sarah (from Applegate) and Simon (from Lintonbray) are both outsiders, but it is essential to point out the difference between them. She is an outsider in a different way from him for she transgresses gender appropriate behaviour adopting the behavioural pattern of the *dominant* sex, which could also explain why she has no allies among the girls.

Despite the complexities it is meaningful to speak of a 'girls' world' and a 'boys' world' within each school.

Spatial and Verbal Dominance

As a result of the 'worlds' of girls and boys, the children developed amongst themselves relationships of status and power based on gender, the analysis of which interrelates crucially with the wider institutional features, thus differentially structuring opportunity, resources and power.

Domination of space within schools operates as an expression and mechanism of social control. This is imposed by 'dominant' groups — specifically by males upon females; whether they be teachers, ancillary staff,[8] or pupils, however here I will concentrate on the latter.

Within the School Building

In Dock Side, space and who dominated it was an important issue. One of the reasons for this was the lack of it, being a cramped, Victorian edifice. Within the classroom, despite limited space, there was some attempt to provide a 'play area'. Specific corners were marked out in each infants' class which varied according to the size of the room and the number of children present. It became apparent that it was mainly boys who tended to occupy this space with girls restricte to their desks and the surrounding area. I assumed that there would be some interchange with regard to the utilization of space but, as the days turned to weeks and months, the pattern remained consistent. The boys dominated the area, expecting first choice of toys and going to particular lengths to keep at bay either the girls or another group of boys. I must point out that the tactics used to repel other groups of boys or the girls were different in that though physical tactics were used to 'repel all borders', with girls there was also sexual ridicule combined (as I will show later). Girls did venture into the 'play area' when it was vacant or to retrieve an item of equipment. Lisa tended to be the only girl who appeared to have free access in this space and was on particularly 'good' speaking terms with the boys, along with her best friend Katy. I soon found out why. Lisa was prepared to threaten any contentious boy with violence, not only from herself but her 'big brother' who happened to be in the second year juniors and who was not squeamish about beating up little boys from the infants.

Long Meadow provided a strong physical contrast with Dock Side. It was the largest and most spacious of the four schools; sex-segregated toilets and corridors made available the exclusivity, by sex, of facilities. In both the infant and junior classes some of the teachers encouraged the extensive use of numerical and play equipment, seeing it as a problem solver, since it diminished the amount of disruption amongst the boys, who were able to dominate more space with their verbal and physical activity.

In Applegate and Lintonbray, as in Dock Side, space tended to be an issue strongly contested between the girls and boys. In the middle (7-9-year-olds) and senior (9-11-year-olds) classes of Lintonbray there was no space set aside for play areas, whilst in the infants (5-7-year-olds) class some attempt was made to provide space for play. There were the usual constructive toys and books occupying makeshift shelves in this space. The infants' teacher ensured that most of the children were involved in some form of activity or project and in this way there appeared to be 'equality' in the use of the play space between the boys and the girls. However, observations revealed something quite different which shows that analysis must include not only *who* occupies space but also *how* such space is occupied. Before the end of the school day the children in this particular class gather in the playspace for their 'end-of-the-day' story. There was the usual rush for places and during the ensuing scuffle which accompanied such jostling for positions it became clear that the low-lying book-cases and who sat on them represented high status within the class. On a number of occasions when some girls attempted to occupy such places they were invariably pushed off with screams such as 'it's only for us boys'. The teacher did rebuke the boys for their harsh behaviour in certain circumstances — when a kick or a punch accompanied the 'scream' — but they were not for insisting on occupying such an 'exalted position' in the play space. She was to all intents and purposes, unaware of the aspects of power being acted out in this form of spatial dominance.

In Applegate such forms of dominance were also being acted out in the recreation spaces provided. This was particularly apparent in the middle juniors where there was a fair sized room adjoining the classroom for activities 'of a less serious nature'. Harsh physical behaviour from the boys towards the girls was frowned upon, in accordance with the ethos of the school, but this did not pre-empt certain forms of spatial dominance being enacted. Researchers have noted that ridicule is used as a means of control by male pupils in schools (Shaw, 1977; Spender and Sarah, 1980; Mahoney, 1985). On a particular occasion two girls were attempting to retrieve an abacus from one of the many cupboards within the room. Five boys, already ensconced in a project, resented their 'intrusion' and jeered at them: 'I suppose you'll need that seeing as you can't count' stated one. The other boys start to laugh. The girls retorted reminding one boy, Carl Haymers that he'd only 'got nought out of ten for a recent mental arithmetic test'. The boys returned the remark with threats and the girls feeling outnumbered retreated from the room.

This is just an example from a long catalogue of 'masculine' behaviour which undermines girls' skills and confidence. Verbal practice which included jokes and even threats were constantly made as a way of gaining space from the girls, with no fear of disciplinary action. The issue is one of power, and until that is recognised no action to challenge such behaviour will be forthcoming.

Cross-group and intra-group rivalry was apparent in all the schools. Boys in particular made a great show of who was 'top dog' amongst themselves and also banded together in order to express their collective dominance as a group. In addition when an individual boy sought to dominate a girl in some respect, he called on others for support, and in certain cases even used the teacher.

It was 11.30 am and the second year infants class at Long Meadow had resigned themselves to their work books. A group compared each other's work amongst themselves. Paul stated: 'I've done more than you!' 'No you haven't' replied the indignant girl. Paul turned for support from Stephen and Neil 'I've done more than her, haven't I?' 'Yeah, you have, so there ...' The girl shrugged and attempted to get on with her work.

But the boy, Paul would not leave it there, but went on about it and had caused quite a good deal of disturbance around him. He shouted to the teacher 'Miss, Miss, I've done more than her, haven't I?' The harrassed teacher wanted an end to the disturbance and agreed with him in the hope he would return to his work. 'See!' said Paul determined to have the last word.

Some of the boys appeared to have a constant fear of being beaten by the girls. A situation, which an unthinking teacher, exacerbated on a number of occasions. A male teacher informed a games class in Dock Side, who were clambering over items of sports apparatus, that the girls were 'beating' the boys in climbing up the rope. Almost immediately the boys went into paroxysms of activity in order to prove that they were 'better'; they attempted to outrun, outclimb, outdo each other and the girls. To them it was important not only to 'beat' their counterparts, it was also necessary that they should be seen doing so. The girls condemned boys for being rough and aggressive whilst the boys condemned girls for appearing to be the 'good pupils', since it is through the display of reverse qualities of what girls do that boys gain and reward status.

A further way in which the boys were able to dominate classroom life was in being able to gain the teacher's attention much more often. On many occasions when a girl made attempts to show her work to the teacher she was unable to gain her attention. Some degree of forcefulness was necessary to divert the teacher and some girls lacked the confidence to do this. However, one of the most often used means of dominance was teasing and joking. Certain jokes depend upon shared assumptions, which encompass the 'sexual prowess' of men, the idea that women are the objects of derision and the willingness of the audience to ratify these attributes by laughing. The use of sexual ridicule was used as a very effective weapon against the females:

Whilst laying out old newspapers for a painting and craftwork session in a class of 8-year-olds, one of the boys came across the 'Page 3' section of *The Sun*. Giggling to three of this friends he held up the paper to a girl in the class and taunted her: 'This is

what you'll look like when you grow up, Tracy'. The girl felt
offended and turned to the teacher 'No I won't, will I Miss?'

The teacher looked on but not impassively, the ridicule had also affected
her as indicated by her uneasy response: 'I try not to make anything of such
incidents ... you know what children are like'. She then went on to
confiscate the newspaper depicting the semi-nude woman from the boy
who was still flaunting it at a number of the girls. This form of ridicule was
used to lay claim to a specific space and also to confirm the 'physical
inferiority' of women. This kind of sexism cuts across class (Wood, 1984):

> In the first year juniors of Applegate, Oliver was playing with clay
> in the project area. He proceeded to mock the female body by
> affixing clay points to his chest; 'Hey, this what you'll have when
> you get big', to the girl present. The other two boys with him
> joined in the laughter while Claire fled the area humiliated.

Upon hearing so much noise the teacher came to investigate. Claire stated
that the boys were being 'naughty'; she could not express her confusion or
the form of insult aimed at her (and *all* females) despite her articulacy but as
Holly (1985) states girls do understand the nature of sexism and neither have
they accepted its inevitability. Claire did not enter the project area
alone, but always made sure she was with other girls during the rest of my
participant observation in this class.

In ascertaining that boys negotiated space for themselves, it must not
be forgotten that girls attempted to do likewise — although their methods
differed. This was particularly apparent with regard to their relationship
with the male teachers (amongst junior girls). Girls tended to congregate
more at male teachers' desks and stay longer than the boys. They were
often given the task of handing out classroom materials which gave them a
temporary position of power, and one which they sometimes used to
extend their influence further. With the support of the teacher a girl,
Joanna, was able to refuse the demands of a particular boy who was asking
for one of the books she was giving out:

> I'll give you a book when I come to your table.
>
> I want one now! demanded the boy.

The boy was made to return to his seat under the auspices of the teacher:
'Sit down Robert Johnson, the only person who should be out of their seat
should be the one giving out books'. Joanna proceeded to give out the
books to her friends first and made the boys wait 'til last. However, this
particular kind of influence is double-edged, in that duties in question can
be seen as mirroring the 'service' role that women play in the outside
world.

Outside the Classroom

As a result of the overall structural organization of the schools[9] and overt aggression expressed by a minority of the boys, the latter were able to dominate not only lesson content and classroom life in general but also space outside the school; a much noted phenomenon (Wolpe, 1977; Spender and Sarah, 1980; Whylde, 1983; Holly, 1985; Mahoney, 1985). The boys' games of 'superman', cowboys and Indians, and football can keep the whole playground in a state of tension and excitement as they 'charge' and 'whoop' their way through the ranks of other children. This does not mean that girls cower at the edge. The boys dominated the available space in most forms of play in the playground (although in Dock Side, playgrounds were separate). If by chance the girls wandered into what was seen as the space of the boys, they were viewed as intruders who do not know 'their place' and who try to take that which is not theirs.

Differences of power and status are closely tied to gender differences in both verbal and non-verbal behaviour. In all four schools, sports activities were carried out on a sex-segregated basis with boys taking up the greater amount of space for football and with girls mainly playing netball. In the modern world the two sports cannot be compared in terms of the cultural prestige afforded to them. The school is no exception. Far greater facilities and privileges were given to football and those who played it (Whylde, 1983; Holly, 1985).

In theory, all sports are open to both sexes but the boys very rarely played netball and the girls were not included in the structured sports' periods of footballs. However, they did attempt to join the lads' game during playtime (especially in Dock Side and Applegate) or, instead have their own game of football (Lintonbray). Usually both forms of attempt were frustrated due to the fact that, in the former case, the lads refused to let them join in and, in the latter, they obstructed the girls' game by appropriating as much space as possible for themselves.

The girls in the schools were aware to varying degrees that things were more than a little unfair. When trying to share in the privileges allotted to the boys in relation to sports and games, most of the girls voiced their complaints on an individual basis or jointly in a spontaneous fashion:

> The top junior teacher, Mr. Smales, announced that the boys were to be taken to the park for football practice. The girls protested:
> 'That's not fair Sir, why can't we go?'
> 'Because you aren't in the football team' replied Mr. Smales.

Some of the girls carried on voicing their opposition but most resigned themselves to the situation. There were some girls who consistently got together and posed quite a problem for the boys (and even the teachers). The example has previously been discussed of the four girls in Applegate.

Together they formed a force which the boys felt quite incapable of taking on:

> Elizabeth and Sally proceeded at morning playtime to move into a boys' game of football, having had their own game spoiled by this same group the previous day. The boys became angry and one, Gavin, made a move towards Sally, but Joanne took the boy by surprise and made a counter-attack and promptly Gavin took to his heels.

When girls collectively organized to contest the areas of male power and privilege it can be seen, in certain situations, that the boys do back down. But they can and did always fall back on the structure that exists to admonish those girls who were labelled 'deviant'.

In the Dock Side playground my attention was drawn to a group of boys who were indulging in social and sexual gestures modelled on the sexual power relationships of the adult heterosexual world (Rich, 1980; Friedman and Sarah, 1982). On particular occasions an unsuspecting girl was forced into the doorway of the boys' toilets and her underclothes were interfered with. On another occasion one boy exposed himself to a girl in the same toilets, whilst two of his friends held her. This form of physical and sexual aggression was the most basic display of the boys' attempts to dominate the girls. It does not follow that *all* the boys indulged in such behaviour; they do not have to for it to have the effect of maintaining control over the girls, who avoided particular areas of the playgrounds lest they should fall prey to that kind of harrassment. This kind of 'behaviour' was by no means restricted to Dock Side but also existed in Applegate:

> On one occasion whilst observing playground behaviour I was nearly knocked over by a terrified girl who took up a position behind me in order to protect herself from a pursuing boy;
>
> 'Miss, he's trying to lift my dress up' she yelled.
>
> 'I'm only playing' was his reply.

For the most part, girls inevitably tended to avoid direct confrontation with the boys and confined themselves to bridled indignation, especially when the boys had a way of making them 'run the gauntlet' to the toilets in Dock side (Clarricoates, 1981). But towards the end of my time of observation in this school the boys had been checked to a certain extent, especially outside the toilets. This was mainly due to Kerry, whom I have mentioned previously. It was she who had the notion of posting 'look outs' in the strategic parts of the playground not only to have a clear run to the girls' toilets but also to avoid some of the worst forms of sexual harrassment that the boys indulged in. However this kind of resistance is only limited unless challenges are made against the structures within the schools.

Conclusions

Throughout this section I have shown that in all the schools there existed a dominant/subordinate relationship between the male and female pupils and have itemized some of the differing mechanisms of that power relationship.

It was noted that gender was a category which defined haviour as 'appropriate' or 'inappropriate' to the members of groups and that this contributed to a pupil's acceptance or rejection by the peer group. Conformity and deviation varied within the school (or group) as it did between the schools, with social class, on certain occasions, being an important factor behind these variations.

The focus of attention has been upon the exclusion of girls by boys from those areas that represent status and power, the forms of exclusion used and the ways in which the girls adapted to these forms, together with the status that an individual or a group manages to acquire. 'Silly' and 'thick' though the low-academic and disruptive boys may appear to the girls, nevertheless the boys' 'gang' is 'the club' and the main route to power. Girls were excluded and encouraged to grow up taking other people's needs (mainly males) and wishes into account; to service others. The tasks that the girls undertook within the class and which they saw as a way of gaining some form of influence were usually connected with servicing others. They were excluded from male association — whether in the form of games, play and 'masculine' rituals which enhance male domination.

Although boys constantly made attempts to subordinate the girls this does not mean that girls are necessarily passive. In some ways, in fact, they are more active than the boys in that they have to work out:

(a)   what is going on;
(b)   how to deal with the boys; and
(c)   how to redirect their ambitions

Within each school notions of 'femininity', were an important part of the cultural repertoire and it was these notions that helped (in part) to construct the differing positions between the male and female pupils. In the case of the working class pupils, the interaction of class and gender categories took a particular form: the boys celebrated their 'masculinity' and manifested this in their general behaviour, inside and outside the school itself, by dominating verbal and physical space whenever and wherever possible.

In the middle class school of Applegate there was a suffusion of rigid notions of 'femininity' which exacted greater 'gender-appropriate' behaviour from the girls than did the other schools, whilst the manifestations of 'masculinity' amongst the boys appeared less 'brutish'. It was obvious that a gender power relationship did exist between male and female pupils in this school. Verbal and physical space was dominated by the boys in and around the school confines.

The boys, whatever their social class, have learned to mark themselves off from the girls, and construct a status hierarchy from which they exclude the girls by various means. This status hierarchy has greater credence than anything that the girls create as an alternative because that status hierarchy both functions within the school (through its organisation, the curriculum and subject content) and is expressed and authenticated by the macro-structure of the culture in which we exist. However, we can also see that the girls are not necessarily compliant and passive in the face of male antagonism. Aware of the confrontation and ridicule that they have to contend with (especially sexual), the girls not only segregated themselves off from the boys but were working out ways of resistance to combat male power.

Notes

1 The last ten years have produced considerable theoretical and empirical work illustrating gender differentiation in schooling (see for example Sharpe, S. (1976) *Just Like A Girl*, Harmondsworth, Penguin; Deem, R. (1978) *Women and Schooling*, London, Routledge and Kegan Paul; Delamont, S. (1980) *Sex Roles and the School*, London, Methuen; Spender, D. (1982) *Invisible Girls: The Schooling Scandal*, London, Writers and Readers; Stanworth, M. (1983) *Gender and Schooling*, London, Hutchinson).

2 See the collection of papers in Deem, R. (Ed.) (1980) *Schooling for Women's Work*, London, Routledge and Kegan Paul; and Walker, S. and Barton, L. (Eds) (1983) *Gender, Class and Education*, Lewes, Falmer Press, particularly from the latter collection Anyon, J. (1983) 'Intersections of gender and class: Accommodation and resistance by working class and affluent females to contradictory sex-role ideologies' and from Deem's collection see Llewellyn, M. 'Studying girls at school: The implications of confusion'.

3 For an interesting discussion on the loci of decision-making and the 'determinants' of educational structure see Cully, L. and Demaine, J. (1983) 'Social theory, social relations and education' in Walker, S. and Barton, L. (Eds) *Gender, Class and Education*, Lewes, Falmer Press.

4 Nava, M. (1984) has asserted that a critical analysis of the relationship between boys and girls rarely appears and she stresses the importance of such an analysis. See her paper 'Youth service provision, social order and the question of girls' in McRobbie, A. and Nava, M. (Eds) *Gender and Generation*, London, Macmillan.

5 Early research indicated that the social class position of parents determined a child's school career, see Newson, J. and Newson, E. (1977) *Perspectives on School at Seven Years Old*, London, George Allen and Unwin.

6 See Holley, L. (1985) for a more detailed discussion of the exclusion of girls from football and what this means to them.

7 Janet Finch (1983) showed how women actively create and sustain hierarchically arranged social divisions. She goes on to state that 'far from being simply the passive recipients of a social position based on their husband's occupation' the 'respectables' in her study engaged in constructing their *own* position. See her paper 'Dividing the rough and the respectable: Working class women and pre-

school playgrounds' in Gamarnikow, E. *et al.* (Eds) *The Public and the Private*, London, Heinemann.

8 For a more detailed analysis of patriarchal structures in primary schools see Clarricoates, K. (forthcoming) *Gender and Power in Primary Schools*, Cambridge, Polity Press.

9 *Ibid.*

Acknowledgements

I would like to thank the editor of this volume for his patience and constructive criticism on the long overdue and over-long first draft of this chapter. I also owe many thanks to Nicola Griffiths for her helpful suggestions and comments during the final draft.

References

BELOTTI, G. (1975) *Little Girls*, London, Writers and Readers.

BYRNE, E. (1978) *Women and Education*, London, Tavistock.

CLARRICOATES, K. (1978) 'Dinosaurs in the classroom: A re-examination of some aspects of the "hidden" curriculum in the primary schools', *Women's Studies International Quarterly*, 1, 4, pp. 353–64.

CLARRICOATES, K. (1980) 'The importance of being Ernest ... Emma ... Tom ... Jane ...: The perception and categorisation of gender deviation and gender conformity in primary schools' in DEEM, R. (Ed.) *Schooling for Women's Work*, London, Routledge and Kegan Paul.

CLARRICOATES, K. (1981) 'The experience of patriarchal schooling', *Interchange*, 12, 2/3, pp. 185–206.

CLARRICOATES, K. (forthcoming) 'There's no place like home? Fatherhood in the primary school' in POLLOCK, S. and SUTTON, J. (Eds) *Women and the Politics of Fatherhood*, London, Women's Press.

CLARRICOATES, K. (forthcoming) *Gender and Power in Primary School*, Cambridge, Polity Press.

DAVIES, L. (1979) 'Deadlier than the male? Girls' conformity and deviance in school' in BARTON, L. and MEIGHAN, S. (Eds) *Schools, Pupils and Deviance*, Driffield, Nafferton.

DEEM, R. (Ed.) (1980) *Schooling for Women's Work*, London, Routledge and Kegan Paul.

DEEM, R. (Ed.) (1984) *Co-education Reconsidered*, Milton Keynes, Open University Press.

EVANS, T. (1979) 'Creativity, sex-role socialisation and pupil-teacher interaction in early schooling', *Sociological Review*, 27, pp. 139–55.

FRIEDMAN, S. and SARAH, E. (Eds) (1982) *On the Problem of Men*, London, Women's Press.

GRIFFIN, C. (1985) *Typical Girls? Young Women From School to the Labour Market*, London, Routledge and Kegan Paul.

INGLEBY, J.D. and COOPER, E. (1974) 'How teachers perceive first year school children', *Sociology*, 8, 3, pp. 463–73.

HOLLY, L. (1985) 'Mary, Jane and Virginia Woolf: Ten year-old girls talking' in WEINER, G. (Ed.) *Just a Bunch of Girls*, Milton Keynes, Open University Press.

MAHONEY, P. (1985) *Schools for the Boys? Co-education Reassessed*, London, Hutchinson.

POLLARD, A. (1985) *The Social World of the Primary School*, London, Holt, Rinehart and Winston.

RICH, A. (1979) *On Lies, Secrets and Silence: Selected Prose, 1966–1978*, New York, Norton.

RICH, A. (1980) 'Compulsory heterosexuality and lesbian existence', *Signs*, 5, 4, pp. 631–60.

SHAW, J. (1977) 'Sexual divisions in the classroom', paper given at the Teaching Girls to be Women conference, April, Essex.

SMITH, S. (1984) 'Single-sex setting' in DEEM, R. (Ed.) *Co-education Reconsidered*, Milton Keynes, Open University Press.

SPENDER, D. and SARAH, E. (1980) *Learning to Lose*, London, Women's Press.

STANWORTH, M. (1983) *Gender and Schooling: A Study of Sexual Divisions in the Classroom*, London, Hutchinson.

WALKER, S. and BARTON, L. (Eds) (1983) *Gender, Class and Education*, Lewes, Falmer Press.

WEINER, G. (Ed.) (1985) *Just a Bunch of Girls*, Milton Keynes, Open University Press.

WHYLDE, J. (Ed.) (1983) *Sexism in the Secondary Curriculum*, London, Harper and Row.

WOLPE, A. (1977) *Some Processes in Sexist Education*, London, Women's Research and Resources Centre.

WOOD, J. (1984) 'Groping towards sexism: Boys' sex talk' in McROBBIE, A. and NAVA, M. (Eds) *Gender and Generation*, London, Macmillan.

13 Stories Children Tell

Veronica and John Lee with Maggie Pearson

The Swann Report (DES, 1985) challenges teachers in all schools and perhaps particularly in all-white schools to create and operate a multi-cultural, multiracial curriculum. It notes that:

> Britain is a multiracial and multicultural society and all pupils must be enabled to understand what this means, . . . [and that] . . . it is . . . necessary to combat racism, to attack inherited myths and stereotypes, and the ways in which they are embodied in institution-al practices. (para. 418)

This chapter offers a description of the work of three teachers — two class teachers and a polytechnic lecturer — in very different schools, attempting to meet the challenge of Swann. It focusses on the teachers' and children's perspectives, and is thus very much the viewpoint of insiders. The authors of the paper, Veronica and John Lee, worked collaboratively in Veronica's classroom at Riverside Primary School, not merely on the project but on other areas of the curriculum. Collaboration between Veronica Lee's work at Riverside Primary School and Maggie Pearson's work at Park Primary School was established by a deliberate attempt to follow a similar curriculum with their classes of mixed third and fourth year juniors and by the development of inter-school visiting.

The Situation

The schools were very different. Park School, a recently amalgamated junior mixed and infants school, was racially and culturally mixed, but almost entirely working-class. It has Afro-Caribbean black children, Sikh children, Moslem children, whose parents came mainly from Pakistan, and working-class white children. Although housed in pleasant new build-ings, this was a typical inner-city school.

Riverside School was socially but not racially mixed. A small junior mixed and infants school, it was housed in rambling old buildings on the edge of a very fashionable inner-city suburb. The population of the school was split between the children of the professional middle classes and working-class children from nearby council flats. There was only one black child in the school; the daughter of a doctor. Interestingly, the incidence of family break-up and single parent families was higher in Riverside and was most common amongst middle-class children, somewhat belieing the stereotype of 'inner-city schools'.

Both class teachers were and are personally committed not merely to multicultural education but also to positive action against racism. Maggie Pearson from Park works in a school already committed to the multicultural ideal. It is clearly the sort of school where multicultural curriculum practice is easiest to establish. Such practice can be seen to be directly relevant to the lives of the children in the school and they provided a rich resource of cultural diversity. It was of course in the interest of the school to foster good cultural and race relations. The question of anti-racist practice was, though, more problematic; as politicized education it had not gained the total agreement of the staff of the school and in this Maggie Pearson and one or two other teachers in the school had been identified as at best radicals, at worst extremists. The situation for Veronica Lee was very different. She was in the positon of having to argue forcibly for a multicultural and anti-racist approach since it had no 'natural constituency' in her class and school. In a curious way, the Swann Report was more relevant to her situation in that it provided authoritative backing for her arguments. It also needs to be stressed that unlike Maggie Pearson's classroom, Veronica Lee's classroom did not have an immediately recognizable resource of cultural diversity.

A common problem the two teachers shared was posed by the problematic nature of educational theory in the field of multicultural and anti-racist education and here we have in mind the polarised debate between anti-racist education and multicultural education.

We can take Chris Mullard (1982) as representative of the anti-racist critique of multiculturalism. He has argued that multicultural education is underprinned by the liberal ideologies of integrationism and cultural pluralism and this represents a deliberate attempt to cool out black opposition to injustice (cf. Mullard, 1982 and 1984). The counterpart of this is that it can have little effect on white pupils since the incorporation of other cultures simply bolsters the status quo. It is the insistence on a politicized education (by politicizisation we mean that both teacher and children should articulate their positions with respect to the issue of racism), that makes anti-racism action different; it demands a commitment from the teacher to oppose racism and, in order to do this, Mullard (1984 p. 43) argues for: '*an orientation to the new black definitions (of reality)*' by both white teachers and pupils.

We take Jeffcoate to be representative of the proponents of multicultural education (Jeffcoate, 1979 and 1984). He argues that it is indeed a liberal movement and that we must seek to deal with all cultures even-handedly. The classroom is the space in which cultural differences and similarities can be explored and, hopefully, a tolerant and fair-minded citizen may be developed. His argument is fiercely against the committed politicization of anti-racist theorists:

> (if) in the possession of relevant facts, some children argue that white people are as a group intellectually superior to black people, or come out in favour of repatriation and oppose racially mixed youth clubs or whatever, we have to accept that as their privilege. (Jeffcoate, 1984 pp. 161)

As teachers we faced the problem of remaining committed to anti-racist action whilst at the same time sustaining and developing progressive primary school pedagogy in the classroom, since a progressive primary pedagogy with its emphasis on child centredness and exploration seems to be at odds with the political and moral stance of anti-racist education. With its apparent insistence of holding a 'current perspective', how can the two be reconciled? We shall return to these problems at the end of the chapter.

The two teachers decided on inter-school visiting, believing that giving the children the opportunity to meet each other would be extremely valuable, on both social and educational grounds. This kind of carefully structured inter-school visiting, it was felt, would encourage the children to share and explore each other's social perspectives, particularly those relating to race. In the ensuing discussions it was felt that such visits ought to have a common focus. Both teachers, therefore, decided to do a considerable amount of work on stereotyping, name-calling, sex roles and the general analysis of bias in the media, believing that this could contribute towards a social awareness which would be supportive of an anti-racist perspective. They both watched Thames TV's *Middle English* programme which pays particular attention to such issues. In Park School, the work on stereotyping took the form of discussing how conclusions about people were drawn from minimal evidence such as photographs and what effect captioning had on interpreting them. These children were particularly interested in how newspapers and TV presented the sort of area they lived in and they contrasted their knowledge of their locality with the view that inner-city areas are riot-torn centres of criminality. They also watched *Walrus*, a BBC programme which partly focusses on how judgments about people are made on the evidence of their voices. In Riverside School, the children also watched Yorkshire TV's *Tomorrow's People*. Tomorrow's People deliberately uses the cultural and racial variety of England as its explicit content. It uses the voices and lives of real children both to describe their own cultures and to comment on how they are received by the English community at large. Veronica Lee's records of work with one such programme are indicative of how children can, by discussion, begin to consider stereo typing and bias.

> Tomorrow's People — The programme showed a lad claiming his dislike of blacks must be hereditary as his dad didn't like them either and that football wasn't for girls. There was a sharp intake of breath and a hiss from the class — racist! sexist!

> Andrew wrote: 'I think that the child in a black jacket is a racist skinhead. How would he like it if a black person came up to him and said, "Hi, Mr. Chalky?" and thumped him?'

> Eleanor felt that: 'the boy in the jacket is racist, sexist and stupid to say what he said. I think it's good that they have girls' football teams. I think we, in our school, should have a mixed one — girls and boys. I did not like that boy at all.'

At both Riverside and the Park School considerable work was also done on bias and stereotyping in the media.

There are various points about the pedagogy employed that need clarification. The work was conducted through a continuing discussion as both teachers took the view that talking is learning and that talk is not merely teacher-to-child but child-to-child and needs considerable time. The children shared not merely content but also styles of learning and as a result we would suggest had roughly similar curriculum experiences. The curriculum and pedagogy the children shared based as it was on an educational philosophy of talking as learning, entails a belief that children are able to hold and express sophisticated social views. What we are suggesting is that children's ability to utilize powerful social perspectives can be developed through particular curriculum initiatives.

The classes joined each other on four different occasions. Park School entertained Riverside to a Diwali celebration which included a shadow puppet play, the cultural resources of Park School being presented positively to the Riverside children. Later, Park hosted an urban nature trail for Riverside, to some extent working against the stereotype of the inner city as concrete and bricks. Riverside hosted an urban trail focussing on the history and architectural environment round their school. On the second occasion they set up problem-solving activities involving collaboration between children from the different schools and also interviewed each other. In brief, this is the curriculum that the schools shared. We must now turn to what the children said and make some tentative connections with the work of Martin Francis.

What The Children Said

Francis (1984) in one of the few accounts of anti-racist primary practice, states '... that in one sense, we are merely talking about good primary practice — but in another we are talking about radical change' (p. 95). In his description of his own classroom he stresses its progressive nature, in particular upholding the importance of talk. As a result of this he shows that the children and particularly the black children are able to discuss the issue of racism (1984 pp. 99–100).

John:	Usually, when it happens (being called a name) you just want to get the person that said it, really.
Francis:	You were really angry and shaking and crying, weren't you?
Kim:	It weren't really only me that said it, it was Cheryl as well, but Cheryl got out of it so that I got all the blame.
Francis:	But what do you feel about the way we dealt with that, was it better or not?
John:	That's the best way to deal with it really. Have a talk with each child and see what you can do and when you can see which one is right or which is wrong, let that person who is wrong say they're sorry or whatever …
Francis:	Kim, do you really think you were wrong that time?
Kim:	Yea.
Francis:	And what did you think when you wrote the letter to John? Did you *feel* that or were you just doing it because you were told to?
Kim:	I weren't doing it because I was told to. I shouldn't have done it in the first place.
Francis:	What did you think, John, when you got the letter back?
John:	Yes, it's alright but usually you can't take an apology for a few minutes can you? It sticks in your mind … usually you don't like taking a letter; you like hearing it personally. Like when Kim gave me the letter I made her read it all out to me and say it first.
Lorraine:	You know, when you tell teachers something, like if you had a fight, they look at you as if they don't know you, as if you came from Mars or Jupiter or something.
John:	Yes, like you're an outer-spacer, like they've never seen you before.

Francis stresses that this is typical and John's closing remark is representative of the reality of black children.

The children in Park School, in their discussions of race and bias, showed themselves to be as aware as Francis's children, as the following typical extract shows:

Mervyn (black child):	The men that do the newspapers, they just make stories up so they get money and go to different places.

Christian:	They take pictures of some black one holding a stick, Miss, and put up riot.
Lisa:	They make it look like a bad place.
Maggie Pearson:	Is it?
Lisa:	Not really, Miss.
Mervyn:	They make you move Miss … whites. Like last time when the police shot that lady they say it was accident.
Girl (in Afro-Caribbean voice):	(teeth suck). Lies … too much lies … and don't do nothing and if it happened some other place and the colour was different.
Maggie Pearson:	Do you think it is a colour thing?
Lots of voices:	Racial.
Maggie Pearson:	Do you think it is racial?
Shazad:	If it was a black policeman shot somebody white, they'd go on about it. It like that for us.

We would expect that, having had these sorts of discussions, these children would comment strongly on the whiteness of Riverside School. This, however, was not the case. The prime focus for these children in talking about Riverside was not race but class.

Shazad:	Miss, they had different accent.
Maggie Pearson:	The way they spoke was different, was it?
Jamie:	They talk posh … ooo like that. Most of them come from Hillton.
Maggie Pearson:	Do you think all people in Hillton are posh?
Children:	Posh … Yeah, most of them.
Child:	When my dad does taxis that's the most place he goes to pick up people.

Bearing in mind the startling visual contrast between an all-white school in an all-white area and a multiracial school in a multiracial area, we would surely suspect some references to race. It is even more puzzling since Maggie Pearson provided a curriculum in which explicit reference was often made to race and racism and the children had discussed the issue on many occasions. Yet on no occasion did these children make any explicit reference to race. What these children had selected to comment on was the most important facet of their existence in these circumstances, i.e. class differentiation.

This focus on class involved them in consideration of their own stereotypes of class. Like practically all working-class children in our experience, they identified middle-class children as 'soft'. Yet the reality of Riverside is very different.

> *Shazard:* When we were playing games, the rugby game sort of like ... well, they were really rough and they said to me, Sam said to me that we didn't know how to play it and this kid, I don't know his name, and he had two bumps on his head and this is what Colin did.
>
> *Shakhil:* Miss, when we was playing American football on the floor they was all piling on me for nothing.
>
> *Lisa:* Yes, they was. They was fighting for the ball. You had the ball in your hand.
>
> *Shakhil:* To get the ball some of them pulled me along.
>
> *All:* Yeah. They're rough. They gang up on everybody. They think they're tough.
>
> *Mervyn:* When they came here a little boy he thought he was boss and if we said no ...

Would these same children have commented on the roughness of children they identified as working-class? We have no way of knowing, but a reasonable interpretation here seems to be that they are viewing things powerfully in class terms, as they comment on this soft — tough polarity. This becomes even more apparent in their discussion of the clothes of Riverside School children.

> *Liza:* Miss, the children in Riverside School. The girls wear sort of like gypsy clothes. But the boys wear fashionable clothes just like the people in this school.
>
> *Maggie Pearson:* Can you describe what you mean by gypsy clothes?
>
> *Liza:* Well, Miss, they sort of wear like long skirts and multi-coloured jumpers.
>
> *Andrea:* I think their clothes were horrible.
>
> *Maggie Pearson:* Every single one?
>
> *Andrea:* There was one girl called Beat ... no Beatrice, er, Elly, she wore quite nice clothes.
>
> *Maggie Pearson:* Do you think that's important?
>
> *Shazad:* ... big school where you have to have a uniform. Like you can have nice clothes at home but you might want to wear horrible clothes at school.
>
> *Rebecca:* Some of them in Ms. V's class ... their clothes were, I don't know how to put it, some of the boys wear nice clothes and some of them didn't and that's the same as girls as well.

Maggie Pearson: How about in this class?
Andrea: They wear fashionable.

What the children are commenting on is in their view a contradiction. Middle-class children are expected to be wealthy and this ought to be reflected in their clothes. It is obviously puzzling to these children from Park School that anyone who could afford it would not be fashionably dressed. Many of these children live in relative poverty and by comparing the Riverside School children with gypsies they were making what amounts to a moral judgment whilst at the same time revealing a lack of comprehension. Clothes are a highly significant symbol in their lives, to view others treating those symbols with apparent disrespect seems to be quite disturbing for them. We noted that they often returned to these themes of dress and accent over the period of the work.

The central puzzle remains, though, why no explicit references to race? Is the lack of such reference an indication of the failure of the curriculum described above? We do not believe so. The fact that black children in our society must constantly interact with white people is significant. In contrast to the white children's reality, as will be shown later, the black children's reality includes a consideration of a white perspective. The black children did not meet white children *per se* but white children who were not overtly racially antagonistic or patronising because of their school experience and, for some, home experience. We contend that what was important was the effect of the curriculum on the white children. The effect of this was that the black children had no need to state the obvious about race, but were enabled to broaden their discussion to tentatively locate themselves in class terms.

Thus, having begun our discussion of the way Park School children viewed their counterparts by expressing surprise as to the lack of racial reference we are reminded that meaningful contrast across class boundaries may be rarer in our society than across racial groups. We now turn to consider the impact of inter-school visits on the children of Riverside School.

Davey's (1983) work demonstrates the early acquisition and subsequent maintenance of racial prejudice. Arising from this sort of work we would expect personal prejudice to be present in all-white Riverside. One of the reasons for Veronica Lee's curriculum was to tackle precisely this problem. Racial prejudice in the area around the school was often explicit and racist remarks from children while not regular were certainly present. We would expect, then, that the contact of these white children with black children would produce comments on race and it did. We noted, though, that it produced little comment on class.

Emma: And also the coloured people go round with the coloured people.

Veronica Lee:	Do we call them coloured people or what? 'Cos I'm coloured.
Emma:	Blacks. They go round with their own.
All:	They don't.
Emma:	They do.
Anna:	They don't.
Emma:	When I went round they did.
Eleanor:	There was a load of a group of girls and about three of them were black and the others were white.

Emma asserts here, we believe, two different things. First a generalized idea that black people behave like that. It is a child's version of the adult's thoughtless racism. 'They live there because they want to be next to each other' regardless of the deliberate process of ghettoization in our society. Veronica Lee's intervention objects to the adjective 'coloured', she reminds Emma that Black is the preferred term. These children have had a great deal of experience discussing the issue of nomenclature. Such discussions are typical of anti-racist education. Emma, though, sticks to her guns. We would interpret the succeeding argument as operating for the children as an attack on stereotyping. What Emma is asserting is what she saw; the children do not seem to be denying that, they are simply rejecting it as a universal truth. It is Eleanor who by offering a contradictory bit of evidence enables the point to be made. The question of inter-racial friendships and racially mixed grouping was the subject of a good deal of discussion but what puzzled these children most was that the black children did not seem to notice that they were all white. Jo's comment exemplifies this:

Jo:	I was with Eleanor most of the time, well all of the time, and there were . . . it was odd you would have thought that it . . . they would find it weird that there wasn't any black or brown people in our class and it was odd they didn't at all; they just sort of came up to you.
Veronica Lee:	Do you thing it makes a difference what colour you are?
All:	No.
Veronica Lee:	As to what sort of person you are inside?
Rowena:	It might make a difference if you keep on being teased on your colour so you may be a bit more aggressive than white people. They don't get teased so much so they might be easily aggravated.

These white children seemed to be reaching out to try to discover the black children's reality. From their white perspective black children ought to find the situation strange; we would suggest that this was a tentative move toward reorientation. It went beyond the personal and included an appreciation of why black people live in specific areas:

> *Jo*: In the area ... if you went to a place where you get houses — estate agents — they just sort of dump the black people in one area.

Evidence of the structural nature of racism was clearly presented here. What these children did not yet appreciate is that in our society the reality for black people is that the world is predominantly white. Jo then went on to insist 'They were black and white together' in a somewhat puzzled tone. Eleanor interpreted this in the following way: 'They weren't racist. They may have been sexist, but they weren't racist.' Here Eleanor seemed to be acutely conscious of the claim of many adults that black people are equally culpable of racism against whites. She asserted evidence to the contrary but had no difficulty naming a different sort of social judgment.

Although the children from Riverside commented regularly on the question of race there is no evidence in their talk of racist judgments. It might then be argued that they were simply taking the teacher's line, not criticizing as a matter of politeness. This explanation is not borne out, we believe, in the light of the criticism they made of the other children regarding gender relations.

> *Sam*: You can also see how the boys hang around with the boys and the girls hang around with the girls.
> *Anna*: (sotto voce) ... sexist ... uuh., because they're sexist.

This theme of sexism parallels the children's comments on race but on almost every occasion they are condemnatory.

> *Rowena*: Well, when they last came to our school and it was playtime they all went — all the girls went together — and all the boys were joining in with each other.
> *Veronica Lee*: So our boys were just as sexist as their boys were they, Rowena?
> *Rowena*: Yes (giggle).

The children's perceptions very much matched those of the teacher. We noted that at Riverside, probably because of its small size, but also because sexism was an issue in the community, the older children played together regardless of sex. In effect, school playground football was not a male-dominated game. The introduction of Park School into the children's territory had the effect of redefining the games along gender lines. This was the subject of much comment from the Riverside children, both boys and girls. Significantly, perhaps, the girls from Riverside also commented unfavourably on girls' behaviour. They viewed whispering about others as a sign of sexism.

Rowena: It's a bit sexist. Emma was playing with two girls, and I was playing with a girl called Kamalesh and I wanted to know the names of the two girls Emma was playing with, so I asked one of them what her name was and they took me off in this corner and said 'Don't tell Kamalesh what her name is' and they whispered this girl's name in my ear and then started to say really horrible things about Kamalesh.

General 'girlish giggly' behaviour was also condemned as sexist.

Conclusion

What sort of curriculum have these children been offered and what underpins it? In general curriculum terms, we must now return to the polarised debate between multicultural and anti-racist education and the nature of progressive primary school practice.

We would gloss one version of progressivism in the following manner. The Plowden Report's (CACE, 1967) famous statement: 'At the heart of the educational process lies the child' (para. 9) defined a specific version of child-centred education. In this account, 'The child is an agent of his own learning' (para. 529), for whom learning proceeds by individual discovery through first-hand experience. Knowledge is not to be divided into separate compartments rather it is integrated and as a consequence the teacher is not an initiator but rather a guide, an arranger of the environment, thus putting children in the way of things to be learnt. Crucial in this account of progressivism the state of childhood is privileged. The school 'is a community in which children learn to live first and foremost as children and not as future adults' (para. 505) We argue that the Report's emphasis on both the child as child and the child as individual makes this form of progressivism a liberal position which inevitably rules out anti-racist education as the imposition of correct opinions on children.

This version of progressivism, we would argue, underpins multicultural education. In Jeffcoate's (1984) account which we take to be representative, he lays great stress on children exploring the issues of racial and cultural diversity and drawing their own conclusions based on '*good educational experiences*'. As a liberal educator he rightly rejects the idea that exchanging the 'right' for 'wrong' content will make any significant educational change. He rejects the teacher as instructor entirely.

I asked a 12-year-old girl who had produced an admirable piece of work on the Indian independence movement what she made of it all. 'Nothing much', she replied, 'we only copied it down off the board'. She might as well have studied the Tudors and Stuarts.

We would agree with Jeffcoate that learning is different from mere intention and that children ought to be active agents of their own learning. We would also agree that the process of education should be a democratic procedure. It is in his rejection of anti-racist education as the imposition of correct views that we part company with him. His insistence on liberal individualism, we argue, colludes with the racism that as a liberal he abhors. What is needed is a different gloss on progressivism which is capable of incorporating an anti-racist stance.

A major problem for the progressive ideas presented in the Plowden Report is the presentation of childhood as a special separate state. We argue that the child ought not to be viewed in this undifferentiated way. It is clear to us that children are differentiated, as adults are, by race, class and gender and that this is highly significant. In the work reported above the children speak not merely from the perspective of the child but from the perspective of the black child, or female child or working-class child. Once children are viewed in this manner then the nature of progressive practice is subtly changed. The idea that children can and should learn by exploration is different when that learning is not merely a matter of individual interest but at least reflects the experience of the social group to which the child belongs. A significant consequence of this is that the teacher can no longer simply be a neutral chairperson. It is incumbent on us as teachers to express a value position, to take a stance against racism.

We want to argue that the idea of progressivism we are briefly presenting is a revision of the Plowden position. The focus of this variety of progressivism is a commitment to talking as learning. In accepting this position we recognize that the way people argue and what they argue for reflects their social and historical experience. Thus, we wish to state that in discussions of racial issues both teachers and children recognize each other as black and white.

The insistence of anti-racist educators on the rectitude of their political and moral stance would seem to rule out this form of progressivism. If anti-racist education takes the course of the instruction of children in 'correct perspectives', then Jeffcoate's criticism that it is merely a form of indoctrination is justified but we argue that such practices cannot form the basis of anti-racist education. We take the view that racism stands in total opposition to democracy and that to engage in anti-racism education involves us in a democratic struggle. It is basic to anti-racist teaching that children can and should engage in democratic processes and we would argue that the primary school classroom is an important site for such involvement. If the children are to explore the issue around race and racism the classroom must be so arranged that children can share each others' perspectives.

Mullard (1984) argues for a strategy and practice of anti-racist education as having three broad aims viz: orientation, observation and opposition. He calls first for a reorientation of white children towards a new reality, a Black perspective, and states that this can only come about by observation that is by listening and learning from black children's experience, by trying to understand their perspectives. This would be purely academic if opposition to racism is not engendered by the process. We agree with these aims but note that both the tone of Mullard's writing and its non-engagement with issues of pedagogy make its anti-racist education seem like a process of instruction rather than one of education. In the work we report here we have stressed that children are able to operate powerful social concepts and that they can articulate their own perspectives. It seems to us that to establish anti-racist education as a democratic process it must be underpinned by a progressive pedagogy. In our reviewed form we tentatively suggest that progressive practice values cooperation and collaboration through talk rather than simply individual exploration and opens the way to critical enquiry.

References

CENTRAL ADVISORY COUNCIL ON EDUCATION (1967) *Children and Their Primary Schools*, (The Plowden Report), London, HMSO.

DAVEY, A. (1983) *Learning To Be Prejudiced*, London, Arnold.

DEPARTMENT OF EDUCATION AND SCIENCE (1985) *Education For All*, (The Swann Report), London, HMSO.

FRANCIS, M. (1984) 'Anti-racist teaching: Curricular practices', *Challenging Racism*, London, ALTARF.

JEFFCOATE, R. (1979) *Positive Image*, London, Writers and Readers.

MULLARD, C. (1982) 'Multi-racial education in Britain: From assimilation to pluralism' in TIERNEY, J. (Ed.) *Race, Migration and Schooling*, London, Holt.

MULLARD, C. (1984) *Anti-Racist Education: The Three O's*, London, National Association for Multicultural Education.

14 Towards an Anti-racist Initiative in the All White Primary School: A Case Study

Geoffrey Short and Bruce Carrington

In this chapter we address the need for an anti-racist intervention in the all white primary school and suggest how facets of primary teachers' pedagogic discourse may be inimical to its implementation. The major ideological constraint upon which we focus is 'sequential developmentalism' (Alexander, 1984) — the belief that children pass through a series of qualitatively distinct and hierarchically ordered cognitive stages and can only master a given type of intellectual activity when they have reached the appropriate stage. Piaget (1924), for example, asserts that most children at primary school are unable to think in the abstract. If he is correct, then such children should experience difficulty in understanding the concept of racism, especially if they live in a mono-ethnic environment. We examine this hypothesis by describing and evaluating an anti-racist project undertaken with a fourth year class at an all white junior school. Issues raised by anti-racist teaching (ART) will be discussed with reference to the case study.

Although endorsed by a growing number of LEAs, ART remains the subject of controversy and debate. In contrast to less overtly political approaches to race and ethnicity in education, (ie. forms of multicultural education — MCE), ART has aroused considerable passion among practitioners, academics and politicians and has also attracted unfavourable comment in the press (see, for instance, *The Times* editorial, 28 March 1986). Similarly, at the chalk face, far more resistance has been shown to ART than to MCE (Troyna and Ball, 1985). Schools in all white areas, however, have tended to eschew both types of intervention (DES, 1985)

Whilst it may be misleading to depict these diffuse ideologies as mutually exclusive or implacably hostile (Leicester, 1986; Lynch, 1985) they clearly differ in tenor and thrust. Whereas multiculturalists are principally concerned to celebrate cultural diversity, overcome curricular ethnocentrism and increase inter-group tolerance, anti-racists stress the need for schools to play a more active role in combating forms of racism at an institutional as well as an individual level. They also advocate fundamental reappraisal of both the formal and hidden curriculum and insist that all schools teach about racism and take steps to promote racial equality and justice.

Although the Swann Report (DES, 1985) has been criticized for offering at best only limited support for anti-racist principles and practices (Naguib, 1986; NAME, 1985), it does acknowledge the need for all schools, *irrespective of phase or ethnic composition*, to deal openly and directly with the issue of racism and to consider its origins and manifestations as part of a wider programme of political education (DES, 1985, p. 336).

The Need for Anti-racism

There is abundant evidence for asserting that racial attitudes in many children are well advanced by the time they start school. Much of this evidence originated in the United States where the conclusion reached by Horowitz (1936) has consistently been supported. He claimed that:

> the development of prejudice against Negroes begins very, very early in the life of the ordinary child ... boys barely over 5 years of age demonstrated a preference for whites ... Some few attempts at testing special cases at 3 and 4 elicited such comments as (from a 3 year old) 'I don't like black boys' and (from a 4 year old) 'I don't like coloured boys'. (pp. 117–8).

A relatively recent British study that corroborates Horowitz's findings was conducted by Jeffcoate (1979) in a Bradford nursery school. It was undertaken in order to refute the widely held and 'commonsensical' view that children below statutory school age are incapable of articulating racist sentiments. Predictably, he found that when the teacher invited children to comment on a set of pictures representing Black people in 'a variety of situations and in a respectful and unstereotyped way' their response could not possibly be construed as racist. However, when the same set of pictures were left 'casually' around the room, (but in locations close to concealed tape recorders), the remarks made by a different but equivalent group of children, in the assumed absence of an adult audience, were undeniably racist in tone. This study not only highlights the existence of racism in the very young, but shows that such children are well aware of its taboo status. They know that teachers are likely to censure any form of racist expression.

For those who doubt the value of experimental data, there exists the press accounts of primary school children's involvement in racist activity (see, for example. Stephens, 1983), the reported experiences of primary school teachers (for example, Francis, 1984; Galton, 1986), and the fictionalized accounts of such experiences by those likely to have witnessed them at first hand. A good example of the latter is '*The Trouble with Donovan Croft*' by Bernard Ashley, headteacher of a multiracial primary school in London. The book includes several vignettes of racist name calling by 10 year-olds and sensitively describes how Donovan (an Afro-Caribbean of the same age) reacts to it.

> (He) could think of many times when his mother had comforted him so; when as a little boy he had fallen out with a good friend and been surprised to be called unpleasant names with so much feeling; when, older and more sensitive, other boys who liked him ... affectionately called him Sambo or Blackie instead of Donovan. (p. 85)

That children as young as three years of age are able to construe the world in racial, (and indeed racist) terms is no longer in dispute (Thomas, 1984). Moreover, this potential for incipient racism is continually nurtured by the myths and stereotypes that abound in popular culture (Lawrence, 1982). For this reason, ART has clear relevance at primary level and especially, as the Swann Committee recognized, in all white areas:

> Whilst most people would accept that there may be a degree of inter-racial tension between groups in schools with substantial ethnic minority populations, it might generally be felt that racist attitudes and behaviour would be less common in schools with few or no ethnic minority pupils ... we believe this is far from the case. (DES, 1985, p. 36)

A number of factors, however, militate against ART in the primary school, particularly in all white areas, and it is to a consideration of these factors that we now turn.

Obstacles to Anti-racist Teaching

Alexander (1984) contends that:

> Nobody familiar with the culture of primary schools can doubt the pervasiveness of ... the language of child-centredness, the verbal expression of an ideology which remains in the 1980s as powerful ... as it was in the 1960s. (p. 15)

Empirical support for this contention is provided by King's (1978) study of three infant schools. He claimed that the teachers operated within a clearly articulated child-centred ideology having four components, two of which may function as obstacles to ART. First is the belief in childhood innocence — the idea that whilst children of primary school age, and especially infants, can behave in socially unacceptable ways, they nevertheless remain free from malicious intent. Noxious influences on behaviour are assumed to reside in the outside world rather than within the child who has, therefore, to be protected from a pernicious reality. Ross (1984) makes much the same point when discussing the reluctance of primary school teachers to involve their pupils in political education. He writes:

> It would be fair to say that most primary school teachers have never considered politically educating their children. For many of them this is because they would (correctly) regard the notion of politics as being necessarily concerned with ... conflict and a lack of consensus, and feel that such harsh realities have no place in the comfortable view of the world that their primary schools propagate to children. (p. 131)

In addition to childhood innocence, King identified amongst his sample of infant teachers a belief in 'sequential developmentalism' and the allied notion of 'readiness'. The former refers to a stage-related conception of cognitive development; the latter to an acceptance that stages define the limits to a child's intellectual competence. In so far as political education is seen as demanding the ability to grasp abstract concepts, children below the age of 11/12, and who, in the main, have yet to attain the Piagetian stage of formal operations, may be thought incapable of benefiting from any sort of political intervention. An over-rigid adherence to sequential developmentalism is thus the second major constraint on ART in the primary school. A further constraint affects only those schools in all white areas where there may well be a feeling that 'we have no problem here' ('problem' in this context referring to the presence of children from ethnic minorities). However, the active recruitment of secondary school pupils by neo-fascist groups in these areas (see *Times Educational Supplement*, 20 June 1986) should, in itself, alert local primary schools to the possible dangers of non-intervention. In the light of this stricture, we now report on our own experience of anti-racist teaching at an all white primary school.

The Case Study

Rationale

In recent years, many criticisms have been levelled at Piaget's research findings (for example, Donaldson, 1978), and thus at various implications of sequential developmentalism. We were primarily interested in this project to explore the extent to which these criticisms apply to ART, for one of the latter's untested assumptions is that primary school children *are* able to cope conceptually with teaching about racism. We were also concerned at the tendency for classroom practitioners to spurn the findings of much educational research on account of its artificial nature and its perceived pedagogical irrelevance. For this reason, the project was carried out as part of the normal curriculum of a fourth year junior class taught by Geoffrey Short. Bruce Carrington visited the school throughout the year as research consultant.

The School

The project was undertaken at Oldtown primary — an SPA school located in the heart of a mining area with current levels of adult and youth unemployment well above the national average. The school's intake is almost exclusively working class.

Whilst relationships between members of staff (including the head) and between staff and children were generally relaxed, there was little about the school that would merit the epithet 'progressive'. Despite the bonhomie of the staffroom and the accessibility of the head, there was no evidence of coordinated initiatives in any sphere of curriculum development. Race was no exception, although it should be noted that a few individuals had made modest concessions to cultural pluralism in their teaching. [The children involved in our project, for example, had been acquainted with some of the tenets of the world's major religions.]

Pedagogical Considerations

In planning this work, we took cognizance of the stance adopted by pluralists and anti-racists alike against strong forms of relativism (Zec, 1980). Accepting the view that some beliefs are so morally abhorrent and at variance with rational universals as to be actively proscribed by the teacher (see Lynch, 1983; Milner, 1983), we ensured that racist beliefs were unequivocally challenged during class discussion. This did not, however, inhibit us from making a concerted effort to democratize the classroom, believing, along with Allport (1954), that issues of social justice and equality can only be meaningfully explored where a serious attempt is made to 'reduce the unequal communication rights between teachers and learners' (Edwards and Furlong, 1978, p. 242)

The Project — 'In Living Memory'

The project had its origins in work done on the Second World War during the spring term. This had entailed introducing the children to the concepts of democracy and dictatorship and had also offered an obvious opportunity to broach the issue of racism when an abridged version of *The*

Diary of Anne Frank had been read to the class. 'In Living Memory' began the following term and was essentially an examination of economic, cultural and social change in post-war Britain. Employing a variety of media (fiction, drama, autobiography, film, other artifacts and museum visits), it dealt with different aspects of popular culture and lifestyles. It also explored changes in the structure of the labour market.

We chose to teach about race as part of an integrated project for two reasons. The first was to avoid the danger of artificiality stemming from a lack of a broad historical perspective; the second was to prevent the children from feeling that they were being 'got at'. We were aware of examples of ART proving counterproductive (for example, Miller, 1969; Verma and Bagley, 1979; Robertson, 1986) and we thought that if the children interpreted our teaching as preaching, they would resent it and react either with indifference or outright opposition.

We approached the issue of racism via changes in the world of work. The children were asked to question their parents and grandparents about the various jobs they had had since leaving school and during a follow up discussion these reminiscences were examined in the context of changing employment patterns since 1945. The class later divided into small friendship groups which were given the task of 'solving the present crisis of unemployment'. Some of the ideas that flowed from this exercise were subsequently resurrected in the form of improvized drama. Here the children revealed considerable maturity in their understanding of unemployment in terms of its social and personal ramifications. In one group, for example, the 'father' was at pains to distinguish between getting the sack and being declared redundant in order to convince his 'wife' that he was not responsible for his predicament.

On a second occasion, the groups were asked how they would solve the acute labour shortage of the immediate post-war years. It was this activity which led, quite naturally, into the area of race and immigration for, in every group, one proposed solution was to seek workers from overseas. We felt that this link between unemployment and immigration was important on two counts. First, because it permitted the issues of immigration and racism to arise spontaneously; secondly, because we suspected that some of the children had had their first acquaintance with racist 'logic' in the context of unemployment. In other words, parents, (in the presence of their children), blaming Afro-Caribbean and Asian workers for the loss of jobs. In support of this speculation, one pupil, Terry, prior to any discussion of immigration, actually said, 'my dad thinks it is all the Blacks here that causes unemployment'. This misconception was immediately contested by Bruce Carrington. [The frequency of such scapegoating among young people in all white areas has recently been demonstrated by Mould, 1986].

We illustrate below some examples of children's written work on the topic of 'Solving the Labour Shortage'. The extracts betray a predictably limited understanding of basic economics but the critical need to attract workers from overseas — an idea that was not in any way prompted by either Geoffrey Short or Bruce Carrington — featured prominently in *every* child's proposed remedies.

> *Jenny*: We could solve (the labour shortage) by getting the people who emigrated to come back and work in the old jobs. Ask people from an over-populated country such as China and let them work here.
>
> *Kevin*: If I was the government, I would move businesses to other countries or bring other workers from America and all over the world, give them free accomodation and free board . . .

By making no reference, either direct or indirect, to the New Commonwealth, these representative comments suggest that the class, initially, failed to appreciate the racial dimension to post-war labour migration. Such lack of awareness was especially evident when Allison, one of the more academically successful pupils, attempted to evaluate immigration as a solution to the problem.

> A good way to solve over (full) employment is to bring people from other countries to come and work in Britain. A good way is to ask men to come over and have children. It is a good idea because when the children grow up they will go straight for a job. It is a bad idea because some women might not be able to have children.

In order to undermine further the myth of immigration as a cause of unemployment, the children were informed, with the aid of archive photographs, of London Transport's recruitment drive in the West Indies. They were then asked to design their own posters inviting workers to come to Britain. Kathy, appreciating the need to offer potential migrants a range of incentives, referred in her poster to the prospect of better accomodation in Britain. She then proceeded to contrast mud huts and brick built houses. The unwitting racism of the picture was privately pointed out to her and, in a later session, the class discussed the role of the media and of comics in particular, in transmitting unflattering images of the Third World.

Having examined issues surrounding the labour shortage — how it arose and how it was solved — we then explored the nature and experience of the migration to Britain from Europe, (including Eire), and the New Commonwealth. The children were provided with background information on the sending countries, the scale and timing of the migration and the main areas of settlement in Britain. Motives underlying the migration and the different types of work undertaken on arrival were also mentioned, but our chief concern in this and subsequent sessions was with the children's untutored understanding of the issue of racism. They were given two tasks. The first was to imagine that they had recently entered Britain from either the West Indies or the Indian sub-continent and were writing a letter home to a close relative or good friend who was thinking of joining them. The class discussion that preceded the writing was intended to excavate the ideas which the children already possessed; no attempt, at this stage, was made either to refine them or to suggest more plausible alternatives. In these 'letters', various references were made to manifestations of racial violence, racist name-calling and discriminatory practices in housing and work. The following extracts are typical of the children's response.

John: ... us Black people get beat up as soon as we get off the ship. Would you fancy having to take your luggage everywhere by yourself while people just look and laugh at you as you go from house to house trying to get a place to spend the night? Just guess what their reply was after me begging for a bed. It was 'sorry, it's already been took' or just a simple 'no, get lost. We don't give rooms to niggers like you.' In the end, when you get a house, they throw you out just because you were not used to their terrible food that they call pasties. And what about the jobs that you said were very good for someone like me? Oh, I got a job alright. It was a dishwasher in a rotten old fish and chip shop where the dishes must have been at least twenty years old. Then I got kicked out for dropping an old chipped plate by accident.

Clare: ... I never thought it would be like this as we all get on so well back in India. I advise you to stay at home and forget about Britain. The other day I decided to start looking for a job. As you know, I have plenty of skills. I thought even if nobody likes me, I'll be sure to get a good decent job but I was wrong. Instead, I got an awful job cleaning toilets. Over here, that's all they seem to think we're good for. Anyway, I started this job today. It was horrible, people pushing you around. One person even flushed my head down the toilet. I wish I never brought Julian, our son, to school. All he ever does is get picked on. He came home the other day covered with bruises and cuts. I am having second thoughts about staying here. Most people are prejudiced.

Despite occasional strains on the credulity, ('... get beat up as soon as we get off the ship'), these imaginative accounts provide clear evidence of the children's awareness of racism in its various forms. John's allusion to food is of particular interest in that it shows how some children of primary school age are able to grasp the relationship of racism to ethnocentrism. Clare's 'letter' in common with many others, is noteworthy in that it demonstrates some cognizance of stereotyping, ('that's all they seem to think we're good for'), — a concept which had not been mentioned in the previous class discussion. Her 'letter' is also of interest because it refers directly to the gap between the immigrant expectation of life in Britain and the actual experience. In drawing the session to a close, the children were given an opportunity to compare their own piece of writing with black autobiographical accounts of the period (see Husband, 1982).

The second task we set the children was not only an alternative means to gaining insight into their understanding of racism; it was also an attempt to show them that British born Afro-Caribbeans and Asians face many of the difficulties which had earlier confronted their parents and grandparents. We were further concerned at this juncture to counter populist racist rhetoric which utilizes the word 'immigrant' both as a symbolic marker to separate 'them' from us and to support the claim that people of Afro-Caribbean and Asian origin do not belong in this country.

The task itself was modelled on Nixon's (1985) 'direct approach' to racism awareness teaching. This ideally involves presenting the children 'with a clearly defined situation and a central character with which they could easily identify'. The class then engage in small group discussion in order to deal with problematic aspects of the situation. Nixon asserts that:

> The one essential requirement governing (use of the direct approach) is that the teacher should have achieved a good working relationship with the group and that the pupils should be capable of sustaining frank and open discussions with one another. (p. 76)

With our commitment to redressing the 'unequal communication rights between teachers and learners', every effort was made to meet this condition.

The actual cameo read to the class was as follows:

> You are playing in the street where you live when a pantechnicon draws up and unloads. Mr. Taylor, a lorry driver from Birmingham, gets out. He says he's gots a couple of 11-year-old children and he wants advice about this school. What will you tell him?

Almost as an afterthought, the researcher then added:

> Oh, by the way, the family is black, from the West Indies, but the kids were born in England.

The children discussed their response in small groups before pooling their ideas in a plenary session. One of the more interesting aspects of the class discussion was the length of time which elapsed before any reference was made to race. To begin with, the children 'presented Mr. Taylor' with seemingly innocuous information about school meals, the demeanour and gait of the headmaster and the control strategies of Geoffrey Short. Their tendency to eschew the question of race suggests either that the issue, (as in Jeffcoate's study), was considered an embarrassing and improper subject for public discourse or, more simply, that these particular children, under 'normal' circumstances, just do not construe the world in racial terms. The latter explanation may be the more convincing in view of the clamour to express an opinion on race following John's remark:

John:	I wouldn't count on anyone liking your kids.
GS:	What do you mean?
John:	They'll be black and everyone else in the school's got a different colour skin and won't mix with them.
Everybody:	The lads and lassies will skit them (poke fun at them) all the time.
Patsy:	I think the teachers will ignore them as well as the other children.
GS:	Why do you think that?
Patsy:	I just don't think the teachers would like them or get on with them.
GS:	Do you think the teachers would see the black children as different from the white children in some way?
Patsy:	Yes, they might think that they're going to start trouble.
GS:	What do you mean?
Patsy:	Start going round children's desks, getting books out and throwing them back on the floor.
Samantha:	I don't think it's fair how they get picked on because the whites think they're different in all ways. But it's just the colour that's different not the personality.
Terry:	You can't judge people by their skin. It's the way they act (that's important).
Peter:	I'd be friendly with them cos they've as much right as white people to be in this school even though they're coloured.
Derek:	I don't think they should be picked on because they are just human beings like us. It doesn't matter what colour they are.
Samantha:	Most people (in this school) wouldn't play with them but quite a few would.
GS:	Why do you think that some white children would play with them whilst others wouldn't?
Samantha:	Because some of them could feel embarrassed about playing with coloureds.
GS:	Why?
Kathy:	Because their friends weren't playing with them so they wouldn't and if Samantha did go over and play with them, her friends would pick on her for playing with them.

GS: Why are white people so different?

John: Well I think they would get skitted even more when we're doing geography and talking about where they come from and they can answer all the questions.

At this point, Bruce Carrington intervened to stress that not only had the Taylor twins come from Birmingham but that they had also been born there. Despite this interjection, the children continued to think of the twins as in some sense alien.

Carol: Some white people are too stuck up to play with them. They don't want to play with them just because they wear different clothes to us.

Allison: They might think they're poor because they've been reading some comic. They might think they live in mud huts.

GS: That's right. That's what we discussed earlier in connection with Kathy's poster.

Terry: If I was playing with a black person and a white person came up and called them names, I'd say what do you think you'd feel like if you moved away and had to go to a school where there was a lot of coloured children? You wouldn't like it.

Patsy: I think that sometimes the mums and dads are to blame because maybe the kids have been brought up not to speak to black children.

Liz: I think the reason why white children won't play with them is ... that they like different types of things.

GS: What do you mean? What sort of things do they like?

Liz: We like pop groups in this country and they like pop groups in their country.

Peter: ... half the people in this country don't like black people because we can't go over there because we get beat up in Africa by black people.

A number of interesting points emerge from this discussion. First, the children seem to have internalized the language and logic of racist discourse which sees blacks as aliens (for example, Liz '... they like different types of things'), and physical differences as necessarily implying cultural differences, (for example, Carol 'they wear different clothes to us'). There was also evidence of confused thinking as in Peter's attempt to legitimate white racism by referring to 'white people get(ting) beat up in Africa'. Rather than perceive these comments as embryonic racism, primary teachers, committed to the notion of sequential developmentalism, may be tempted to regard the myths that they embody as supporting the view that young children are intellectually incapable of handling the issue of racism. However, opposed to this interpretation and the argument for non-intervention to which it gives rise, a number of children displayed relatively sophisticated insights. It was recognized, for example, that Blacks will often 'get skitted' and physically threatened solely on the basis of their colour; that teachers may perceive black children as trouble makers (cf. Rampton Report, DES, 1981); that white people cannot be treated as a monolithic entity and, as Samantha pointed out, that skin colour is not automatically associated with personality. The crucial role of parental precept as a determinant of children's racial attitudes was also acknowledged. But perhaps of most importance were those comments indicating an ability to view racism from the standpoint of the victim, (for example, Terry: 'I'd say what do you think you'd feel like if . . . you had to go to a school where there was a lot of coloured children?') without this ability, no anti-racist intervention can hope to succeed.

Not surprisingly, the children's written work on 'The Taylor Twins' First Day at School', reflected many of the themes mentioned in the class discussion. For example, Kathy's story reveals some understanding of individual racism and an awareness that not all white people succumb to it. Although her story may also reveal an inclination to combat racism, she nonetheless chooses to give the children non-English first names as symbolic markers to differentiate them from others at the school.

> One day two new children started at Oldtown School. They were coloured children and so they got picked on. The other children thought these children were going to be white like them, but when the children walked in, everybody stared at them. They felt very strange when they walked in. Even the teacher was astonished to see coloured children, but the teacher never bullied them like the children did. They told them the wrong way to the tuck shop, kicked them and then called them names. There was one girl in the class called Samantha who felt sorry for them. She made friends with them and showed them the right way to the tuck shop. During lessons the boys threw paper at them. The children's names were Saria and Tariq. They were very kind and did not understand why people were being nasty to them. When they were doing geography, the twins answered all the questions. That night Samantha took them to her house and introduced them to her mum. Her mother was delighted because her child had made friends with two coloured children. The children's mother and father were also very pleased.

We now turn to the final part of the project which involved reading to the class Bernard Ashley's novel, *The Trouble with Donovan Croft*. This book was considered suitable largely on account of its convincing portrayal of life in a multiracial junior school and in the surrounding catchment area. Individual racism within the white community (among children, teachers and ordinary residents) was contrasted with the strenuous efforts made by others within the same community for racial harmony. Other reasons for selecting the book included its non-tokenistic treatment of the black characters, its optimistic message with regard to inter-racial understanding and the ease with which fourth year juniors could identify with Donovan and his white friend because of the similarity in age. The children, (interviewed in pairs), discussed their reaction to the book with BC. The were unanimous in having enjoyed it and the element of suspense appeared to be the main reason. It was not, however, the only one.

> *Patsy*: When Donovan started talking the whole classroom just went up and everyone was hoping and hoping for Donovan to talk.
>
> *Kathy*: It was good because it explained his feelings.
>
> *Sarah*: I enjoyed it. I thought it was good with a black person instead of a white person.
>
> *Samantha*: I liked the way that he never spoke right the way through until the last page.

When the children were asked about the book's value ('Would you recommend it to other fourth years?') none of them initially appreciated its· potential as a medium for combating racism. Indeed, when this possibility was suggested to them, many, like Linda, were sceptical.

> *BC*: Would you recommend it to another fourth year class?
>
> *Linda*: Yeah
>
> *BC*: Why?
>
> *Linda*: It's good to listen to.
>
> *BC*: Would it help change the attitudes of people who are prejudiced?
>
> *Linda*: Not really, cos it's only a book.

Conclusions

The material presented in this chapter shows clearly that the children concerned were able to cope conceptually with both individual racism and with structurally determined forms of racial inequality. Despite living in an all white area and, (perhaps as a result), tending to construe the world in non-racial terms, the children could certainly not be described as 'colour blind'. In this respect, our research confirms numerous studies (see, for example, Davey, 1983; Thomas, 1984) and thus we feel confident in asserting that most children aged between 10 and 11, regardless of the ethnic composition of their school, have the cognitive ability to benefit from an anti-racist initiative. Pedagogic competence, however, may be more important, in respect of ART, than the age of the child. As Allport (1954) noted more than thirty years ago:

> The age at which these lessons should be taught need not worry
> us. If taught in a simple fashion all the points can be made
> intelligible to younger children and, in a more fully developed
> way, they can be presented to older students ... In fact ...
> through 'graded lessons' the same content can, and should, be
> offered year after year. (p. 511)

He goes on to stress the importance (for what would now be termed ART),
of classroom relationships and the general school environment.

> If segregation of the sexes or races prevails, if authoritarianism and
> hierarchy dominate the system, the child cannot help but learn
> that power and status are the dominant factors in human rela-
> tionships. If, on the other hand, the school system is democratic,
> if the teacher and child are each respected units, the lesson of
> respect for the person will easily register. As in society at large,
> the *structure* of the pedagogical system will blanket, and may
> negate, the specific intercultural lessons taught.

In heeding this advice, we deliberately restricted the amount of didactic
teaching and encouraged the exchange of ideas and an openness to others.
Collaborative learning groups were introduced as a means of achieving
these ends.

Although our data are consistent with calls for ART, we would maintain
that they also support those critics (like Lynch, 1985; and Leicester, 1986)
who perceive no necessary incompatibility between anti-racist and multicultural education. Many of the children gave evidence of inaccurate
information about ethnic minorities, and if these inaccuracies are allowed
to pass unchallenged, they could provide a fertile breeding ground for
individual racism. We are certainly not advocating the sort of 'soft, folksy
tokenism' so disparaged by Lynch (1983), among others, but rather a form
of multicultural education that is, at the same time, anti-racist. Francis
(1984) makes the same point.

> It should be recognized that an across-the-board multi-ethnic
> approach can be developed into anti-racist teaching where the
> teacher sees this as viable, correcting misinformation or ignorance
> over other cultures ... (p. 229)

Leicester (1986) argues that the essence of an anti-racist, multi-cultural
education is the provision of 'genuine "internal" understanding of a variety
of cultural traditions'. She stresses cultural differences, but rightly objects
to treating these differences as 'exotic' or 'strange'. We do not wish to
undermine this aspect of multicultural education but would contend, on
the basis of comments made by some of our children, that equal consideration be given to the similarities in lifestyle and access to power between
working class Asian families in the East End of London and their Afro-

Caribbean and white counterparts in Toxteth and Newcastle respectively.

The most obvious policy implication of our study is to give the green light to anti-racist innovations in the all white primary school. In making this recommendation, we are, of course, aware of the exploratory nature of our own investigation and recognize that the response to similar initiatives may vary with the age and social class of the children and the location of the school. For this reason we would urge that further case studies of anti-racist education be undertaken with a wide range of primary aged children.

References

ALEXANDER, R.J. (1984) *Primary Teaching*, London, Holt, Rinehart and Winston.

ALLPORT, G.W. (1954) *The Nature of Prejudice*, Reading, MA, Addison-Wesley.

ASHLEY, B. *The Trouble with Donovan Croft*, Harmondsworth, Penguin.

DAVEY, A. (1983) *Learning to be Prejudiced*, London, Edward Arnold.

DEPARTMENT OF EDUCATION AND SCIENCE, (1981) *West Indian Children in Our Schools* (The Rampton Report). London, HMSO.

DEPARTMENT OF EDUCATION AND SCIENCE (1985) *Education for All* (The Swann Report) London, HMSO.

DONALDSON, M. (1978) *Children's Minds*, London, Fontana.

EDWARDS, A.D. and FURLONG, V.J. (1978) The *Language of Teaching*, London, Heinemann.

FRANCIS, M. (1984) 'Anti-racist teaching in the primary school', in STRAKER-WELDS, M. (Ed.) *Education for a Multicultural Society: Case Sudies in ILEA Schools*, London, Bell and Hyman.

GALTON, M. (1986) 'Attitudes and the infant teacher', *Child Education*, June, pp. 15-18.

HOROWITZ, E.L. (1936) 'Development of attitudes towards negroes', in PROSCHANSKY, H. and SEIDENBERG, B. (Eds) (1965) *Basic Studies in Social Psychology*, New York, Holt, Rinehart and Winston.

HUSBAND, C. (Ed.) (1982) *Race in Britain; Continuity and Change*, London, Hutchinson.

JEFFCOATE, R. (1979) *Positive Image: Towards a Multiracial Curriculum*, London, Writers and Readers Publishing Cooperative.

KING, R. (1978) *All Things Bright and Beautiful? A Sociological Study of Infants' Classrooms*, Chichester, Wiley.

LAWRENCE, E. (1982) 'Just plain commonsense', in CENTRE FOR CONTEMPORARY CULTURAL STUDIES *The Empire Strikes Back*, London, Hutchinson.

LEICESTER, M. (1986) 'Multicultural curriculum or antiracist education; Denying the gulf', *Multicultural Teaching*, 4, 2, pp. 4–7.

LYNCH, J. (1983) *The Multicultural Curriculum*, London, Batsford.

LYNCH, J. (1985) 'Human rights, racism and the multicultural curriculum', *Educational Review*, 37, 2, pp. 141–52.

MILLER, H.J. (1969) 'The effectiveness of teaching techniques for reducing colour prejudice', *Liberal Education*, 16, pp. 25–31.

MILNER, D. (1983) *Children and Race — Ten Years On*, London, Ward Lock.

MOULD, W. (1986) 'No Rainbow Coalition on Tyneside', *Multicultural Teaching*, 4, 3, pp. 9–13.

NAGUIB, M. (1986) 'Racism as an aspect of the Swann Report: 'A black perspective', *Multicultural Teaching*, 4, 2, pp. 8–10.

NAME (1985) *NAME on Swann*, Walsall, National Antiracist Movement in Education.

NIXON, J. (1985) *A Teacher's Guide to Multicultural Education*, London, Blackwell.

PIAGET, J. (1924) *The Language and Thought of the Child*, London, Routledge and Kegan Paul.

ROBERTSON, W. (1986) 'Generating change: Approaches to teacher education at Sunderland Polytechnic', *Multicultural Teaching*, 4, 3, pp. 43–5.

ROSS, A. (1984) 'Developing political concepts and skills in the primary school', *Educational Review*, 36, 2, pp. 133–9.

STEPHENS, D. (1983) 'Who are the Paki baiters?', *New Society*, 4 August.

THOMAS, K. (1984) 'Intercultural relations in Classrooms', in CRAFT, M. (Ed.) *Education and Cultural Pluralism* Lewes, Falmer Press.

TROYNA, B. and BALL, W. (1985) *Views from the Chalk Face: School Responses to an LEA's Policy on Multicultural Education*, Warwick, Centre for Research in Ethnic Relations, Policy Papers Paper 1.

VERMA, G.K. and BAGLEY, C. (1979) 'Measured changes in racial attitudes following the use of three different teaching methods', in VERMA, G.K. and BAGLEY, C. (Eds) *Race, Education and Identity*, London, Macmillam.

ZEC, P. (1980) 'Multicultural education: What kind of relativism is possible?', *Journal of Philosophy of Education*, 14, 1, pp. 77–86.

15 Anxieties and Anticipations - Pupils' Views of Transfer to Secondary School

Sara Delamont and Maurice Galton

> I am sad to have to leave because I have got used to the people at St. Michaels. But I know why we have to change because we need more knowledge. 12 is the right age.

In this quotation from Bryan's (1980) study of pupils transferring to secondary school lies the central theme of the chapter. Pupils are ambivalent about transfer. They have regrets about leaving their primary school, some anxieties about their new school, and some anticipations.

This chapter uses data from the ORACLE project[1] plus that of Measor and Woods (1984) and Bryan (1980) to reveal what pupils about to transfer to a bigger school were looking forward to, and what they feared. The data used are drawn from observation, informal and formal interviews with pupils and teachers and essays written for the researchers by pupils.[2] All the schools that pupils were leaving are called feeder or lower schools and those they were moving to are termed destination or transfer schools in this chapter. The features of the schools which pupils anticipated with pleasure, and the fears they had were the same in all three studies, and appear to be remarkably constant across time and space.

Children look forward to transfer with a mixture of enthusiasm and anxieties about features of their new schools. Many of the fears would be recognized as reasonable and 'rational' (even when unfounded) by, say, teachers and parents; others are couched in terms of more lurid and scarey 'horror' stories passed on by other pupils about phantasy features of their destinations. Aspects of the destination schools that pupils looked forward to with pleasure are examined first, before turning to their fears.

Eager Anticipations

All three samples of pupils were found to have clear ideas about positive features of their destination schools before transfer, but individual children had very different enthusiasms. Everything that was mentioned by any one pupil as fearsome was mentioned by another child as a delight. For example, an horrendous cross-country trail for one pupil was viewed as a fantastic opportunity for serious training by another.

Among the things which were regularly mentioned as plus points about the destination school were improved games facilities, better music, new subjects, better dinners, a larger playground and a bigger library. There was also a generalized feeling that current schools had become too small and tame, and pupils were ready to move on. Bryan's (1980) sample of essays contained the followng anticipatory comments:

> I'm looking forward to my new school because there are lots of facilities such as squash courts and badminton ... cooking rooms and science rooms.

> I think there's a big library there and I will enjoy that. ... the drama studio, that's one good thing because I want to be an actor when I grow up.

> I believe Rowland Hutty can no longer train us sufficiently for future life. Our science labs are insufficiently equipped and our sports equipment is old and worn out.

> In the nexed (*sic*) school you can learn better things like chemistry and physics.

Measor and Woods (1984, p. 41) report similar anticipations, such as:

> They have got great big sports halls like down the town in the leisure centre, they have got a great big place where you play basketball.

> You walk through the library here, and their library's a big one, as big as the one in the town centre!

> I am really looking forward to using all the equipment in science.

> The good thing was in a big school there is loads of equipment, especially metal work equipment.

The ORACLE pupils showed a similar range of enthusiasms. So, for example, Lionel and Jack both looked forward to cross-country, athletics and football; Fleur and Victor valued the gym apparatus; Martina and Terence anticipated the better choice of school dinners; Felicity and Brendan were keen to start playing new instruments; Camilla admired the big school library; Howard had been impressed by the tuck shop and the large playground; and Randal relished the chance to 'do more work'.[3]

Daphne was looking forward to maths and social studies, Wanda to science, Petunia to French, Odette to maths and PE, Eunice to English, Fern to PE and home economics, Errol to French and science, Craig to 'PE, design, social studies, French, English and science', and Fida to everything because 'all the lessons we did in the junior school were very boring'. Greg was one of the enthusiasts:

> The lessons I was looking forward to was (*sic*) science, social studies and the disine (*sic*) work because I had never done them before. The PE was alot (*sic*) better two (*sic*) because there was alot more subjects to do for e.g, rugby, cricit (*sic*) basket ball, base ball, athletics and other various things — there is a lot more things to do, and alot more fasilatyes (*sic*)

Similarly Bronwen wrote for us:

> I liked games because we do the disco's (discus) but we didn't do the disco's at our old school — are (*sic*) old school didn't have a gym nor a woodwork room or a metalwork for design.

Her classmate, Gaynor, told us:

> And we have lots of exicted (*sic*) lessons for instants (*sic*) we have needlework and woodwork and maths is very good.

Greg's desire to explore and enjoy the 'fasilatyes' of the bigger school, and Bronwen and Gaynor's enthusiasms for 'exicted' lessons capture the anticipations that the ORACLE children had. Such enthusiasms can be created by well-organized pre-transfer programmes, which we evaluate in Delamont and Galton (1986). As well as pleasurable anticipations, children have fears, to which we now turn. The anxieties that pupils had about their destination schools can be grouped into four general areas: fears about the building, the curriculum, the staff and the pupils. As we examine each fear, we show how in addition to the widely expressed anxieties there are also a series of myths, horror stories or urban legends, which children tell each other, but rarely voice to adults.

The Buildings

Pupils anxious about the buildings at their destination school were usually focussing on their size and complexity. Thus the essays written for us included comments such as:

> Dan wrote: I remember the first time I came up to maid marion it semd very lonly and the school seemd very big. (Dan's spelling retained.)

> Maid Marion was a lot bigger than I expected, my sister had been

here in previous years but I didn't think it was as big as she told me, (Greg).

When I came to Maid Marion, on intake day, I was amazed at the size of the whole place. The teacher who was taking us around speed (*sic*) round saying 'Now this is the . . .' (Heather)

When I first came to Maid Marion I thought it was a large school with many classes. I found it difficult to find my way around. (Daphne)

This can be paralleled by the child who told Bryan (1980):

I've seen my new school and its very big there's corridors every-where you look and an endless supply of classrooms and its very easy to get lost in a school like this.

Measor and Woods (1984, p. 9) were told:

It is so big — so many places that I have to go and see, it will take me a whole year to learn all the places . . .

It will probably be strange at first, getting used to things, how big it is. It looks big, and people always walking around and every-thing.

The ORACLE children's anxieties about their destination school's build-ings and facilities were mainly general — the new institutions were so much bigger they feared getting lost. However some children were scared of specific facilities, such as Karena who had been alarmed by her new school's four storey 'tower' block because she had a fear of heights. Similarly some children feared the science labs to which their peers were looking forward.

There is one particular type of location in the school that seemed to give rise to special fears, and which crystallized a number of horror stories or urban legends (Brunvand, 1983 and 1984): the *lavatories and the showers*. Measor and Woods (1984, P.12) report one boy saying:

I don't get the idea of having a shower after games. Why do we have to take a shower?

and a girl said:

I'm not really looking forward to the showers, that will be difficult to get used to, that will be a new experience.

Fida, an ORACLE pupil, was afraid of showering after PE. These an-xieties provide fertile ground for a myth to flourish. Measor and Woods (1983 and 1984) collected several versions of the story and it was reported in the *Times Educational Supplement* in 1986:

someone has been spreading those rumours about first years having their heads flushed down the toilets by the third year again. (Phillips, 1986)

This myth, though known by both boys and girls, describes a threatening event which is only believed to happen to boys, and only boys actually tell it (Measor and Woods, 1983 and 1984). The most crude version of this scare story is that:

they flush yer head down the toilet on your birthday.

But there is an allied, cleaner version, that on your birthday you are thrown into the shower with all your clothes on. We also collected a variant from Denzil, who had been told that:

You have to clean the toilets out if they flood, Miss.

Measor was able to establish such good rapport that pupils felt they could tell her stories as 'dirty' as the lavatory one. Bryan's data and ours, being mainly written, did not include explicit reference to it. As Bauman says, pupils are often reluctant to discuss 'dirty' stories with adults:

> The free peer group activity of children is by its very nature a privileged realm in which adults are alien intruders, especially so insofar as much of the children's folklore repertoire violates what children understand to be adult standards of decorum. (Bauman, 1982, p. 178)

Bryan (1980) was told a 'clean' variation on the myth:

> I am hoping that when it is someone's birthday some of the older pupils do not break eggs over the person's head like they do at Waverbridge.

In the USA a variation on the shower myth is that smaller pupils changing are thrown naked out of the locker rooms into the public corridors, and as well as the lavatory myth there is a version in which big children stuff small ones into rubbish bins. In the USA the torture of having one's head forced into the flushing toilet is called a 'swirly' and can be clean or dirty depending on the state of the lavatory (Fine, 1986). In this set of stories the recurring themes are: larger children bullying smaller ones, victims being forcibly immersed in a polluting container (lavatory or rubbish bin), or humiliated by nakedness, and the desecration of a special day — the birthday. The secondary school is, in these myths, a dangerous, impersonal place where pollution and humiliation can occur.

The Curriculum

The size of the destination schools was related to their specialist facilities, which emphasized to the children the wider curriculum that they would soon be facing. Pupils had anxieties of two kinds about the curriculum in the transfer schools: that the work would be hard, and about specific new subjects. Thus an anonymous essay from a boy transferring to Kenilworth School mentioned that:

> In my first term I expected to come bottom of the class in every subject.

Clyde summarized both types of anxiety about the curriculum:

> When I first came to Kenilworth it seemed easier than I expected ... The lesson that I was most nervous about was French, but it hasn't been too bad.

Gilbert agreed:

> One subject I thought I wouldn't be any good at is French but I think I'm quite good at it.

Similarly Eunice (at Maid Marion) was 'dreading maths' and other pupils feared science, P E, craft, English and cooking. Measor and Woods (1984, p. 11) report a girl telling them that she felt:

> sometimes when we learn new things I won't learn it straight away. I am worried about maths really, because I am not very good.

Another girl told Measor (*ibid*, p. 38) :

> I am worried about their way of doing physics, and I am no good at it, the hard part.

Some boys also objected to needlework including one who wrote:

> The only thing I don't like is needlework.

Bryan (1980) reports pupils' essays containing comments about the curriculum at their transfer schools, which were equally divided between those who looked forward to a 'secondary' curriculum and those who dreaded it.

There is one item in the anticipated curriculum about which pupils' more extreme fears crystallize — the dissection of a rat. The Laboratory Rat Myth is told by both sexes and seems to be regarded as applying to both sexes. Simply, there is a persistent story that all new first-year pupils will be forced to dissect a rat, which in the more vivid accounts is pregnant and/or still alive. Anxieties about this future endurance test was apparent from the questions pupils asked during their pre-transfer programmes. For example when a master from a destination school was answering pupils' questions we noted:

> Another boy asked what they actually did in science, would they do any dissections? Mr. Southern said, 'Sometimes, but not directly after lunch.' which the boys all found apparently funny.

Measor and Woods (1984, pp. 24–5) report a boy telling the laboratory rat myth about his pre-transfer visit to Old Town with relish:

> The best bit was two boys about 14 or 15 were dissecting a rat. They had pinned its legs, feet and tail down, and cut it open, then folded the skin back.

As another boy commented on his visit:

> Yeh, the rat didn't scare me though. But it did the girls, you could hear them all going 'Urgh!', when they heard about it.

Stacey told the myth this way:

> Sometimes they do it alive so you can see the heartbeat, I don't like rats, but I don't think that's very nice.

This myth is told to frighten or revolt girls, who are expected to go 'Urgh!', but may also scare some boys.

The Staff

Alongside the richer, more varied curriculum, pupils realize that they will be meeting a greater range of teachers, including more men, and subject specialists. There were anxieties about how fierce and strict the staff would be, and concern that there were so many different teachers that it would be impossible to sort them out, remember their names and adapt to them. As Gail and Eunice recollected:

> On my first day I was very scared when I met all the new people. My worst thing was when I met all the new teachers.

> I was very nervous when I saw all the teachers ... I also dreaded my teacher with a name like Mr. Slaughter.

Eunice had misheard her new formmaster's name, which was actually Salter. Royston and George commented:

> When I first came I was shown round by Mr. Salter. My first impressions were that it was a huge school with a much stricter set of teachers than where I had come from.

> When I first came I thought all the teachers would be stricked (*sic*) and tell you off if you got something wrong ...

Measor and Woods (1984, p. 10) report pupils anticipating that:

> they are quite strict ther (*sic*). If you do something wrong, you get a wallop.

> The teachers will be stricter than here, they're soft here.

> I've never had a man teacher before, so I don't know what it's like.

> it's gonna be a lot more difficult to talk to teachers there than here

> Will they teach me, or will they just expect me to do it?

Similarly Bryan (1980) was told that:

> I will be frightened because there are more people and more teachers than at St. Michael's.

> Having different teachers all the time does not improve your work because you cannot guarantee that they are all good teachers.

This last fear is only reported by Bryan, but otherwise pupils in all three studies share similar worries about the staff in their transfer schools.

It transpires that there is one category of staff who give rise to horror stories among pre-transfer pupils. The activities and demands of physical education teachers give rise to The Five Mile Run Myth.

The Five Mile Run Myth is told by both sexes, but only boys expect to have to suffer the torture of a five (or even ten) mile cross-country run, which has to be completed under the surveillance of savage PE staff who beat or humilate laggards. Measor and Woods (1984, pp. 21–22) say:

> Many boys repeated with some alarm the view that, at the new school, you were frequently expected to go on long distance runs, especially if there was (*sic*) snow on the ground. Mark said, 'And they say you have to run to Brookfield and back.' And Bruce; 'some kids told me, in PE you run to Brookfield and back — its nearly five miles!'

Other variations of this story were the eight minute mile:

> The thing that bothers me most ... is to run a mile in under eight minutes, and if you do it in over eight minutes, you get sent back to do it again.

Coupled to these exhausting demands is a belief that the PE masters are fierce:

> One of them hits you with the corner post if you're not out of the changing room in one minute (*ibid*, p. 22)

In the ORACLE project we found that boys going to Guy Mannering feared that they would be sent to run round a large local park, and girls that they had to run several times round the playing fields before lessons. Bryan does not report any PE stories by his respondents.

The Pupils

There were two types of anxiety about the pupils who would be the children's companions in their new schools: fears about having friends; and about being bullied. Pupils were anxious about losing the friends they had in their feeder schools and about whether they would be able to make new ones. For example, Josh and Luke told the ORACLE interviewer:

> they had been very worried about finding new friends here and were very scared that they would not make friends easily and get very left out.

> *Daphne*: When I first came I had got no friends and I had to find my way around on my own. But I soon got to no (*sic*) the other people in my form

Stephanie said in her interview she did not know how she would get friendly with children from other schools and she worried about that. Karena and Fida felt worried that they would not meet new friends in Maid Marion and would be left on their own. These pupils can be contrasted with those like Nathan who knew his particular friend, Amos, would be in the same class, and felt no worries of any kind. Certainly, once people had made some friends, their whole attitude to the school improved. For example, Kirsty was 'not all that keen on the school at the very beginning ...' however, once she had met new friends she found things were 'not too bad'. This sentiment was echoed by most of the children. New friends *were* found and school became more bearable. Bryan (1980) found similar anxieties:

> One thing I won't like is leaving all my old friends who are going to different schools.

> I don't really like leaving because in this school ... all my friends and people I know are here.

> When I first went into the school a teacher took me into the hall ... I was scared I might not be in the same class as some of my friends.

Measor and Woods (1984, p. 14) state that:

> the pupils' greatest anxiety was whether they would be 'split up' from their friends and placed in different classes. Philip hoped he would have 'someone I know in the class, 'cos you have to start all over again making new friends, and it can be pretty bad sometimes. You get left out of everything.'

One of the reasons children are anxious about having friends is that mates serve as a protection from potential bullies. As one of Measor and Wood's (*ibid*) informants explains bullying was less likely to happen when: 'your mates are there, especially if they are good mates'. Fears about bullying were certainly widespread in all three samples. For example, Measor and Woods (*ibid*, p. 12) were told:

> I'm not looking forward to being a first year. I don't fancy being bullied. If you get in their way, they call you 'first years', and 'stupid little first years', and call you names.

> there might be somebody there who is a bit of a bully, so I don't like the idea of that.

Bryan (1980) found similar anxieties:

> I expect big boys and girls biger (*sic*) than me to pick on me and bully me.

> I do not think large comprehensives are a good idea because ... there will be a lot more bullying.

So too with the ORACLE pupils, such as Joscelin who had heard a rumour about children being beaten up, while Bart said he:

> were bothered about coming here, Miss, because friends had told me it were bad. They said you got beat up a lot!

Dawn had been frightened by rumours that on the first day 'You got kicked in, Miss'. An anonymous pupil at the school told us in an essay:

> On the first day I was very nervous, afraid of being bullied by older children.

Both boys and girls are frightened by tales of gangs of older pupils at their destination school who roam unchecked terrorising newcomers. The Violent Gang Myth is told by both sexes but believed to be more dangerous for males. Boys are warned that marauding gangs of older boys will attack them, punch them with spiked gloves on, roll them down banks or into bushes, steal their money and crisps, or in their words 'kick us in, Miss'. Bryan (1980) was told:

> I have horrible thoughts of my new school which is Seacombe High. I think there is no disciplin (*sic*) from what my friends have told me. They told me that groups of lads go around battering people up, they are supposed to be from the dreaded BEBB which stands for the Brightsea Estate Boot Boys.

These fearsome Boot Boys are clearly a close associate, in the myths, of a gang at Old Town:

> There's these boys, and if you have a fight, they wear punch gloves with spikes, and they hit you and leave punch holes in your face.

At least one of our informants had heard such stories, and asked a visiting master from his destination school if boys at Kenilworth could carry knives. Mr. Southern gave a shocked answer of 'No, of course not,' but did not enquire why any 11-year-old in a Midlands suburb would even consider doing so. It is clear to us that the child had heard of gangs carrying knives there and/or wanted to carry one himself for protection.

These, then, are the four main myths that pupils scare each other with.[4]

Discussion

Because the buildings are larger, the curriculum wider, the discipline tougher, and other pupils fiercer in the destination schools, pupils awaiting transfer form a perfect audience for scarey stories about the fate that awaits them. Older children (neighbours, siblings, cousins and friends) delight in spreading a set of urban legends, which the pupils facing transfer then repeat among themselves. Morin *et al.* (1971, p. 101) has called adolescent girls 'natural myth conductors', but boys are equally adept at telling and re-telling a set of folk tales about the horrors that await new pupils in their destination schools.

In this section we use the American literature on urban legends, and especially children's urban folklore, to illuminate the four myths (lavatory, rat, cross country, and violent gang) outlined above. The best known urban legends include 'The Hook':

> Outside of McPherson, Kansas, . . . is an old road . . . a traditional parking spot for the kids. A fellow and his date pulled in to listen to the radio and do a little necking, and over the radio came an announcement that a crazed killer with a hook in place of a hand had escaped from the local insane asylum. The girl got scared and begged the boy to take her home. He got mad and stepped on the gas and roared off. When they got to her house, he got out and went around . . . to let her out. There on the door handle was a bloody hook. (Brunvand, 1983, pp. 47–8)

Brunvand is an expert on urban folk tales and legends, such as 'the hook', 'the vanishing hitchhiker' and 'the spider in the beehive hairdo'. There is ample evidence that such stories have been circulating for over fifty years, and are a genuine form of folklore.[5] A particular sub-set, which include 'the hook', 'the boyfriend's death', 'the babysitter and the man upstairs' and 'the roommate's death', are regularly told by, and to, adolescents, for whom necking in parked cars, babysitting and adventures with college roommates are real experiences made frightening by the stories. Brunvand himself explains the social role of the urban legend for the adolescent as follows:

People of all ages love a good scare. Early childhood is full of semi-serious spooky stories and ghastly threats, while the more sophisticated black humour ... enters a bit later ... favourite stories at summer camp tell of maniacal axe-murderers and deformed giants lurking the dark forest to ambush unwary Scouts.... One consistent theme in these teenage horrors is that as the adolescent moves out from home into the larger world, the world's dangers may close in on him or her. Therefore, although the immediate purpose of many of these legends is to produce a good scare, they also serve to deliver a warning: Watch out! this could happen to you! (*ibid*, p. 46)

Urban legends, told by teenagers and adults, are not just an American phenomenon, but exist in Europe as well. A set of urban legends parallel to those in the USA were recorded in Orleans, France by Morin and his colleagues (1971), centring on an accusation that the teenage fashion boutiques were kidnapping girls and selling them into white slavery. However, the academic study of urban legends in general, and children's folklore in particular has been much more firmly established in America by authors such as Brunvand (1983 and 1984), Knapp and Knapp (1976), Fine (1986), and Bauman (1982).[6]

Brunvand (1984, p. 69) says that American teenagers tell their repertoire of bloodcurdling legends 'at slumber parties, on camping trips, or in dormitory bull sessions and the like.' His informants are students, somewhat older that the pupils involved in school transfer. Pupils of 9–13 tell tales about school rather than lovers' lanes or college dorms. Older children scare younger ones with stories about their destination school, which are essentially the same all over the country, but always contain tiny local variations to give an air of authenticity. Knapp and Knapp (1976, pp. 248–9) found this was a common feature of younger children's folklore and argue that:

the neighbourhood story which gives a certain glamour — some literary resonance — to the otherwise unremarkable places where children grow up ...

The Knapps found two stories about schools current among their informations:

One boy from Kansas City told us that at his school the little kids believed that the former principal was buried under the mound at the base of the flagpole, which came right out of her grave. Other children told us of a teacher who looked like a witch; if she touched you, you would get warts.

We did not find any stories about dead vampire principals who had to be staked through the heart, or wart-giving witch-teachers, but the four commonly found themes in pupils' pre-transfer stories, are of the same general type.

The myths deserve adult attention because they are important to children. We may wish to discover if the stories report actual incidents and events in the destination schools, and if the children believe them. Schools need to decide whether to address them in their pretransfer programmes. Folklorists should study the function and significance of such urban folklore among adolescents. Measor and Woods (1983 and 1984) offer one explanation, and Brunvand (1983) another, but although in the UK the Opies (1959) found versions of some of these myths, British ones have received little attention. However, as this is an article about pupils and not folklore, our focus shifts now to the three questions already posed: are they true; do children believe them; and should schools try to tackle them?

Brunvand (1983) reports that many of the raconteurs of urban legends believe them to be true stories, and are surprised when shown that precisely similar tales have been reported from all over the USA for forty years and no actual incident has ever been reported. Checks with hospitals, for example, never reveal patients dying of spiders in their beehive hairdos or killed in the road accident that supposedly produced the vanishing hitchhiker, or lunatics with hooks escaping. The four school myths are less easily dismissed. It would be foolhardy to state that no boy in any school has ever been dowsed in a lavatory, thrown into the showers clothed, or rolled down banks. There may be fierce teachers, longer cross country trails than pupils can manage, and compulsory dissection of rats. Hanna's (1982) American study of an elementary school, found that

> Toilets are for toughs . . . an unpleasant area of teasing and harassment.

Children told Hanna of physical and verbal attacks in the lavatories, and many pupils tried never to use the school toilets at all. In particular boys objected to the lack of doors on the cubicles, and the fact that:

> Teachers and aides rarely enter the restrooms. Most are female and the boys claim they get embarrassed.

Consequently boys could be harassed by other male pupils without any adults intervening. If this is generally true of schools, then the lavatories would be a space where bullying can take place, and we have to accept that the lavatory torture *could* happen. Poorly supervised playgrounds could allow gangs to attack smaller boys, and push them into the showers or down banks. The rat is most likely to be dissected by the teacher, but a survey of first-year science teaching would enable us to discover what dissection, if any, pupils have to do. The myths describe things that may happen in schools (such as that studied by Beynon, 1985) but their power is not dependent on their facticity any more that the historical authenticity of Vlad the Impaler 'explains' the success of Hammer Horror films. Children will tell them even if reassured that such events are unheard of. When questioned the majority of pupils say that they do not believe them. Some children may be really credulous and made miserable by them, but the majority are not. Measor and Woods (1984, p. 20) quote one boy on the 'lavatory' myth as follows:

Interviewer: Do you believe it?
Darrell: I've 'eard me mates talk ... an' they say ... I doubt it really ... well ... it could happen, I suppose (pause) It could ...

Similarly in our research when Ellen told us that her sister had scared her with 'horrrible stories' about Waverly, she was laughing and the interviewer interpreted her laugh to mean Ellen had known her sister was teasing. We need data on how seriously pupils take these stories.

Destination schools are, therefore, faced with a dilemma. Should they gear their pre-transfer programmes to reassuring their prospective pupils that the myths are only myths, or ignore them as part of the children's private lives? Similarly, should the class teacher of the 'leavers' open up the myths for rational discussion? Most of the teachers involved in the pre-transfer programmes run by our ORACLE schools dealt with the factual anxieties of the pupils — such as getting lost — and did not address the myths in their speeches or in the pupil tours and visits. For example, lavatories were rarely included on tours, and the lavatory myth was rarely included in talks. The types of pre-transfer programme which were operated by schools in the ORACLE project differed in their effectiveness; and we feel this was because only some of them allowed pupils to test some of their myths to destruction (see Delamont and Galton, 1986).

Conclusions

The pupils we studied, like those observed by Measor and Woods (1984) and those who wrote essays for Bryan (1980) wer facing transfer to a bigger school with mixed feelings of anticipation and anxiety. Myths, or horror stories, circulate among them, adding a layer of fantasy to the genuine, practical concerns they have. Schools design pretransfer programmes to calm their prospective pupils' fears, and these address many of the practical concerns but not several of the phantasies fanned by the urban legends. The policy implication of this is that destination schools should think carefully about opening up the urban legends to rational discussion.

However it should also be made clear that for nearly all the children, the fears, both rational and fantastic, had vanished by the end of the first month in their new schools. By the end of their first year in the schools pupils were re-telling the urban legends to younger children, and looking forward to being old hands. As Paige wrote in her essay for us:

> It is now getting close to the summer holidays and we become second year girls. Then we can boss the first years about.

> And as Jenny told us: On my first day I felt a little scared about the second and third years, but as time past (*sic*) I haven't felt scared for a long time. Their (*sic*) are a lot of nice boys come from the other schools ... For the people who are coming next year I hope they have a nice time like I have.

In short, any anxieties quickly fade, and are replaced by more long-term concerns about schooling in general.

Notes

1   The Observational Research and Classroom Learning Evaluation (ORACLE) Project ran at the University of Leicester School of Education from 1975 to 1980 funded by the then SSRC. This chapter focusses on one very small part of the findings and the reader unacquainted with the project can consult the five published volumes (Galton, Simon and Croll, 1980: Galton and Simon, 1980: Simon and Willcocks, 1981: Galton and Willcocks, 1983: and Delamont and Galton, 1986) and papers (eg, Galton and Delamont, 1980, and 1985). A version of this chapter was prepared for the 1984 10th British Educational Research Association Conference held at the University of Lancaster, 30 August — 3 September 1984. We are grateful to the SSRC for funding the ORACLE project. The Project was directed by Brian Simon and Maurice Galton, and employed Paul Croll, Anne Jasman and John Willcocks fulltime, plus Margaret Greig, Janice Lea, and Sarah Tann in the phase we discuss here. Diana Stroud and Jaya Katariya were the project secretaries, Lillian Lewis typed this chapter in draft. We are grateful to them for their work. The children studied in this phase of the ORACLE project were moving schools at either 9, or 11, or 12 depending on which of the three LEAs we studied they were in, and we had observed them for a year before transfer. The sample studied by Measor and Woods (1984) were moving at 12, and had also been studied intensively for a year. Bryan's (1980) pupils were moving schools at 11,12, or 13 and his data are only from essays. The five different LEAs, all in England, had different school systems (for example, some had middle schools) but all the children were transferring to a larger building, with more staff and a more varied curriculum. We have therefore combined the data and treated all the pupils and all the transfers as essentially similar.
2   Full details of all the methods used in the ORACLE project and how those data have been analyzed can be found in the publications listed above.
3   The names of all LEAs, schools, teachers and pupils quoted in this chapter are pseudonyms, which are the same as those used in the ORACLE publications (see Delamont and Galton, 1986). The names used by Bryan, and by Measor and Woods are also pseudonyms.
4   There is also a fifth myth that Measor and Woods (1983 and 1984) found, again among boys, that there is a homosexual teacher (and/or a homosexual older boy) at the destination school who must be avoided. We did not find this myth among the ORACLE pupils.

5 Brunvand (1984, p. ix) explains the term 'urban legend' as follows:

> highly captivating and plausible, but mainly fictional, oral narratives that are widely told as true stories. We folklorists call them urban legends, although modern legends might be a more accurate term.

Stories of the type collected by Brunvand are mostly told and retold in cities and towns, and many depend on interactions between strangers for their dramatic point.

6 Alison Lurie (1986) reveals how well-established the study of children's folklore is in the USA by making the heroine of her novel *Foreign Affairs* an expert in that subject. Virginia Miner is so conventional that she would never profess a subject that was not respectable.

References

BAUMAN, R. (1982) 'Ethnography of children's folklore', in GILMORE, P. and GLATTHORN, A.A. (Eds), *Children In and Out of School*, Washington, DC, Centre for Applied Linguistics.

BEYNON, J. (1985) *Initial Encounters in the Secondary School*, Lewes, Falmer Press.

BRUNVAND, J. (1983) *The Vanishing Hitchhiker*, London, Picador.

BRUNVAND, J. (1984) *The Choking Doberman*, New York, W. Norton.

BRYAN, K.A. (1980) 'Pupil perceptions of transfer', in HARGREAVES, A. and TICKLE, L. (Eds) *Middle Schools*, London, Harper and Row.

DELAMONT, S. and GALTON, M. (1986) *Inside the Secondary Classroom*, London, Routledge and Kegan Paul.

FINE, G. (1986) personal communication.

GALTON, M., SIMON, B. and CROLL, P. (1980) *Inside the Primary Classroom*, London, Routledge and Kegan Paul.

GALTON, M. and SIMON, B. (1980) *Progress and Performance in the Primary Classroom*, London, Routledge and Kegan Paul.

GALTON, M. and DELAMONT, S. (1980) 'The first weeks of middle school', in HARGREAVES, A. and TICKLE, L. (Eds) *Middle Schools*, London, Harper and Row.

GALTON, M. and DELAMONT, S. (1985) 'Speaking with forked tongue', in BURGESS, R.G. (Ed.) *Field Methods in the Study of Education*, Lewes, Falmer Press.

GALTON, M. and WILLCOCKS, J. (1983) *Moving from the Primary Classroom*, London, Routledge and Kegan Paul.

HANNA, J. (1982) 'Social policy and the children's world', in SPINDLER, G. (Ed.) *Doing the Ethnography of Schooling*, New York, Holt, Rinehart and Winston.

KNAPP, M. and KNAPP, H. (1976) *One Potato, Two Potato*, New York, W. Norton.

LURIE, A (1986) *Foreign Affairs*, London, Abacus.

MEASOR, L. and WOODS, P. (1983) 'The interpretation of pupil myths', in HAMMERSLEY, M. (Ed.) *The Ethnography of Schooling*, Driffield, Yorks, Nafferton.

MEASOR, L. and WOODS, P. (1984) *Changing Schools*, Milton Keynes, Open University Press.

MORIN, E. *et al.* (1971) *Rumour in Orleans*, London, Weidenfeld and Nicholson.

OPIE, I. and OPIE, P. (1959) *The Lore and Language of Schoolchildren*, Oxford, Clarendon Press.

PHILLIPS, N. (1986) 'Sean is Sean', *Times Educational Supplement* 4 July, p. 32.

SIMON, B. and WILLCOCKS, J. (Eds) (1981) *Research and Practice in the Primary Classroom*, London, Routledge and Kegan Paul.

STILLMAN, A. and MAYCHELL, K. (1984), *School to School*, Windsor, NFER-Nelson.

Notes on Contributors

Steven Bossert is an Assistant Professor of Sociology at the University of Michigan. His book, *Tasks and Social Relationships in Classrooms*, was published in 1979.

Bruce Carrington worked in primary schools in London and is now a Lecturer at the University of Newcastle-upon Tyne.

Katherine Clarricoates has wide-ranging research experience with a particular interest in gender and primary education and has recently completed research on traveller women in West London.

Bronwyn Davies is a Senior Lecturer at the University of New England, Australia, and author of *Life in Classroom and Playground* (1982).

Sara Delamont is a Senior Lecturer in Sociology at University College, Cardiff. She has published widely including *Interaction in the Classroom* (1976), *Sex Roles and the School* (1980) and *Inside the Secondary Classroom* (1986) (with M. Galton).

Sue Duxbury has extensive experience of working in nursery schools and now lectures in education at St Helen's College.

Maurice Galton is a Professor of Education at the University of Leicester. A co-director of the ORACLE project, he and his collaborators have produced a series of reports, including *Inside the Primary Classroom* (1980), *Progress and Performance in the Primary Classroom* (1980), *Moving from the Primary Classroom* (1983) and *Inside the Secondary Classroom* (1986).

David Hartley is a Lecturer at the Centre for Continuing Education at the University of Dundee. His book, *Understanding the Primary School*, was published in 1985.

Martin Hughes has researched extensively on the thinking of young children and is currently a Lecturer at the University of Exeter. Among his books are *Nurseries Now* (1980) *Young Children Learning* (1984) (with B. Tizard) and *Children and Number* (1986).

Margaret Jackson is a former primary school teacher who currently works at Bristol Polytechnic. She is particularly interested in early literacy.

John Lee lectures at Bristol Polytechnic and has a long-standing interest in anti-racist education and primary school practice.

Veronica Lee is a deputy headteacher who works in a primary school in a central area of a major city.

Maggie Pearson is an experienced primary school teacher. She currently teaches in a multi-racial inner-city school.

Andrew Pollard has taught across the primary age range and is currently a Reader in Primary Education at Bristol Polytechnic. His books include *The Social World of the Primary School* (1985) and *Reflective Teaching in the Primary School* (1987) (with S. Tann).

Thea Prisk is headteacher of RA Butler Infant School, Saffron Walden. She is particularly interested in language development and also works as a supervisory tutor at the Cambridge Institute of Education.

Stephen Rowland has taught and researched in primary schools, one outcome of which is his book, *The Enquiring Classroom* (1984). At present he is a Lecturer at the University of Sheffield.

Geoffrey Short has extensive teaching experience in primary and middle schools and a long-standing interest in race and education. He is now a Lecturer in Education at Hatfield Polytechnic.

Andy Sluckin published *Growing Up in the Playground* in 1981. He is now a Clinical Psychologist and Psychotherapist at the Bethel Child and Family Centre, Norwich.

Barbara Tizard is a Professor of Education at the University of London and Director of the Thomas Coram Research Unit. Among her books are *Early Childhood Education* (1975), *Involving Parents in Nursery and Infant Schools* (1981) and *Young Children Learning* (1984) (with M. Hughes).

Peter Woods is a Reader in Education at the Open University. His books include *The Divided School* (1979), *Sociology and the School* (1983) and *Inside Classrooms* (1986).

Subject Index

Name Index